People who can't remember their shoe size don't forget what they got on the SAT. In this long-overdue look at the Educational Testing Service, one of the least understood and most powerful institutions in America, David Owen challenges the facade of scientific infallibility the company has erected between itself and the public. He documents numerous defects in the conception, construction, scoring, and interpretation of the SAT and reveals that most colleges requiring the tests don't even use them. And although ETS claims that the test takers cannot be coached, Owen tells which coaching systems can raise scores significantly and which are worthless. His book also provides information to help students raise their scores substantially.

Although the SAT is the best known of the ETS tests, it is only one of dozens that help determine the futures of millions of students, teachers, businessmen, lawyers, physicians, professional golfers, CIA agents, insurance salesmen, travel agents, and many others in a variety of unlikely professions and occupations.

Among its nontesting activities, ETS designs routes for school buses and sells lists based on information students supply when they take the SAT. For a price, customers can buy lists of students broken down by a number of characteristics, including sex, race, financial background, and religion. Although ETS, a nonprofit company, claims to be above economic interests in evangelizing its tests, *Forbes* once called it "one of the hottest little growth companies in U.S. business."

Because few of us can escape this company's power over our careers and over the way students in secondary schools

continued on back flap

None of the Above

None of the Above

BEHIND THE MYTH OF SCHOLASTIC APTITUDE

David Owen

Houghton Mifflin Company
Boston • 1985

Library of Congress Cataloging in Publication Data
Owen, David, date
None of the above.

Bibliography: p.
Includes index.
1. Scholastic aptitude test.   2. Prediction of
scholastic success — Evaluation.   I. Title.
LB2353.57.094   1985   378'.1664   84-25262
ISBN 0-395-35540-0

Printed in the United States of America

P 10 9 8 7 6 5 4 3 2 1

Parts of this book appeared originally in *Harper's,
The New Republic,* the *Washington Post,*
and the *APF Reporter,* in different form.

For Ann

Acknowledgments

This book began as a short assignment for *Harper's,* grew into an endless article, swelled into its present form, and threatens to become a permanent obsession.

Before it swallows my life completely, I need to offer special thanks to Michael Kinsley, who suggested the subject; to the Alicia Patterson Foundation, which paid for much of my research; to Frances Tenenbaum, my excellent editor; to Julia Coopersmith, my incomparable agent; to my parents, the world's best clipping service; and most of all to Ann Hodgman, my wife, who put up with everything.

All of the following were helpful above and beyond the call of duty: James Crouse, John Katzman, Adam Robinson, George Gelman, Jill Haley, Walt Haney, Douglas Porter, Warner Slack, John Weiss, Steve Solomon, Mary Ann McLean-Austen, Banesh Hoffmann, Dale Trusheim, Jan Drews, Helen Rogan, Mickey Kaus, Robert Asahina, Jefferson Morley, Tamara Glenny, Jeffrey Schaire, Jamie Baylis, James Wolcott, Alice Digilio, Dorothy Wickenden, John Owen, Cornelia Hodgman, Paul Hoffman, Rick Lyon, David White, Ruth Barton, John Marquand, and many others, some of whom can't be named.

Thanks also to the public relations staff of the College Board, whose members were often helpful and usually civil. No thanks to most of the people I dealt with at ETS, who were generally neither.

Contents

Introduction

High Anxiety

It was already evening when I suddenly remembered. I rummaged through my desk and then emptied a kitchen drawer, turning up several ambiguous candidates. Is a Woodclinched Eberhard-Faber Blackwing the same as a No. 2? My wife buys the pencils in our household, and she favors exotic leads. Suddenly gripped by an old but familiar fear, I hurried to the corner drugstore and bought a package of Harvard Squares.

College-bound high school students may have guessed the reason for my moment of panic: I had signed up to take the Scholastic Aptitude Test the following morning, and a No. 2 is the only pencil whose mark is legible to the machines that score it. The instruction sheet I had received with my admission ticket advised me to bring two No. 2's to the test. I sharpened four and put them beside my wallet on the bureau. Then I holed up in the dining room, called for silence in the apartment, and took two practice tests before I went to bed.

Early the next morning I left home without breakfast and joined two or three hundred teenagers on the sidewalk in front of Julia Richman High School on Manhattan's Upper East Side. The school is an ironic symbol of American social progress: thirty years after *Brown v. Board of Education*, Richman's students commute daily from Harlem to attend a black high school in a white neighborhood. But on days when the College Boards are given, white faces outnumber black ones. The sons and daughters of the privileged, who now attend private schools like Dalton, Trinity, and Collegiate, temporarily reclaim the building they have otherwise abandoned.

It was a frigid Saturday in December, but we weren't allowed to wait inside. Shadowy figures occasionally peered out through the grated windows. A few girls smoked cigarettes. Most of the boys just milled around. About a dozen of the sort of students who volunteer to clean erasers after class were clustered around the locked front door, perhaps hoping to secure some small advantage on the test by thawing out first. Some students thumbed through test review books. Most had come to take Achievement Tests, not SATs, and many were still trying to decide which subjects to try.* A boy standing near me said French and biology were the easiest. I patted my pencils to make sure they were still in my pocket. I was trembling slightly; was it just the cold? Finally, fifteen minutes after the announced starting time, the door creaked open and we filed inside.

There are a great many miserable experiences that adults might very well consent to relive if offered the chance — first date, high school prom, adolescence itself — but taking the Scholastic Aptitude Test is not one of them. Several years ago, *Esquire* asked me to call up a few dozen prominent media types and ask them to submit, all in good fun, to a special administration of the SAT. The idea was to find out whether New York's cultural lions were

---

*The Admissions Testing Program of the College Board, administered by ETS, comprises the two-hour Scholastic Aptitude Test (SAT), the thirty-minute Test of Standard Written English (TSWE), and fourteen one-hour Achievement Tests. The SAT, which is supposed to measure general "aptitude" for schoolwork, is almost entirely a vocabulary and arithmetic test. The Achievement Tests, which are intended to measure specific learning in thirteen subjects (there are two tests of English composition, one with a short essay and one without), are geared directly to coursework. The TSWE, which is virtually identical to the multiple-choice Achievement Test in English composition, is supposed to be used in college course placement. Most students take just the SAT and TSWE, which are given together. Applicants to very selective schools may also be required to take two or three Achievement Tests. All of these tests will be discussed in greater detail later.

really everything they were cracked up to be. *Esquire* planned to throw a big party at the Harvard Club and publish everyone's scores in what was then its annual college issue.

The project was a spectacular failure. Of all the people I talked to, only one — P. J. O'Rourke, then editor of the *National Lampoon* — agreed to take the test. Everyone else was horrified. David Halberstam: "That's the cruelest idea I ever heard of. Not since the Chinese water torture . . ." George Plimpton: "You must be crazy! I'd be too scared." Frances FitzGerald: "How simply horrid. What a horrid idea. That's a ghastly idea." Jules Feiffer: "Not on your life. Not even as a gag, not even for *money* would I do it." Susan Brownmiller: "NO!!!! I'm coasting on my high school IQ." John Simon: "It would bore me to tears." Midge Decter: "Oh, my God!" Wilfrid Sheed: "Oh, the humiliation would be too intense. Could I send my son instead?" Gail Sheehy: "Oh, Jesus! Oh, God! I don't think I can take this! I'd do anything for a cause, but I don't think I can do this!" Irving Kristol: "That is too humiliating. No! I won't! God forbid, no! It would be a *trauma*!"

It's quite astonishing, really, this fear and trembling about the SAT. The people I called were scholars and best-selling authors and winners of Pulitzer Prizes. Their careers had been enviably successful by almost anyone's definition. And yet they were afraid to take a short multiple-choice test whose content doesn't stray far beyond a high-school-level vocabulary and simple arithmetic. Surely someone like Irving Kristol, distinguished professor of social thought at New York University, would have a leg up on such a test.

But of course most people's feelings about the SAT and other standardized tests are not entirely rational. The tests have a power out of all proportion to their actual content, and they awaken smoldering insecurities in the people who take them. The intensity of their anxiety doesn't have much to do with the size of their scores. Low scorers worry that the tests are definitive and binding; high scorers worry that they are not.

For people who do poorly on standardized tests, low scores are a heavy burden. A psychoanalyst I know told me that low SAT scores are one of the most common and powerful sources of unhappiness in his young patients. A low grade in a course is just one teacher's judgment, but a low SAT score is a brand for the ages. Even when reality seems to contradict them, the numbers cast a spell of their own. I once heard a high school student refer to a bright classmate who had just scored 420 on the verbal SAT as a "retard." Before the SAT, he said, he had thought his classmate was smart. Now he knew he was dumb. The idea that the test might have been wrong never occurred to him. Most of us are insecure or uninformed enough to be cowed by measurements that seem to have the weight of science behind them.

For those who do well, high scores are an intellectual security blanket, a charm to ward off uncertainty and self-doubt. Mealtime conversation in Harvard's Freshman Union traditionally revolves around the low quality of the food and the high quality of the speakers' SAT scores. Even in adult life one occasionally encounters people who, in anxious moments, find ways of inserting their scores into casual conversation. People who can't remember their shoe size don't forget what they got on the SAT.

The inevitable corollary of test anxiety is an excessive reverence for the scores. Over the last sixty years or so, mental measurement in the United States has been less a science than a cult, a sort of secular religion. "IQ" is the psychometrician's equivalent of the soul. Our insecurity about tests gives them a mastery over us. Are we saved or damned? We defer to the tests because we think they see what we cannot.

Nearly twenty-five years ago, Banesh Hoffmann, a noted mathematician and former colleague of Albert Einstein's at the Institute for Advanced Study, unsettled the thriving measurement industry with a book called *The Tyranny of Testing*.[1] For several years, Hoffmann had been annoying his wife with complaints about multiple-choice tests, which he thought were unfair and simpleminded. She finally said that if the tests upset him so much, he ought to write something about them. He put aside his other work and wrote articles for *Harper's* and *The American Scholar*[2] that later became the basis for his book, which begins with a letter from the March 18, 1959, edition of *The Times* of London:

> Sir,——Among the "odd one out" type of questions which my son had to answer for a school entrance examination was: "Which is the odd one out among cricket, football, billiards, and hockey?"

I said billiards because it is the only one played indoors. A colleague says football because it is the only one in which the ball is not struck by an implement. A neighbour says cricket because in all the other games the object is to put the ball into a net; and my son, with the confidence of nine summers, plumps for hockey "because it is the only one that is a girl's game." Could any of your readers put me out of my misery by stating what is the correct answer, and further enlighten me by explaining how questions of this sort prove anything, especially when the scholar has merely to underline the odd one out without giving any reason?

Perhaps there is a remarkable subtlety behind it all. Is the question designed to test what a child of nine may or may not know about billiards — proficiency at which may still be regarded as the sign of a misspent youth?

Yours faithfully,
T. C. BATTY[3]

In succeeding editions, *The Times* printed numerous solutions supplied by readers: billiards, because it's the only one that's not a team sport; football, because it's the only one played with a hollow ball; billiards, because it's the only one in which the color of the balls matters; billiards, because it's the only one played with more than one ball at a time; hockey, because it's the only one that ends in a vowel.

"The question of the four sports makes a fascinating party game," Hoffmann wrote. "There are many reasons for picking the various answers, and one has only to read the questions aloud to start a party off in high gear, with everyone joining in the fun. Any number can play. There is only one drawback: after a while the fun suddenly stops and the party becomes indignantly serious. This happens as soon as someone asks what sense there is in giving children such questions on tests."[4]

Unfortunately, we tend to be better at concocting excuses for giving tests than we are at making sense of the results. A test score is a number to conjure with. We see in it what we want to see, enabling us to capture a child in a three-digit "index" or make sweeping moral judgments based on answers to a few dozen ambiguous multiple-choice questions. No one would presume to describe a child's mind in a single sentence; but a number — 124? — can say it all.

Your child's standing in the eyes of his elementary school

teachers may be determined in part by how he answers the following question from the Wechsler Intelligence Scale for Children (WISC-R), a popular IQ test published by the Psychological Corporation and used in many schools: "Why it is usually better to give money to a well-known charity than to a street beggar?" If he says, "The beggar may be rich" and "It's tax deductible" — two of several acceptable answers listed in the test's manual — he'll earn the maximum score of two points. If he is less cynical than the author of the test or if he happens to see nothing wrong with giving money to beggars — because, say, he lives in a city like New York or Philadelphia and knows that "well-known charities" don't help the homeless — he'll receive no points, and his "IQ" will be lower. Nor will he receive any points if he gives what for many people would be the only truthful answer to the question: "Because then you don't have to look the beggar in the eye."[5]

When I was in the second or third grade, a visiting graduate student tested the "intelligence" of my classmates and me by taking us aside individually and counting how many times we were able to tap one finger on a desk in the space of fifteen or thirty seconds. We never learned the results of this test. Perhaps there weren't any results. But the exercise is typical of the psychometric mentality. Faced with the baffling complexity of human thought and behavior, the testers yearn for a short cut to comprehending them, a Northwest Passage to the mind. Perhaps the most telling fact about the cult of mental measurement is that it can't define the ultimate object of its devotion. "Numerous attempts have been made to define intelligence," says one popular textbook, "yet educators and psychologists have never been able to come to complete agreement on the term or on the concepts it involves. Substantial progress has been made in the measurement of intelligence, however. . . . Actually, our definition of intelligence is circular, since we are in effect saying that intelligence is what intelligence tests measure. . . ."[6] They don't know what it is, but they're getting better and better at measuring it?

Even if they don't know what it is they're looking for, the testers know what to do when they find it. The educational futures and even the lives of millions of children are influenced by the results of tests not much more sophisticated than the finger-tapping test I was given. In some public school systems, a low score on a single IQ test can condemn a child to years in classes for the "retarded." In virtually all schools, teachers' perceptions of their students are colored by a bewildering collection of test scores whose meanings they understand dimly if at all. Many school transcripts have room for test scores but not for the full names of the tests or the dates on which they were given. Testing companies tout their products as "objective" and "scientific," but most teachers and other test users interpret scores pretty much the way phrenologists once interpreted bumps on the skull. Since not even the testers can define what they are testing, their results become a sort of mirror for the prejudices and predilections of score users.

There is no better illustration of our national test mania than the response of otherwise rational people to the decline in SAT scores that began in the early 1960s and apparently ended in the early 1980s. As the average scores dipped year after year, dozens of explanations were advanced: nuclear fallout, junk food, cigarette smoking by pregnant mothers, weather ("Every state with an average of the math and verbal SAT scores of 510 or above also had an average high temperature in January of less than 42 degrees," according to *Psychology Today*),[7] food preservatives, declining church attendance, television ("Is television a cause of the SAT score decline?" asked a College Board advisory panel in 1977, answering without hesitation, "Yes, we think it is."),[8] the military draft, the assassination of President Kennedy, the increased incidence of marriage among female teachers, communism, pornography, the NAACP, the reduced number of eldest children in the testing population, teenage alcoholism, the American Civil Liberties Union, fluoridated water, women's liberation, witches, the civil rights movement, the war in Vietnam, the increased use of anesthesia in childbirth, and hippies.[9]

The score decline was a handy symbol for anything anyone happened to believe was wrong with the world. Experts and amateurs alike read the numbers as though they were tea leaves. Some saw the scores as evidence of divine displeasure, as punishment for a decadent way of life. Others viewed them as harbingers of the impending disintegration of society. The SAT stood in silent judgment, and it clearly didn't like what it saw. Some even believed that the test had brought about its own decline, by dulling the wits, year after year, of the students required to take it.

When SAT scores "turned around" in 1982, the prophets of doom became heralds of salvation. Even though the increase was tiny — the math average rose one point on a 600-point scale; the verbal average rose two — the *New York Times* could scarcely contain itself. "The public schools are clearly paying more attention to teaching skills, discipline and quality control," declared the paper's editors. Similarly, the *Washington Post* decided that the rise in scores was "a reliable sign that young Americans are learning more of what they need to know to be productive citizens." The future, which had looked gloomy the year before, turned out to be bright after all. "There has been a marked return to required courses in place of electives, a reaffirmation of the value of science courses and a renewal of mandatory foreign language teaching in these grades," continued the *Post*, extracting richer and richer ore from the same microscopic statistic. "The folly of laissez-faire grammar and reliance on oral rather than written reports has been exposed."[10]

Despite all the fanfare, the tiny increase revealed less about the state of the schools than it did about the credulity of editorial writers. One year later, SAT soothsayers scrambled to make sense of an unexpected twist. "High school seniors," wrote the Associated Press, "scored slightly lower on the verbal half of the Scholastic Aptitude Test in 1982–83 but improved their math scores for the second consecutive year, sending mixed signals on whether public schools are really recovering."[11] Had all those new academic requirements, which the *Washington Post* had so skillfully divined, been abandoned after just one year?

And were they embraced again the following year? When verbal and math scores rose 1 and 3 points, respectively, in 1983–84, George Hanford, president of the College Board, declared, "We seem to have turned the corner in seeking to improve American education." T. H. Bell, the secretary of education, agreed. "The gain in SAT scores," he said, "reflects the movement toward excellence in our schools that is sweeping our nation." Half our nation, anyway; the math gain was accomplished almost entirely by girls. (Do only boys drink fluoridated water?)

The point is not that our schools are either better or worse than we thought they were but that the SAT is incapable of telling us much about them. The content of the test, as even ETS admits, is only minimally related to the main curricula of schools. Both the test and the test-taking population changed significantly during the course of the twenty-year decline. The drop itself was actually fairly small, working out, in the case of the verbal test, to just one additional question missed every four or five years. To the extent that the SAT score decline had anything at all to do with the deterioration of American schools, it probably underestimated it. But commentators lose all perspective when confronted by numbers they don't understand.

Keeping the numbers in perspective is very difficult. In the fall of 1983, students at Eleanor Roosevelt High School near Washington, D.C., were thrilled to discover that their school's composite SAT average was one point higher than that of rival Walt Whitman High. "We're the best — I mean, what can you say?" the president of the senior class announced. She might have been less at a loss for words if she had realized that the entire margin of difference between the two schools would have disappeared if 17 Roosevelt students (out of the 337 who took the test) had guessed wrong on one additional vocabulary question and one additional math problem.[12]

It doesn't take very long for the tests to begin to seem more important than whatever it was they were supposed to measure. At Cobb Middle School in Tallahassee, Florida, eighth-graders attended "beat the test" pep rallies before taking standardized exams in 1983. The school's principal promised to paint himself blue if scores improved and to buy pizzas and supply quarters for video games to students with perfect scores.[13] Elsewhere, teachers and school administrators improve their students' performances by shopping around for easier tests guaranteed to yield higher scores. In Dallas, where teachers are awarded $1,500 bonuses if their students' scores go up, a dozen third-grade teachers in 1984 were accused of having given their classes the answers to a standardized test. The cult of mental measurement beguiles us into forgetting that the numbers are less important than the learning they are supposed to represent.

*   *   *

This book is about standardized testing. Because the testing business is dominated, both economically and philosophically, by the Educational Testing Service, it is a book about ETS. Because ETS is best known for its Scholastic Aptitude Test, much of the book focuses on the SAT.

ETS isn't the only testing company in the world. The American College Testing Program, based in Iowa City, tests roughly the same number of college applicants as ETS, and its ACT is far and away the most popular college admissions test in some parts of the West and Midwest. For-profit companies like McGraw-Hill, the Psychological Corporation, and the company that published this book also sell tests. But none approaches ETS in size or power. From the moment of its founding in 1947, ETS has set the standards, the tone, and the agenda for standardized testing in America. More than any other organization, it has been responsible for maintaining the cult of mental measurement.

ETS is the largest testing company in the world, publishing not only the SAT but also the Graduate Record Examinations (GRE), the Graduate Management Admission Test (GMAT), the National Teacher Examinations (NTE), the National Assessment of Educational Progress (NAEP), parts of the Law School Admission Test (LSAT), and dozens of occupational certification and licensing exams used in this country and abroad. Many people think ETS is a government agency. It is not. Many others think it is a subsidiary of Princeton University. There is no connection. ETS is a private, autonomous, tax-exempt corporation whose revenues in fiscal 1983 exceeded $130 million.*[14] What started forty years ago as a small company performing a narrow service for a handful of colleges has taken on a complex and enormously powerful life of its own.

---

*ETS is classified as an "organization exempt from income tax" under section 501(c)3 of the Internal Revenue Code, which deals with schools, churches, and other organizations that function exclusively for educational, charitable, religious, scientific, or similar purposes. Such organizations are also called nonprofit because the IRS requires them to reinvest excess revenues and pay no dividends to stockholders. The only difference between profits and excess revenues is that the latter are not taxed. ETS earns substantial excess revenues on many of its programs; it retains its tax-exempt status by recycling these de facto profits into higher salaries, free housing for its presidents, public relations campaigns, lobbying, landscaping, and other activities.

Although ETS does not hire its own executives on the basis of test scores, its guiding philosophy is that people's positions in society should be determined by their scores on a series of multiple-choice tests. The company's executives believe that human superiority and inferiority can and should be measured scientifically and rewarded accordingly. In promoting this notion through the sale of its approximately five hundred different tests,[15] ETS plays a significant role in determining who gets ahead in America and who falls, or stays, behind. ETS is one of the most powerful institutions in the United States.

It is also one of the least known. Throughout its existence, ETS has insisted that its work is too complex and too important to accommodate the scrutiny of outsiders. By cloaking its exams in statistics and technical jargon, it has kept the public at a distance. Although the company's spokesmen frequently and vocally celebrate their commitment to "openness" and "public accountability," their operative attitude is that the real story of testing is none of the public's business.

In fending off unwanted public attention, ETS plays on the insecurities it cultivates. It maintains its power by manipulating anxieties. Outsiders who wonder about the quality of the tests or the motives of the test-makers are often reluctant to pursue their suspicions very far. To ask questions is to risk revealing one's own weakness. What if the test-makers respond that the surest sign of low intelligence is a propensity to doubt the results of intelligence tests?

But just as war is too important to be left to the generals, testing is too important to be left to the test-makers. We all owe it to ourselves and especially to our children to swallow our anxieties and take a look at what actually goes on behind the façade of scientific infallibility that ETS has erected between itself and the society it helps to shape. Despite ETS's protestations and assurances, an inside look at the company reveals that the test-makers aren't what they pretend to be. The scientific mystique on which their power depends is an illusion.

None of the Above

1

The Kettle Defense

THE NOT-FOR-PROFIT are different from you and me. Tennis courts, a swimming pool, a baseball diamond, a croquet lawn, a private hotel, 400 acres of woods and rolling hills, cavorting deer, a resident flock of Canada geese — I'm loving every minute here at the Educational Testing Service, the great untaxed, unregulated, unblinking eye of the American meritocracy.

Just now I'm stretched out in ETS's coed sauna, dabbing my beaded forehead with a hankie. Less than an hour ago, as the sun was sinking in the west, I stood beside the skating pond and watched a pair of distant riders cross a snowy field on horseback. In the early 1970s, ETS had plans to build a golf course here. During an hour of tramping around I managed to find neither it nor the Laurie Chauncey Nature Path, a meandering forest byway that, according to an ETS brochure, "provides an idyllic setting for a quiet stroll or conversation."[1] The late Laurie Chauncey (the beloved second wife of Henry, ETS's first president and abiding institutional deity) is immortalized not only in her sylvan jogging trail but also in Laurie House. This is an enlarged and lavishly renovated nineteenth-century dwelling that served as the Stoney Brook Hunt Club during much of the Great Depression and, after its purchase by ETS, as the Chauncey family residence from 1955 to 1970. Today Laurie House is part of the Henry Chauncey Conference Center, a hundred-room, $150-a-night convention facility whose pillowcases, bath towels, and shoeshine mitts are emblazoned with ETS insignia and whose rooms are decorated with artwork of the signed and numbered variety. Guests at the conference center are invited to enjoy both "a variety of potables" and "a proud selection of comestibles," the splendor of the latter being "limited only by a client's imagination."[2]

In the innocence of youth, a No. 2 pencil trembling in my fingers, I pictured the Educational Testing Service not as the passable vacation spot it is but as a dusty, cramped, and spinster-staffed department of Princeton University. In truth, ETS owes Princeton only the scholarly heft of its return address, which itself is a mere postal courtesy: ETS's rustic headquarters actually lie in Lawrence Township, not in Princeton.* Nor are the company's employees the crotchety old maids I once imagined; they're smooth-talking ministers of mental measurement, people who more than once have taken solemn pleasure in describing their company as "the nation's gatekeeper."[3]

The business of deciding who goes where in American society is so vast and various that during peak grading season, ETS's "scanners," the machines that automatically score answer sheets at the rate of 200 sides a minute, are never turned off. Day after day, night after night, ETS's computers process an unceasing stream of information, giving the company one of the largest compilations of private data about individuals in the world. "Maybe only the C.I.A. has greater and better capacities," an ETS memorandum once asserted with pride.[4]

The Central Intelligence Agency may have greater capacities, but even that resourceful institution knows when it needs outside help. The CIA buys tests from ETS. So do the Defense Department, the National Security Council, the government of Trinidad and Tobago, the Institute for Nuclear Power Operations, the National Contact Lens Examiners, the International Council for Shopping Centers, the American Society of Heating, Refrigerating and Air-Conditioning Engineers, the Commission on Graduates of Foreign Nursing Schools, the Wood Heating Education and Re-

---

*A great many people who ought to know better, including a substantial number of teachers, test-takers, and even admissions officers, actually believe there is some connection between the company and the university. ETS had an office in the town of Princeton many years ago, but its continued use of the name is strictly for public relations.

search Foundation, the Malaysian Ministry of Education, the Institute of International Container Lessors, the National Board of Podiatry Examiners, the American Society of Plumbing Engineers, and the Institute for the Advancement of Philosophy for Children.[5]

You can't become a golf pro without passing an ETS exam; sample item: "The distance from the center line of a shaft hole to the farthest front portion of the face is the (A) hosel offset (B) loft (C) lie (D) face progression (E) length."* In at least some parts of the country you also can't become a real estate salesman, a certified moving consultant, a certified auto mechanic, a merchant marine officer (the same holds true in Liberia), a fireman, a policeman, a travel agent ("with the ultimate expectation of improving public confidence in the travel industry," according to ETS),[6] a certified business form consultant, or, in Pennsylvania, a beautician or a barber.

Old-fashioned thinkers may wonder whether a multiple-choice test is really a better measure of barbering skills than a haircut, or what great social cost would be exacted if a few untutored individuals were suffered to trim the sideburns of Pennsylvanians. But no such befuddlement hampers executives at ETS. A company pamphlet makes prominent mention of the barber exam as well as tests for, among others, office managers, architects, social workers, and gynecologists.

Over the years, ETS has made wider and wider forays beyond the limits of its original mission. Many profitable programs have little or nothing to do with testing. One division designs routes for school buses. Another helps teachers and school districts decide what kind of personal computer software to buy. Another sells a computerized guidance counseling program called System of Interactive Guidance & Information (SIGI, pronounced "Siggy"), which asks students about their interests and then suggests careers. (SIGI has a special fondness for certain occupations; it told both ETS president Gregory R. Anrig and me that we ought to be clergymen.) ETS also receives substantial funding from the federal

*Answer: D.

government and various foundations in the form of grants, test purchases, and research contracts. Past research projects have included "Sex Chromosome Anomalies in a Male Prison Population," "Relationship of Height to Anti-Social Behavior," and a study indicating that although it will stare at either, a baby will smile more at a normal face than at a cyclops.[7]

The single largest program at ETS, in terms of candidate volume, has nothing at all to do with testing. This is the College Scholarship Service (CSS). In 1983, CSS published and processed 2.6 million Financial Aid Forms (FAF) and other applications for institutional, state, and federal aid, including scholarships, grants, and loans. The forms, which require total financial disclosure, are analyzed by ETS employees, who calculate "the level of each applicant's need" and forward this estimate to colleges and government agencies.[8]

CSS not only provides substantial revenue[9] but also produces one of the largest collections of financial information about American citizens. This information, which is stored on computer tape at ETS, includes balances of savings and checking accounts, previous year's income, medical and dental expenses, welfare benefits, disability payments, rent, investments, and cash gifts from grandparents.

Another nontesting program is the Student Search Service (SSS). Through SSS, ETS collects information about participants in its Admissions Testing Program and sells it to colleges, foundations, military recruiters, and other "institutions, consortia, and scholarship agencies." For $150 per search plus 14 cents per name, customers can buy lists of students broken down according to any combination of more than a dozen characteristics, including sex, grade level, Zip Code, SAT or PSAT scores, high school grades, financial background, inclination to live in a dormitory, intended major, and race.[10] SSS customers have even used the service specifically to buy mailing lists from which blacks and other minorities have been deleted.[11] Additions to SSS this year will allow customers to select students by religion as well.

Students are included in SSS only if they consent beforehand, but ETS is considerably less than candid about the true nature of the program. Nowhere, for example, are students told that the information they supply will be *sold*. In the 1983–84 *Student Bulletin* for the SAT and Achievement Tests, students are told only that the names and addresses of SSS participants may be "given" to colleges and scholarship programs.[12] In fact, ETS earns substantial profits from SSS by selling this information — after making students pay (through test fees) for the privilege of providing it.[13]

ETS also misleads students about the nature of the information it supplies to SSS customers. In the questionnaire used to compile the SSS data base, students are asked if they "plan to apply for financial aid at any college" and are told that their answers "will not be included in the reports that are sent to you, your school, and the colleges you designate." They are also asked to estimate, in consultation with their parents, their family's pre-tax income from the year before and to state how many people depend on their parents for support and how many of those dependents are in college. "Your individual responses," ETS assures students, "will not be reported to anyone. Only summary responses for groups of students will be reported to colleges and high schools." Furthermore, ETS says, this summary information will be used only "for research and planning by educational institutions."[14] But this is quite misleading. ETS uses precisely this information to arrive at an "estimated annual parental contribution" figure *for each student in SSS;* it then sells student lists based on *its own estimate* of the student's family's ability to pay for a college education.[15]

ETS has big plans for the future. Its researchers are working on a computerized version of the SAT that will take only a few minutes to administer. "We have the technology virtually ready to go," an ETS executive said in 1982. "We expect we're going to be getting rapidly out of the paper transfer business." President Anrig is looking forward to a day when Americans will be able to take ETS tests on their television sets. Other people at ETS are working on computerized teaching programs that will make the testing company a powerful presence in the schools, enabling it both to teach what it tests and to test what it teaches. Still others are tinkering with scoring systems that will replace numbers with "narrative," providing test-takers with computer-written paragraphs detailing all there is to know about their "aptitude." The day is coming, the company hopes, when you'll hardly be able to get out of your bed without some ETS statistician offering his considered opinion on whether you've really got what it takes.

Historically and in spirit, ETS is a product of the American Century (circa 1945–1973). When returning soldiers besieged American campuses at the end of World War II, the College Entrance Examination Board, an institution that since 1901 had been quietly giving an admissions test for a few selective colleges, found itself with more testing traffic than it could handle. In 1947 it got together with the American Council on Education and the Carnegie Foundation for the Advancement of Teaching and created the nonprofit Educational Testing Service to take care of the new demand.

In the beginning, ETS was a nickel-and-dime operation that did little more than administer the College Board's Scholastic Aptitude Test, which in 1948 was taken by 75,000 students. But ETS grew quickly and soon dwarfed its parent. (Today many people at ETS privately refer to the Board as though it were some mildly retarded younger brother, only reluctantly included in big-boy games.) Although ETS executives like to claim that, insofar as the Admissions Testing Program is concerned, their company is merely the humble servant of the Board, in fact virtually all of the power is held by ETS. In the confidential contract between the two organizations, the Board agrees to give ETS up to three and a half years' notice before taking its business elsewhere (a possibility a Board president once described as "so hypothetical and improbable that it's not worth discussing").[16] The Board pays all of ETS's expenses in the programs for which it contracts, and it guarantees a fixed profit margin plus an escalating incentive bonus based on test volume.[17]

The contract also gives ETS "authority and primary responsibility" not only for "design, prototype development, and operation of programs and services" but also for "the monitoring of ETS performance in the field."[18] In other words, ETS itself is responsible for determining whether it is living up to its contractual obligations. Naturally ETS approves of its performance, and of the College Board's as well, and the College Board approves of ETS.

Indeed, the two organizations spend an extraordinary amount of time and money patting each other on the back and whispering sweet nothings in each other's ears. In 1971, in a "technical report" on the College Board paid for and published by the Board itself but actually written by ETS, a pair of ETS researchers went so far as to quote a forty-five-year-old College Board annual report (which had concluded that the College Board's own SAT "does contribute something to the prediction of college grades") as evidence that the SAT, now written and administered for the College Board by ETS, had consistently "demonstrated that it makes a unique contribution to the prediction of college success."[19] In other words, ETS, under the sponsorship of the Board, was praising itself by praising the Board for praising *it*self in regard to a test now produced for the Board by ETS.

ETS is a monopoly, probably the most powerful unregulated monopoly in America. People who wish to advance in almost all walks of life have no choice but to pay its fees and take its tests. Corporations and institutions with far less power have had to submit, in the public interest, to government regulation over the last half century, but ETS has managed to resist, flourish, and spread into markets where none but the brave would have imagined a need to exist.

ETS had tax-free revenues of $133 million in fiscal 1983, nearly half of it from College Board programs alone.[20] Virtually all of these proceeds (not to mention most of the College Board's own substantial revenues) came from people required to pay for the privilege of submitting to multiple-choice examinations in order to pass various checkpoints in America's social hierarchy.

As a "nonprofit" institution, ETS does not make profits as such. But the company's revenues support a very comfortable life and generous salaries for many of its 2,200 employees. Gregory Anrig, who was paid $70,790 in his first year as president, received a 54 percent raise the next year, bringing his salary to $109,055 in fiscal 1982.*[21] He also received $37,930 worth of fringe benefits from ETS's "flexible" benefits program, a comprehensive plan based on half a dozen mandatory perks and as many as seventeen

---

*This number is from the IRS. ETS wouldn't tell me Anrig's current salary.

optional ones, including tax shelters, dental insurance, and day care.[22] In testimony before a 1979 joint hearing of the committees on higher education of the New York State Senate and Assembly, a former ETS executive described the company as "an educational country club" designed to "pamper over-priced researchers who sit all day and contemplate their psychometric navels."[23]

Forbes magazine called ETS "one of the hottest little growth companies in U.S. business" in 1976.[24] The ETS staff includes a large crew of full-time groundskeepers whose duties range from maintaining the pristine state of the turf jogging trails to skimming leaves from the swimming pool to tending bushes "selected for their ability to attract songbirds."[25] Employees eat subsidized meals in the company cafeteria. Top executives and distinguished guests can make use of the company's chauffeured motor pool. In 1973, at test-taker expense, ETS built its president, William Turnbull, a $150,000 house whose "extravagant use of glass makes the most of its five acres of woodland."[26] Turnbull was grateful, although the house was and is a public relations embarrassment for ETS. When I tried to find out whether Anrig lives in it now, I was told that this information was not "easily and publicly available."[27]

The most conspicuous addition to the ETS country club was the construction, for $3 million in 1973, of the Henry Chauncey Conference Center, the ETS hotel. When it was first reported — by Steven Brill in *New York* magazine in 1974[28] — that ETS intended to embellish the facility with a golf course, tennis courts, and a swimming pool, ETS responded testily that these amenities appeared "only on an early conceptual site plan done by the landscape architect" and that ETS had no intention of building them.[29] The company changed its mind almost immediately. Today the tennis courts (which are lighted for nighttime play) and the swimming pool not only exist but also brighten the complimentary color postcards that ETS supplies to its guests. The golf course, it is true, has yet to materialize, but ETS's failure to build it should not be viewed as a judgment on the game. A photograph in a conference center promotional brochure depicts a trim sportsman hitting cleanly out of shallow rough on one of the "challenging golf courses a few minutes away." Another photograph shows two guests "bicycling through the spacious campus" on bicycles provided by ETS.[30]

ETS's extravagance with test fees seldom extends beyond its own capacious boundaries. In 1974, the company tried to win a reduction in Mercer County property taxes by claiming that 160 of its 400 acres were "actively devoted" to agriculture and thus were covered by the Farmland Assessment Act. "Who says it's not a farm?" read the caption under a photograph of a field, published under a banner headline on page 1 of the company's in-house newspaper. "Photo shows scene on Rosedale acreage as the 1973 crop of hay was being baled for sale." ETS's attorneys appealed the county's ruling that, in the words of the newspaper, "ETS' primary purpose is educational testing and research and that any farming use is strictly incidental."[31]

Anrig is fond of saying that ETS, unlike certain other institutions that pay no income taxes, "has no endowment, no alumni, and no legislature to call upon for funds."[32] But this is not the case. At the end of 1983, ETS had a de facto endowment of $32 million in cash, stocks, and other investments and owned an additional $25 million in property, plant, and equipment.* It had $2.7 million in unspent revenues for the year, a figure that would have been several times higher if ETS were less extravagant with landscaping, legal fees, lobbying expenses, and frivolous research.[34] ETS has also developed a vast "alumni" network of loyal teachers, professors, and administrators through generous "consulting fees" for its various tests. Former ETS employees abound in the membership of the American Psychological Association, the staffs of other testing companies, university psychology departments, and

---

*Both these numbers are grossly understated, since the investment figure is based on the lower of purchase price or current market, and the property value reflects depreciation for prime real estate that has, of course, appreciated dramatically in the years ETS has owned it. I requested a list of ETS's investments and their current market value, but my request was denied. Even unadjusted, though, the portfolio total does not support Anrig's plea of poverty. According to the National Association of College and University Business Officers, only 116 colleges and universities in 1983 had endowments of more than $32 million. ETS is better endowed than the University of Maryland, Sweet Briar, Reed, Wheaton, Hollins, Connecticut College, Cornell College, Temple, the University of Arizona, Kenyon, Drake, Skidmore, and the University of Massachusetts, to name but a few.[33] Not bad, particularly when you consider that ETS doesn't have to spend a dime on students, athletic teams, dormitories, or scholarships.

other key outposts of the psychometric establishment. And since ETS applies for more than a hundred government contracts each year, it actively lobbies legislators and agency officials; indeed, the company maintains an office in Washington specifically for this purpose.[35] ETS also entertains influential public officials at the Chauncey conference center.

Maintaining this comfortable empire has become a matter of increasingly frank concern at ETS in recent years. After decades of uninterrupted growth in tax-free revenues, ETS suffered its first small deficit in fiscal 1980. The company has more than made up for the shortfall in every year since, but that brief encounter with red ink put the fear of the almighty dollar into ETS executives. The company substantially reduced its research staff in a series of large-scale firings and eliminated an entire layer of vice presidents. As recently as four or five years ago, ETS executives were known to grow pale if unthinking workers described their employer as a "company" instead of an "institution." But in 1982 President Anrig inaugurated his term of office by commissioning a $500,000 "strategic plan" from Booz, Allen & Hamilton, a New York management consulting firm.[36] In connection with the study, Anrig divided ETS personnel into a dozen "revenue growth teams" charged with identifying new opportunities for short-term profits.[37] Anrig also issued a confidential Corporate Plan, calling for, among other things, "corporate intelligence gathering, external relations and government relations focused to provide a positive climate and receptive clients for ETS marketing initiatives."[38]

ETS's unabashed hunger for new profits comes at a time when it is facing its first sustained public criticism in areas it had come to believe were sacrosanct: the quality, meaning, and application of its tests. Vocal critics of standardized testing have been around for years, arguing that tests like the SAT measure little more than the absorption of white upper-middle-class culture and penalize both the economically disadvantaged and the unusually bright. But the recent onslaught caught ETS by surprise.

In 1967, researchers at the University of Michigan discovered a blood test that appeared to be better than the SAT at determining which students would ultimately graduate from school.[39] In 1974, Steven Brill (at the time a student at Yale Law School, now editor of the *American Lawyer*) wrote a devastating article for *New York* magazine in which he described ETS as "a classic model of unaccountable power."[40] (In a confidential memo four years later, ETS president Turnbull dismissed Brill's article as "the first clear expression of the mood of an extremist fringe against ETS *per se*.")[41] The Federal Trade Commission released a report taking issue with ETS's long-standing claim that the SAT could not be coached.[42] A young researcher named Allan Nairn, backed with funding from Ralph Nader, published a scathing 500-plus-page report that accused ETS of, among a great many other things, lying to consumers and grossly misrepresenting its tests.[43] (Nairn's preliminary findings, though roundly denied by ETS, had led directly to the passage of New York's "truth-in-testing" law in 1979.) In 1980, two professors at Harvard Medical School published an article in the *Harvard Educational Review* that disputed ETS's assertions about coaching and test validity and insinuated strongly that ETS had intentionally doctored research findings to make the case for the SAT look stronger than it was.[44]

Several ETS employees told me that they resented the tendency of people like Nairn and Nader to compare ETS to the CIA. But readers with above-average verbal aptitude will remember that the CIA comparison I quoted earlier originated not with a detractor but with ETS itself. In fact, ETS has always cultivated this image, presenting itself as an organization whose work passeth all understanding and whose methodology is not only above reproach but also exempt from public scrutiny. In 1979 it published a pamphlet called *The War on Testing,* in which criticism of standardized tests was referred to as "an attack on truth itself."[45]

Because this aura of mystery is so important to ETS, the greatest blow came in 1979, when New York State passed its "truth-in-testing" law, known formally as the Educational Testing Act of 1979. This law required ETS and other test-makers to release test questions and graded answer sheets to students who take certain standardized tests in New York State. Until 1980, when the law went into effect, no one besides the testing companies could check whether the scores that could determine people's places in life had even been added up correctly, let alone whether the questions were faulty. The legislation also required the test-makers to publish information about the "validity" of their exams, about the meaning of the scores, and about the method by which the scores had been derived.

While the bill was being considered, ETS and the College Board pelted college presidents, high school principals, headmasters, and legislators with letters, mailgrams, and phone calls warning of dire results that would ensue if the New York legislature had its way.* "This bill represents a serious assault on the objectivity and fairness of the admissions process," declared an "urgent" mailgram from the president of the College Board to the chief executive officers of all New York State colleges and universities. ". . . Your immediate and forceful action is needed."[47] In a lengthy and sharply worded "Memorandum of Opposition," ETS declared that passage of the bill would result in "increasingly costly test development procedures, a concomitant loss of service to candidates, increasing fees for tests, and a possible diminution in the quality of the tests themselves."[48] Lest this message fail to seep in, ETS and the College Board also hired a team of high-priced lobbyists.

One year before, in the face of what he called "angry, hostile, and sometimes paranoid attacks on testing and on ETS," President Turnbull had prepared a confidential memo recommending, among other things, the expansion of the company's Washington lobbying office and the expenditure of $450,000 in test-takers' fees on public relations during the next three years.[49] (ETS actually spent $620,170 on lobbying against truth-in-testing alone during those three years.)[50] Turnbull's strategy also called for the development of various "demonstration projects," which would prove to the public that tests weren't so bad after all. One of these was intended to cast light on "ambiguity and error" in tests by pointing out that flaws also existed "in a variety of human 'measurements,' from dental cavities to golf scores."[51]

ETS's most compelling charge against truth-in-testing was that

---

*Shortly after the New York law was passed, Lois D. Rice of the College Board sent a letter to U.S. Congresswoman Shirley Chisholm, asserting that passage of a *national* truth-in-testing law, which was being considered at the time, might even imperil "the national goal of equalizing educational opportunity."[46]

disclosing SATs and other tests would lead to huge increases in fees and a sharp reduction in the number of testing dates, since ETS would no longer be able to reuse questions. In testimony before senate and assembly committees, representatives of ETS and the College Board gravely warned that test fees might swell by 50 percent or more. ETS and the College Board consistently portrayed themselves as defenders of the decent common folk, who take their tests without complaining and don't ask questions about the results. Barbara Demick, writing in *The New Republic,* quoted a memo in which the College Board argued that "truth-in-testing will only advantage — if it advantages anybody at all — aggressive families whose indignation at low reported scores will impose a higher cost on all other families."[52] This notion — that the only real supporters of the legislation were the pushy parents of grade-grubbing high school students — became one of the enduring themes of the campaign to stop the bill.

But ETS's frantic warnings about the financial impact of truth-in-testing were based on little more than the fertile imaginings of its public relations officers. ETS representatives made shocking claims and promised to supply supporting documents, then dragged their feet. In the end they were defeated by their own statistics. Allan Nairn produced a 1972 ETS Activity Analysis showing that the development cost of the SAT amounted to less than 6 percent of student fees: "In the case of the 1970–71 [College Board] tests studied by the Activity Analysis, $.93 of the candidate's $5.75 test fee went to ETS–College Board profit, a margin of 16%. This profit was more than four times larger than the $.23 spent on question writing and nearly three times larger than the $.32 spent for all test development costs."[53] Furthermore, a confidential ETS study in 1977 showed that test development for the 1976 Admissions Testing Program had amounted to less than 3 percent of total expenses, or 17 cents per candidate.[54] Lewis W. Pike, the former head of verbal aptitude test development at ETS, wrote a letter to New York State Senator Kenneth P. LaValle, chief sponsor of the bill, confirming that "item-writing costs are but a small proportion of the total tests costs passed on to the consumer (the college applicant)."[55]

Other ETS positions crumbled in a similar fashion. In an undated memorandum submitted to the legislature, the company had asserted that the law's disclosure provisions would pose an insurmountable burden on limited resources. "Contrary to myth," the document stated, "there is no vast storehouse or computer full of appropriate secure test questions waiting to be placed on a test. Questions must be written and tests assembled by individuals with training and experience in test development as well as appropriate subject fields. It is not, for example, possible to use the same question for both the SAT and the LSAT."[56] Nairn countered this claim with a passage from the very manual used by ETS's test development staff: "Much of the strength and versatility of ETS as a testing organization lies in its 'pool' of more than 300,000 test items, most of which are ETS-owned and available within the limits of certain overlap restrictions, for use in programs other than those for which they were originally developed."[57] Even so, ETS eventually admitted that it seldom reused test questions after all.*

In testimony before New York State legislators, ETS executive vice president Robert J. Solomon said that "the development of tests is a laborious process that requires the scholarly and technical skills of a variety of people, including panels of teachers, men and women, minority and majority, for each of the subject areas, including, of course, teachers from schools and colleges in New York State who help design the tests and write the questions."[59] At one point, ETS said that writing a test item involved "as many as 100 different steps over a period of 24 months";[60] on another occasion, this process was said to require "150" steps.[61] However, five years earlier — before the threat of truth-in-testing — ETS had painted a very different picture. Nairn produced the transcript of an interview with an ETS test development executive named Marion Epstein, who revealed that test construction was handled almost exclusively by a small staff of mostly part-time personnel. In fact, Epstein said, "a couple of people could write all of the ques-

---

*ETS went to extraordinary lengths before giving any ground on this issue. At one point it argued that writing new questions for tests in specific subject areas would be impossible because "there is a finite body of knowledge to be tested" and that this body of knowledge might be exhausted "over a period of five to ten years."[58] But confidential ETS documents proved that despite its anxieties about depleting the world's knowledge reserves, the company had been filling examinations with new questions for years.

tions" for all forms of the SAT, both math and verbal, in any given year.[62]

ETS and the College Board sometimes had trouble remembering exactly why they were upset. In a memorandum labeled URGENT and dated May 11, 1979, the College Board alleged that "the bill encroaches on institutional autonomy by requiring testing agencies to disclose confidential information, such as validity information, which is the property of the colleges and universities."*[63] A year before, however, in a memorandum opposing similar legislation in California, ETS had argued that a provision requiring the release of validity information was unnecessary because "most of that information has been made available by ETS for years."[64]

Both ETS and the College Board consistently misrepresented key provisions of the law. In a statement dated May 1, 1979, the Board said, "The reuse of test questions is necessary to 'tie' the scoring of different forms of the test to the standard score scale — a statistical process known as equating. These procedures are critical to producing examinations that are constructed, administered, scored and evaluated *in the same way for everybody*"[65] (emphasis in original). But the law stated explicitly — and the College Board was fully aware — that all such "equating" items were exempt from disclosure. Even so, the Board and ETS made this objection, and similar ones, again and again. ETS and its representatives also claimed repeatedly that the bill covered "any standardized test given in the State of New York," when in fact the only tests covered were those used in "post-secondary or professional school admissions."[66]

"It was a comedy of errors," says Mary Ann McLean-Austen, a legislative assistant to Senator LaValle. "ETS had these poor lobbyists running around with no information. They would make these statements, and then Allan, who had real information, would counter what they had said. They had to spend all their time on the telephone to Princeton, saying, 'Okay, he just said this; what do I say now?' "

*   *   *

*This was a curious charge in itself, since the studies in question are paid for entirely out of test-takers' fees and are provided free of charge, along with reams of other information, to the colleges and universities that want them. If validity studies are the property of anyone, they are the property of the students who pay for them.

Having predicted the collapse of civilization if the truth-in-testing law passed, ETS did not, in the event, collapse itself. In fact, it adapted easily. The SAT fee in New York is only 50 cents higher than in other states. ETS and the College Board claim that this surcharge is needed to cover the cost of complying with the law. But this is not true. In 1982–83, the New York surcharge produced $106,632 in extra revenues for ETS and the College Board. During the same period, ETS spent $176,274 lobbying against truth-in-testing laws in other states. If ETS had simply ceased fighting the law, it could have *reduced* the fee for the SAT by a small amount and charged New Yorkers the same fee it charged everyone else.[67]

Smiling ETS executives today talk about truth-in-testing as though it had been their idea in the first place.* They claim that ETS's furious response was the work of a few excitable individuals and not representative of the company as a whole. This argument is not persuasive to anyone who has sifted through the bales of official documents that ETS and the College Board churned out while the bill was being considered. In fact, ETS still hands out a pamphlet, published in 1981 (more than a year after the bill went into effect), that purports to tell "the truth about truth-in-testing." The pamphlet, which is printed in the form of a multiple-choice test, points out, among other things, that less than 2 percent "of students identifying themselves as black, Mexican-American or Puerto Rican have requested copies of their SAT questions and answers," a statistic intended to demonstrate that the law has been a failure (and one perhaps not entirely unrelated to the fact that ETS charges $7 for every such report). To the last question in the brochure — "Should other states considering legislation similar to the New York State testing law approve it?" — ETS offers only one possible response: "(A) The only reasonable answer is 'no.' "[70]

ETS has responded to every challenge to its mission and methods in the same way it responded to truth-in-testing. This

---

*ETS president Turnbull spoke the truth when, a few months after ETS had failed in its attempt to have the new law vetoed, he told the readers of *The New Republic* that it would "come as a surprise" to them "that ETS fully supports the objectives of the New York state testing law to inform students and the public about admissions tests."[68] During the next two years, ETS spent $515,113 lobbying againt precisely these objectives.[69]

response takes the form of a series of contradictory assertions, known to lawyers as "arguing in the alternative." A man is accused of borrowing and breaking his neighbor's kettle. His lawyer argues in his defense: (1) my client didn't take the kettle; (2) it was already broken when he took it; (3) he returned it in perfect condition. Whatever the issue, ETS argues: (1) it has done nothing wrong; (2) it has already fixed the problem; (3) nothing has changed. Truth-in-testing makes this elusive stance increasingly hard to maintain.

It would be impolitic for ETS, as a semipublic institution, to refuse all outside scrutiny. But the company is extremely cautious about outsiders, particularly those known to be critical of its policies and procedures. "I see no reason why we should give information unless we can be assured you're not going to write a critical article," ETS corporate secretary Jane Wirsig told Steven Brill in 1974.[71] When, several months after my *Harper's* article had been published in 1983,[72] I mentioned in a letter that I was now writing a book about ETS and that I would "gladly make myself available to any and all ETS representatives who take issue with my article," President Anrig sent a confidential memo to his executives asking them to tell their staffs not to engage in "any further communication with Mr. Owen" and to report either to him or to the company's Information Division "if any inquiry is received."[73]

Even before this ban, when I visited ETS headquarters to research my *Harper's* article, I was accompanied on all my interviews by at least one emissary from the Information Division, who generally took copious notes. Employees of the Information Division do not hesitate to inject themselves into conversations if they perceive that the actual interviewee is being insufficiently ingenious in his defense of his employer. After a while I almost expected passing secretaries to come sailing through open doorways, thrusting sheaves of paper at me and saying, "What he *really* means is . . ." When I interviewed Anrig himself, I was preceded by a bundle of my previous magazine articles, which someone in Information had dutifully dug up. Anrig had also requested a list of the questions I intended to ask him. I replied that ETS doesn't hand out its questions ahead of time, and neither do I.

2

Holistic Grading

THE OLDEST CONTROVERSY involving ETS concerns the soundness of multiple-choice tests. Without such tests, which can be graded by machines, testing millions of people every year would be impossible and ETS would go out of business. More important, widespread acceptance of standardized testing depends on the perception that it is scientifically neutral and objective, which only a test with "right" and "wrong" answers can be.

The original College Boards were lengthy essay tests. The multiple-choice Scholastic Aptitude Test was added to the program in 1926 in response to a sudden popular and academic fascination with intelligence testing. Essays were dropped altogether in 1942. The ostensible reason was that the outbreak of World War II had made it difficult to recruit graders, but the College Board had been considering the move for years, and it had no intention of reinstating written examinations when the war ended. "The passing of the . . . essay-type examination after continuous use for forty-one years marks the end of an era so far as the history of the Board is concerned," reported the executive secretary in 1942. The old exams were simply too difficult to produce and too expensive to grade.[1]

Despite their entirely pragmatic motive for abandoning written examinations, ETS and the College Board have frequently claimed that multiple-choice tests are more than merely convenient. In a 1955 booklet called *College Board Scores: Their Use and Interpretation,* Henry S. Dyer and Richard G. King of ETS wrote that a well-made multiple-choice test, "by forcing the student to consider many different kinds of tasks, can often provide a more adequate sample of his mental processes than is provided by an essay test in which the student may steer around logical problems he finds not to his liking."[2] ETS and the College Board have put forth similar arguments at regular intervals. Both organizations have repeatedly implied that even if all testing methods were equally convenient and equally inexpensive, the ideal examination would still be multiple-choice.

ETS and the College Board have always found this easier to believe than teachers have. At times the controversy has become quite heated. In 1943, responding to teachers who had criticized the new policy, John M. Stalnaker — who had worked on the project to develop the SAT — asserted not only that essay tests were flawed but even that essay writing itself wasn't all it was cracked up to be: "The type of test so highly valued by teachers of English, which requires the candidate to write a theme or essay, is not a worth-while testing device. Whether or not the writing of essays as a means of teaching writing deserves the place it has in the secondary school curriculum may be equally questioned."[3]

Teachers balked at this notion. Hoping to appease them, ETS and the College Board experimented fitfully with several kinds of essay examination — a single one-hour essay; three twenty-minute essays; four fifteen-minute paragraphs — but concluded that all were worthless. For a time, ETS placed great hopes on a "semiobjective" test called the interlinear exercise. This test, which appeared as a section in a multiple-choice examination called the English Composition Achievement Test (ECT), "required the candidates to edit (between the printed lines) an expository passage into which had been introduced certain types of errors."[4] Teachers complained that proofreading was not the same thing as writing, and the interlinear exercise eventually went the way of the fifteen-minute paragraph.

Despite the assurances of experts at ETS, educators found it hard to believe that a multiple-choice test could really be a better measure of essay-writing ability than writing an essay was. How could you test a student's composition skill without having him compose something? The grumbling continued and, in 1951, ETS and the College Board gave in. They created a two-hour essay examination called the General Composition Test (GCT) and, against their better judgment, offered it alongside the multiple-choice ECT, which they had been giving since 1942.

In 1954, dissatisfied with this compromise, ETS and the College Board designed a three-year experiment to compare the GCT with both the ECT and the verbal portion of the SAT. These three tests were judged against general essay-writing ability as measured over a year or more by the actual teachers of the students taking the tests.[5]

Now, ETS has long held that teachers' opinions are deceptive, since they are highly subjective and reflect all sorts of unconscious prejudices and expectations. This, indeed, is the justification for giving SATs. But, faced with the need to measure the tests against something, ETS had nowhere else to turn.

In 1957, when ETS tallied the results of its experiment, the all-essay GCT, as ETS had predicted, came in last. The two multiple-choice tests, the verbal SAT and the ECT, came in first and second, respectively. ETS and the College Board announced the findings triumphantly, shelved the GCT, and proceeded as before.

But there was something very odd about these results, as Banesh Hoffmann pointed out a few years later. If the experiment proved to ETS's satisfaction that its multiple-choice ECT was better than an essay test, it also proved that the verbal part of the SAT was a better test of English composition than the ECT.[6] Yet ETS continued to administer the ECT (to customers who'd already paid to take the SAT), perhaps realizing that if necessary an experiment could be devised to demonstrate the superiority of the ECT. ETS is singularly adept at proving the excellence of whatever test it happens to be peddling at the moment, even if these proofs perforce contradict one another.

Extremism in the defense of multiple-choice tests is no vice at ETS. In 1961, a company researcher named Orville Palmer went so far as to argue that performance on essay tests "all too often will correlate poorly or even negatively" with actual essay-writing ability. In other words, according to Palmer, it all too often happens that the better a student is at writing essays, the worse his essays will be.[7]

But even in Palmer's day the tide had begun to turn. In the mid-1960s, in order to justify including a brief essay section in the ECT, ETS conducted an experiment that proved essay tests were valuable after all.[8] This was especially welcome news, because ETS had been giving an essay test, called the Writing Sample, since 1960. The Writing Sample wasn't graded; ETS had proved that a grade on a single writing sample wasn't reliable. Student compositions were merely passed along to college admissions officers, an arrangement that made students unhappy, according to the College Board, "because in many instances they did not know what happened to the Writing Samples at the colleges."[9] Then, three years after proving the value of essay tests, ETS stopped offering the Writing Sample. (The new version of the ECT, which this most recent experiment had been designed to justify, was abandoned in 1971.)

As the years went by, ETS retreated to the position that multiple-choice tests were only *just as good* as essay tests, and it offered new experimental results to prove it. So, having once proved that a multiple-choice test was better than an essay test, it now set out to demonstrate that the two were exactly the same.* In a 1980 article James Fallows wrote: "Hunter Breland, an ETS research psychologist, explained that to get statistically reliable results from an essay exam, students had to write five separate essays, with five readers each. 'We found we could do as well with fifty multiple choice questions in a thirty-minute test,' Breland said. '*We got the same people in the same order*' " (emphasis added).[11]

The same people in the same order? This must be a typical ETS exaggeration. After all, ETS itself calculates that one SAT-taker in three will score more than 33 points higher or lower than his hypothetical "true score" on any given test. (See Chapters 4 and 10.) Not even two administrations of the SAT would produce "the

---

*In the 1964 *LSAT Handbook*, ETS made the same statement in a very different way, saying that experiments in measuring writing ability with essay examinations had shown "no better results" than similar studies using multiple-choice questions, which is what the LSAT had. Of course, saying that an essay test is "no better" than a multiple-choice one implies that there might be reasons for being dissatisfied with the latter, as the *Handbook*'s authors readily acknowledged. "The act of writing," they concluded, "is far too complicated to be adequately measured in the time and with the testing methods now available." This is something ETS was otherwise reluctant to admit.[10]

same people in the same order." And in a full-scale experiment with two different measures—essay and multiple-choice—the differences would be even greater, since different kinds of tests involve different kinds of measurement error. Hunter Breland, it seems, was trying to make his argument sound stronger than it was.*

But let's ignore this point and address Breland's major assertion, that a statistically reliable essay exam requires five separate essays, each one to be evaluated by five graders.

Strange to report, ETS for years has been giving tests that violate Breland's standard. In 1977, it began to offer, once a year, an optional version of the ECT, with one graded twenty-minute essay in place of some of the usual multiple-choice items. This essay is graded not by the five readers Breland calls for but by two. Both versions of the test last an hour overall, and scores on both are reported as single numerical grades on ETS's familiar 600-point (200–800) scale. On tests with an essay, the essay counts for one third of the score.

Contrary to what you may believe, ETS essay tests are not graded by Irving Howe, Northrop Frye, and whatever other distinguished scholars happen to be passing through New Jersey at scoring time. In fact, ECTs are graded by high school and college English teachers from around the country who are lured to Lawrence Township every year by the prospect of spending five days in a gymnasium reading 1,500 or so one-page adolescent responses to a single question in return for $310. Being selected as an ETS reader carries a certain cachet in the educational world, and many of these readers are enormously dedicated. Some are even required by their school boards to pay for the substitutes who fill in for them at home. They live in a college dormitory, eat in a cafeteria, and work from 8:30 in the morning till 5:15 at night.

"Readers are instructed to read the essays quickly," a College Board publication explains, "and to score immediately while the impression of the total essay remains fresh."[12] Time is money in the testing business. ETS refers to this grading system as "holistic." It requires readers to read each essay only once and not to

---

*I wrote to Breland to request a copy of this research study. He never responded.

be overly concerned with spelling, punctuation, or grammar. "The first thing we tell our readers," an ETS executive told me, "is that this is not creative writing. We don't expect a brilliant political essay." Indeed, readers are "encouraged to look at what students have done well rather than at what they have failed to do," according to the College Board. "The scorer does not mark a paper for errors."[13] Each reader assigns a grade of 1, 2, 3, or 4. The two readers' scores are then added together to produce a final range of 2–8, which, when multiplied by 100, provides a no-frills approximation of the standard ETS scale.

Holistic graders are made, not born. Several days before the scoring crew arrives in New Jersey, the Chief Reader and his or her Assistant Chief Readers get together with consultants from ETS in order to read a few hundred selected essays and develop a sense of the state of teenage prose. Representative papers are selected. Later, when the actual grading begins, the Chief Reader passes out these samples one at a time and asks the group to read them quickly and indicate grades with a show of hands. "Readers who are not scoring with the majority are asked to adjust their scores to those of the majority," says a College Board brochure.[14] When everyone is on the same wavelength, the real grading begins. Calibrating sessions, with more sample essays and more shows of hands, are held periodically to make certain that individual readers haven't begun marking papers according to "personal criteria."[15]

Let's take a holistic look at a College Board booklet called *The English Composition Test with Essay,* which contains the essay assignment from the 1978 exam along with some responses. The assignment was to discuss the quotation, "We have met the enemy and he is us." ("What does this quotation imply about human beings? Do you agree or disagree with its implications?") The first sample essay, which the booklet describes as "a well-written response taking a psychological approach," begins with the following paragraph: "The quotation I am to discuss implies a dual nature for human beings, both at the individual and at the collective level."[16] A bit thick, that, especially when you consider that the quotation under discussion was originally uttered by a talking possum in a cartoon strip about the animal inhabitants of a swamp. On the other hand, the student has clearly demonstrated a thorough knowledge of how to sucker a high school English teacher.

Two keys to doing well on the ECT are verbosity and indentation. According to a 1982 study by Hunter Breland and Robert Jones of ETS, "essay length" has a higher correlation with ECT grades than all but one of twenty-five "essay characteristics" studied, including "statement of thesis," "noteworthy ideas," "supporting materials," "sentence logic," "subject-verb agreement," "precision of diction," and "spelling." (The only factor with a higher correlation — .52 as opposed to .51 — is "overall organization.") "Number of paragraphs" is more important than "tone and attitude," "range of vocabulary," "sentence variety," "precision of diction," "pronoun usage," and ten other characteristics.[17] It also apparently doesn't hurt to begin an essay with a clunker like "The quotation I am to discuss." Each of the compositions described as exemplary in the College Board booklet opens with some variation on this timeless rhetorical device.

Essay topics for the ECT are selected by a College Board committee consisting of three college instructors and two high school teachers. Since students have only twenty minutes in which to scrawl out their answers, the committee tries to find assignments that are as vague as possible. Questions felt to be "needlessly provocative" are avoided.[18] Sometimes the committee outdoes itself, as in this assignment from 1979:

> "Not so long ago, the phrase 'a magic carpet' suggested adventure or fantasy. Now, most of us would think that a magic carpet was one we did not have to vacuum." *Assignment:* Is life so focused on the practical that fantasy and adventure have lost their appeal? Write an essay in which you express your opinion, using one or two specific examples from your reading or observation.[19]

Because the essays are meant to be graded quickly and formulaically (in accordance with standards determined by the raising of hands), students can improve their chances substantially by paying close attention to clues in the assignment itself. If the instructions say "express your opinion" and use "one or two specific examples from your reading or observation," the student should take these suggestions at face value and not stray far beyond them (while of course remembering to fill in all sixty-one lines on the answer sheet and to break frequently for paragraphs). Originality is as likely to be punished as rewarded, since graders do little more than glance at what has been written and can't be counted on to notice cleverness.*

Several college admissions officers I talked with told me they liked the ECT with essay because its score gave them more "information" than a score from the ordinary ECT. But a score on the ECT with essay must actually be *less* informative, since the person interpreting it has no way of knowing how the student performed on its individual components. Furthermore, even ETS admits that the correlation between scores on the two sections is very slight, "because there is only one essay question on which to sample writing ability."[20] This correlation (.47) is even lower than the one between scores on math and verbal SATs (.64), which supposedly measure different things.

Taking the essay version is thus always something of a gamble. A student who has a knack for multiple-choice tests would be foolish to take the essay version, even if he writes well: why risk being stuck with a stupid essay question or a sleepy grader? On the other hand, a student who does worse than average on standardized tests might be wise to take the essay version, even if he isn't much of a writer. ECT essays are compared only with one another — the "standards" are entirely internal and devised *de novo* for every administration of the test — which means that a student can earn a good grade simply by being no worse than most of his peers.

---

*If I were coaching students for the ECT with essay, I would advise them to do the following: (1) practice turning essay questions into introductory paragraphs; (2) learn how to find the outline hidden in any ECT essay assignment; (3) memorize five or six longish but not overly conspicuous all-purpose words (such as "juxtapose," "enigma," and "arguable") and practice using them in any context; (4) buy a copy of *The Ordeal of Change* by Eric Hoffer and read it two or three times. Hoffer's books are ideal reading for ECT-takers, because they are very short and strewn with easily remembered pseudo-profundities that can be applied with ease to any essay topic yet devised by the ECT committee; (5) write and memorize a short essay on some all-purpose topic — like "freedom and responsibility" — and then regurgitate it, with needed modifications, on the ECT.

Is the ECT with essay a better measure of writing skills than the ECT without? This is a thorny question, since giving a definite answer would require throwing out one or the other version of the test. If one test is better, why give the other? If the tests are the same, why give both? In an exercise that is supposed to rank people scientifically on a scale from 200 to 800, how can you offer a choice of tests? But throwing out the all-multiple-choice version would imply what ETS has always denied: that an essay test, especially a teeny one, is *better* than a multiple-choice test. On the other hand, getting rid of the essay would amount to a confession that all this "holistic grading" business is a bunch of hooey; it would also defeat the *true* purpose of the essay, which is to pacify all those skeptics out there who don't believe you can learn very much about students' ability to write without asking them to write something.

So does the essay make the ECT better, worse, or what? "Essentially, we're looking at writing style, not creativity, conceptualization, and what have you," says Richard Noeth, director of ETS's Admissions and Guidance Programs. "That's different, I think — though I'm not saying better or worse — different than an item-by-item analysis of ability to recognize something in a particular sentence, or the ability to restate something in a different way, or what have you. We're looking at essentially a very holistic analysis of a student's ability in this area. So I think that's different, and I think that adds a different component to what we can assess."

The test was fine all along; but the essay makes it different; but it's still exactly the same.

ETS thinks the world of holistic grading. "When used by teachers in a school or district," says a company brochure, "the holistic method has advantages other than speed. It induces teachers to think about writing and to share their views about standards and other aspects of the craft. Thus it helps clarify and unify teachers' ideas of what they expect and can expect from students. The method itself also concentrates teachers' attention on students' skills as well as their deficits."[21] In the olden days, ETS argued that essay tests would be undesirable even if they weren't so cumbersome and expensive; nowadays it argues that essay tests are marvelous even though they're both easy and cheap.*

Despite the manifest virtues of holism, ETS still grades some tests the old-fashioned way. In the College Board's Advanced Placement (AP) Program, for example, graders are actually allowed to read student papers more than once.

In the AP Program, high school students take accelerated courses, offered in thirteen fields, whose general content is specified by the College Board. At the end of the year, the students sit for an ETS examination. If their scores are high enough, the colleges they ultimately attend may grant them credit for the work they did in high school. Some AP students are able to begin college as sophomores.

AP examinations generally last three hours and consist of both multiple-choice and "free response" sections. The multiple-choice questions are graded by machines, but the free responses require human arbiters, who pass judgment on as many as 1,000 papers apiece during their six days in Lawrence Township.

ETS and the College Board like to describe AP grading time as an invigorating intellectual experience that allows teachers to make contact, in the words of one, "with the very best and most talented high school students in the nation."[23] Many graders feel this way, but others paint a different picture. Prolonged exposure to AP essays, they say, can be hazardous to the health.

"At first I warded off brain-death by collecting 'howlers' from the student-essays and stringing them together in a parody essay of my own," a grader named Robert Crosman wrote to me in 1983; "then I'd sneak off 'to the men's room' every hour or so and play Space Invaders, a video game that in any other setting I have always considered to be monotony itself; and finally I amused myself by writing a brilliant essay in the blank exam book of a student too demoralized even to try an answer."

---

*I appeared on a New York radio show with George Hanford, president of the College Board, in 1984. Hanford said that "ideally" the Board would prefer to give *only* essay tests, but that this "just isn't practical anymore."[22] In other words, essay tests would be the tests of choice if they weren't so cumbersome and expensive. I give up. Let someone else figure out what ETS and the Board really think about multiple-choice tests.

Collecting idiotic lines from student compositions is a venerable tradition at grading time. The College Board's official historian even included some in his chronicle of that organization's first fifty years ("The hound rushed over the moor, emitting whelps at every leap").[24] In his letter to me, Robert Crosman kindly enclosed several dozen boners of more recent vintage, including: "In a world of ignorance and waste came a man called Faustus"; "Desdemona loves Othello. Iago also enjoys loving Desdemona, and feels that he could have a pleasant relationship with her if Othello was not in the way"; "realistate"; "A man who cannot pray to God is immoral and deserves to die"; "So we realize, at the end, that Antigone wasn't the immature cretin we thought"; "I prove this through remembrance of the text and with the use of personal opinion"; "pigamy"; "If parricide is the fashion, Edmund has to go along if he wants to remain in the swing of things"; "We cannot help but sympathize with the unfortunate Raskolnikov, since most of us have never had the experience of living in such a run down area"; "nemocracy"; "A character who I feel was definitely evil and immoral was the captain of the whaling ship, in the suspense filled story by Charles Dickens, *Moby Dick*."

Graders are continually urged to hurry. According to Jim Vopat, a college English teacher, the air-conditioning in the gymnasium is kept "on high because cold readers have been found to read faster."[25] Vopat found the pressure debilitating. "In fact," he wrote,

> the stress is such that many readers become so confused and insecure that they regress to the most absurd of scoring stratagems. The ETS places a white label across each score recorded on the back of the pink examination booklets to protect the reader from being influenced by already recorded scores. But after 10,000 or so essays many readers begin feeling the need to confirm their judgments through a quick peek under the label. Some roll the booklet back on itself to pop up the label, others use clips and tops of Bic pens. I have seen many grades crossed out and changed after such a clandestine consultation. At the 1980 scoring session, the table leader two rows over took pity on his readers because they were slicing their fingers prying up the labels. He supplied them with a bowl of paperclips to make it easier.[26]

Unlike their ECT counterparts, AP graders are supposed to do more than merely run their eyes across exam books (although none spends more than a few minutes on an essay). Each reader is supplied with a scoring "rubric" that outlines precisely what an essay must contain in order to qualify for each of nine possible scores (1–9). To make certain that readers are following their rubrics, Table Leaders periodically circulate sample essays that have previously been scored. Graders who differ with the Table Leaders are warned to watch their step. According to Crosman, the safest scoring method is simply "skimming for the features mentioned in the rubric." Although the instructions specify that "a badly written essay *must* be given a score no higher than 4," in practice, prose style is ignored.

Students are also given substantial leeway with subject matter. In 1979, Vopat had to grade an essay by a student who had written about a movie instead of the specified "novel or play of recognized literary merit." "I asked for a ruling from the question leaders as to how the examination should be treated," he wrote. "Eventually the essay was returned to me with the instruction to 'reward the essay for what it did well in response to the question.' "[27] As a result of such leniency, most students come through with flying colors. In 1980, 96 percent of all AP candidates were judged to be at least "possibly qualified" for college credit on the basis of their tests.

Colleges like the AP Program because it enables them to give the equivalent of scholarships without spending any money. Parents like AP because it cuts tuition costs by reducing the time their children have to spend in college. ETS and the College Board like AP because the program turns a tidy profit (the 1984 fee was $46 per examination, reduced to $30 for students able to demonstrate "acute financial need").[28] Consequently, there isn't much pressure on anyone to grade essays very strictly. Low AP scores are bad for everybody. (For everybody, that is, except college instructors; as Vopat points out, professors who grade AP exams are "literally reading themselves right out of their jobs," since students who don't need college courses also don't need professors.)[29]

"The sad thing," says Crosman, "is that this bunch of hundreds of high school and college teachers accepted it all so meekly, eagerly even. But then we were all survivors of the College Boards ourselves, and had reason to approve of the ends, if not the means. In fact, given the mission — to test thousands of elite high school students for possible college credit . . . — could we think of a better way to produce that result? I couldn't. It's the project itself that is the hustle."

Giving away course credits is such a popular idea at tuition-strapped colleges that ETS and the College Board devised another program, the College-Level Examination Program (CLEP), to make it even easier. "CLEP is based on the premise that some people enrolling in college have already learned some of what is taught there," explains the 1982 *Guide to the CLEP Examinations*. "They have done so through noncredit adult courses, job training, independent reading and study, and advanced high school courses."[30] CLEP tests are multiple-choice (although some have optional "free response" sections). Students prove themselves worthy of college credit by successfully answering questions like the following:

The star of *The Sheik* was

(A) Rudolph Valentino (B) Buster Keaton
(C) Charles Chaplin (D) Harold Lloyd
(E) Clark Gable

Which is a group of architects?

(A) George Ballanchine, Agnes de Mille, Martha Graham
(B) John Cage, Aaron Copland, Paul Hindemith
(C) Robert Altman, Ingmar Bergman, Federico Fellini
(D) Allen Ginsberg, Amy Lowell, Sylvia Plath
(E) I. M. Pei, Henry Richardson, Frank Lloyd Wright

The best place to find a list of synonyms for a word is

(A) a catalog (B) a thesaurus (C) an almanac
(D) a rhyming dictionary (E) a literary handbook

The first two questions are from the test in the Humanities; the third is from the test in College Composition.

Holistic or otherwise, human graders have always been a nuisance to ETS and the College Board. In the early 1960s, the Board tried to eliminate the need for them by investigating the possibility of grading essays with computers. The Board gave a research grant to Ellis Page of the University of Connecticut, and Page developed a computer program that analyzed student essays according to thirty quantifiable characteristics.

The best predictors of essay quality (as previously determined by a panel of human readers) turned out to be average word length, use of uncommon words, number of commas, essay length, number of prepositions, and absence of apostrophes. At ETS's annual Invitational Conference on Testing Problems in 1966, Page described computerized essay grading as "this great enthusiasm of ours"[31] and speculated that a computer might one day "learn on its own . . . by reading in and correctly processing a great amount of appropriate text."[32] Page was quite confident of the value of his research, although he noted that some reactions to it had been "embarrassingly favorable" and that "some instructors at the University of Connecticut have called our bureau about grading their midterm exams!"[33]

Page's project finally came to a dead end, although not because the Board lost interest. "We proved the feasibility," he says today, "apart from the input question." Computers can't read handwriting. Typing is expensive. Page remains confident that the problems will eventually be solved, but in the meantime he has moved on to other projects, the most recent of which involves introducing the residents of Bermuda to the science of multiple-choice testing.

Page, the College Board, and ETS always took it as a given that computerized essay grading would be desirable if only the "input question" could be answered. In his address at the ETS Invitational Conference, Page mocked a critic who had claimed, in Page's words, "that *human* essay grading is good *because* it is subjective — that is, because one teacher will not agree with another!"[34] (Page has a marked fondness for exclamation marks, even though his study suggests that their use correlates negatively with writing ability.) Page considered this opinion too silly to rate a response, but it actually suggests one of the central questions about standardized testing.

Implicit in Page's view of computerized grading is the idea that differences of opinion about writing quality can arise only from partial or distorted information: when two human graders give different marks to the same piece of writing, it can only be because they have failed to apply the correct "standard" to what is being graded. A multiple-choice or computer-graded essay test is preferable, Page and ETS would argue, because it will always give the same score to the same response.

No one would deny that human graders succumb to all sorts of unscientific influences and are annoyingly inconsistent in their judgments. But it doesn't follow that mechanical grading is better simply because it is more "reliable." Human readers often disagree because the grounds for judgment are too complex to ensure unvarying, predictable responses. Page's computer program is more "reliable" than a human grader, but only because it grades by counting commas.

The easiest way to make a test "reliable" is to make it crude. Instead of having students write a genuine essay, assign a twenty-minute "free response." Instead of posing a genuine problem, ask a stupid question on a trivial topic. Instead of having graders make careful judgments, instruct them merely to skim.

On the ECT and other ETS tests, consistency is achieved at a very great price.

3

Multiple Guess

IN CONTRAST TO messy essay tests, ETS would have you believe, its multiple-choice questions and answers are scientifically designed and entirely above suspicion. But the truth is that these tests are written by ordinary people who quite possibly didn't do as well on their SATs as you did on yours.

ETS multiple-choice tests have been fixtures in American society for so long that we tend to take them for granted. When ETS refers to such tests as "objective," we seldom stop to think that the term can apply only to the mechanical grading process. There's nothing genuinely objective about a test like the SAT: it is written, compiled, keyed, and interpreted by highly subjective human beings. The principal difference between it and a test that can't be graded by a machine is that it leaves no room for more than one correct answer. It leaves no room, in other words, for people who don't see eye to eye with ETS.

Before New York passed its truth-in-testing law, it was impossible for outsiders to evaluate ETS's tests because only a few sample questions were published. But the law's disclosure provisions allowed test-takers to see what they were being tested on and to assess the quality of individual items.

The first important challenge to ETS came in 1981, when a high school student named Daniel Lowen protested ETS's scoring of the now famous "pyramid problem." The problem showed a picture of two pyramids, one (ABCD) with a triangular base and three triangular sides, the other (EFGHI) with a square base and four triangular sides. All the triangles were equilateral, and all were the same size.

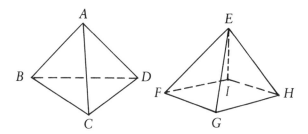

The question asked: "If face ABC were placed on face EFG so that the vertices of the triangles coincide, how many exposed faces would the resulting solid have?"* The answer ETS wanted was seven, since the two touching faces would disappear when the pyramids were joined, leaving seven of the original nine. But Lowen realized that there would be only five faces left, since four of the original triangles would merge into two parallelograms. (Try it yourself if you don't believe him.)† ETS admitted its mistake and raised 240,000 scores, even though few of these 240,000 could have gotten the answer "wrong" for the "right" reason. On the other hand, ETS didn't *lower* any scores, apparently reasoning that students shouldn't be punished for failing to see something ETS didn't see either, even though the answer they chose was demonstrably incorrect. Nor did ETS go back and rescore any of the earlier tests that included the same question.[1]

Admitting it had been wrong about the pyramid problem was especially embarrassing for ETS; less than a week before, ETS executive vice president Robert J. Solomon had published a very sarcastic article, in the form of a multiple-choice test, about New

---

*This item is not only flawed but also ungrammatical. Either "were" should be "is" or "coincide" should be "coincided."
†Most people have as much trouble as ETS in visualizing the correct answer to this problem. A resident of Tokyo wrote me to say that the pyramid problem was keeping him awake at night. "It seems to me plain and clear," he wrote, "that the kid was wrong and the official answer was right. There has to be something like a 16-degree bend where the side faces meet." But this is not, in fact, the case.

York's truth-in-testing law on the op-ed page of the *New York Times*.[2] (This article later provided the basis for the pamphlet against truth-in-testing described in Chapter 1.) ETS tried to save face by implying that Lowen's solution was only "technically" correct and that proving the merits of his objection had required a heroic effort on the part of ETS. In a memorandum sent to high school principals, ETS said that it had decided to rescore the item only after "extensive review by ETS and College Board staff, and after consulting with mathematics teachers and professors at a variety of institutions."[3] But I proved Lowen correct in less than five minutes, using only a piece of cardboard, a pair of scissors, and about eight inches of Scotch tape.

It wasn't long before other solutions to the pyramid problem emerged. As a number of test sleuths pointed out, there was nothing in the wording of the question to prevent a test-taker from joining the two pyramids by placing one of them *inside* the other. "The obvious way to place the face ABC on the face EFG," explained Edward B. Fiske in the *New York Times,* "is to make the vertices coincide in the order given, that is, to place A on E, B on F and C on G. When this is done, the first pyramid is, in effect, placed inside the second one with the tip of vertex D poking through the square base of the second pyramid."[4] The result, in the words of Robert Morris, a mathematician at Bell Laboratories, is a "strange-looking solid with eight faces."[5]

Eight, as it happened, was one of the choices on the test. But ETS was apparently tired of being picked on by amateurs, and it refused to raise any more scores. In defense of this decision, James Braswell, the man in charge of putting together ETS's math tests, said that the eight-faced solution was unacceptable because "in this case the question is such that it makes no difference which face you put on which."[6] Braswell did not, however, reveal what made "this case" different from any other. Nothing in the question made it "such" that the pyramids could not be joined as described. Braswell was merely bluffing. You are wrong, he asserted, because you are not correct. The amateurs must have been as tired as ETS at this point, because they didn't pursue the matter.

For all its bravado, ETS was secretly mortified by the pyramid affair. The company's test development staff, which had never before been on public display, now found itself being chuckled about in the letters column of the *New York Times*. ETS took hurried steps to tighten its question-checking procedures (without, of course, admitting publicly that it had been negligent before or that truth-in-testing laws might be a good thing), but the process was very frustrating. "You know that there's always the belief, I think, that in test development that one more review will find whatever the problems may be," said Arthur Kroll, ETS's vice president in charge of College Board programs, at a closed ETS hearing in 1982. "So you still go on to a number of reviews and you still find pyramids."[7]

Indeed, bad questions continued to surface. Just a month after the pyramid crisis, a high school student named Michael Galligan found a math question on an SAT that had two correct answers. The item presented students with five rows of numbers and asked them to determine which row "contains both the square of an integer and the cube of a *different* integer." The choices were as follows:

(A) 7   2   5   4   6
(B) 3   8   6   9   7
(C) 5   4   3   8   2
(D) 9   5   7   3   6
(E) 5   6   3   7   4

The desired answer was B, since that row contains the cube of 2 (8) and the square of 3 (9). Galligan pointed out that C was also correct; it contains the cube of 2 (8) and the square of -2 (4).[8]

ETS rescored this item but once again tried to deflect criticism by implying that the test-makers, though technically wrong, had really been right. A College Board official confided to a reporter for the *Chronicle of Higher Education* that ETS's test developers "approach these questions on a more sophisticated level" and thus should be excused for forgetting that -2 is an integer and a square root of four.[9] ETS by this time was having trouble keeping track of its excuses. Just a month before, the company had explained away its failure to notice flaws in the pyramid problem by claiming in effect that its item writers had taken a purposely *un*sophisticated approach to the problem. Paul Hoffman, who in the guise of "Dr.

Crypton" writes a monthly column for *Science Digest,* pointed out that the error was particularly amusing because "the commercial courses that prepare students to take the SAT always caution to be on the lookout for negative numbers."[10]

Shortly after this second successful challenge, ETS and the College Board decided to begin disclosing several forms of the SAT nationwide. Students in states other than New York would now be able to buy copies of their questions and answers. Naturally, ETS and the Board denied that this new policy had anything to do with pyramids or negative numbers. But the test-makers clearly realized that their warnings about the evils of truth-in-testing didn't sound quite so convincing anymore, and that other states might be tempted to pass their own laws if something wasn't done to head them off.

In the years since truth-in-testing went into effect, ETS has had to rescore a number of items from various math and science tests. But it has never rescored a verbal item. This is a curious fact, because it would seem logical that writing a foolproof math or science question would actually be easier than writing a foolproof verbal one. Relationships between numbers, after all, are more durable than relationships between words. Two plus two is always four, but is a rose always a rose always a rose? Could it be that bad verbal items are simply easier to bluff excuses for? To answer this question, we need to look at how the tests are made.

One of the first tasks the creator of a multiple-choice test faces is how to make people miss questions whose subject matter they actually understand. This sounds silly, but it's important. One way it's done is by limiting the amount of time allowed for answering questions. Veteran test-takers know, for instance, that the key to doing well on ETS math items lies in finding *quick* solutions; if you have to perform a complex or lengthy calculation, you've missed the trick. You may still end up with the right answer, but you'll have spent a minute instead of ten seconds doing it, leaving you less time for other questions. For example, an item on a recent SAT asked students to estimate the value of the following fraction:

$$\frac{14,995,844}{2,987}$$

This problem may look intimidating, but students who are familiar with the SAT mentality know they would never be asked to work through such a monstrous-looking fraction or even to juggle two big numbers in their heads. They realize that all ETS is really asking them to do is divide 15,000 by 3.[11]

Another way to make students miss questions whose subject matter they understand is to write misleading questions. Test-makers don't always do this intentionally, but they always do it, in part because it's very hard not to. Many of the verbal items ETS calls most difficult are in fact merely ambiguous, since writing a genuinely difficult multiple-choice item that isn't also unfair is much harder than writing a confusing one. This was one of Banesh Hoffmann's main points in *The Tyranny of Testing*. After all, in a multiple-choice test, the answer is always printed right there on the page. The student doesn't have to fish it out of his mind: all he has to do is recognize it. In order to get students to choose the wrong answer, as of course some must if the test is to be useful, another answer must be made to look more (or equally) attractive.

One way to do this is to make the question so hard that students have no idea what the desired response is — using words few students have ever seen, for example. The drawback to this method is that if only a very few students understand the words, more will get it right for the wrong reason or through luck than for the right reason, and it won't be testing what it's supposed to test. The alternative is to make the question ambiguous. It's revealing to note that in the jargon of standardized testing, incorrect answers are known as "distractors."

One of the few scientific studies of test ambiguity was performed in 1980 by Walt Haney and Laurie Scott of the Huron Institute in Cambridge, Massachusetts. Haney and Scott did something that ETS never does in checking its tests: they administered test items to a group of children and then asked them *why* they had chosen their answers. In one of the experimental items, taken from a published Stanford Achievement Test, young children were shown a picture of a potted flower, a cabbage, and a potted cactus, then asked, "Which plant needs the least amount of water?" The desired answer was the cactus, which nine of eleven children chose. But one child chose the head of cabbage, explaining that it would need water "only when you clean it." Since there was nothing in the drawing to indicate that the cabbage was growing in a garden and not sitting in a refrigerator, the child's answer was at least as rational as the desired answer, and it was arguably a good bit more thoughtful, since it indicated that the child had delved further into the question than the other children had. But in an actual test, of course, his score would have been lower.[12]

How many cabbage questions are there on, say, an SAT, ETS's biggest seller? ETS would say none, and it would haul out statistical studies to "prove" it. But statistics can't spot errors of the sort found by the little boy in the Huron Institute study. The only reliable way to evaluate the test-makers is to look at an actual test.

In the days before ETS was required by law to disclose exams, this was impossible. But in 1983 people who could spare $6 could order a College Board publication called *6 SATs*.* This booklet, which was published in 1982, contains six SATs that were administered a year or two before.[13] Since ETS has never thrown out a verbal item, we'll confine our investigation to verbal items. So ETS won't be able to claim we're nitpicking, let's look only at the first test in the booklet. In fact, let's look only at the first section of the first test. It contains forty-five items, has a time limit of thirty minutes, and accounts for half of a student's SAT verbal score.

Here's the first item in this section that caught my eye, a sentence completion:[14]

---

35. Unfortunately, certain aspects of democratic government sometimes put pressure on politicians to take the easy way out, allowing ——— to crowd out ———.

    (A) exigencies..necessities
    (B) immediacies..ultimates
    (C) responsibilities..privileges
    (D) principles..practicalities
    (E) issues..problems

---

*6 *SATs* has since been superseded by *10 SATs*, which is distributed to bookstores by the Scribner Book Company. ETS has also published a new edition of *5 SATs*, containing even more recent tests.

This is a particularly interesting item, because it is an example not only of ambiguity but also of cultural bias.

How you respond to this item will depend on what you think politicians do when they "take the easy way out." Unlike most ETS sentence completions, this one doesn't contain a contextual clue. We are told only that "certain aspects" are at fault, that they only "sometimes" have an effect, and that when they are in force all they do is allow one thing to "crowd out" another.

The answer ETS wants here is B. This produces a plausible sentence, one that is only slightly vaguer and more badly written than the uncompleted version. (Back in my test-taking days, I used to think badly written items and reading passages served some diabolical but scientifically precise assessment purpose; it was something of a shock to learn, as I did upon visiting Lawrence Township, that ETS actually tries hard to write sturdy, well-crafted prose.) *Immediacies* and *ultimates* are dictionary words, the sort that crop up in papers by students who write with thesauruses in their laps. In this context, at least, they don't divulge much solid meaning. I suppose, however, that the finished sentence could be translated into English as something like this: "In a democratic society, considerations of the moment unfortunately sometimes distract politicians from contemplating fundamental principles." Certainly we've all heard a sentiment like this before, perhaps from our high school civics teacher, who was also, quite possibly, the football coach. To get this item "right" requires a dead ear for the language combined with a belief in conventional wisdom.

Is the ETS answer correct? Consider an example from political life. The American government is running a large deficit. Politicians from both parties agree that this is bad. What should be done? One possibility would be to do something "immediate": raise taxes, slash the budget. But these steps affect voters' lives and are unpopular. So instead we have a president who wants neither to raise taxes nor to slash the budget but rather to add a balance-the-budget amendment to the Constitution. A balance-the-budget amendment is an "ultimate," not an "immediacy." It doesn't affect anybody right now. It is a fundamental statement of principle. President Reagan is unfortunately taking the easy way out, allowing an "ultimate" to crowd out "immediacies"—just the opposite of what the ETS sentence says.

By this reasoning, a better answer is D. The president is letting the "principle" of a balanced budget crowd out the "practicalities" of actually balancing the budget. This happens all the time in politics. For example: the sanctity of human life is a principle; dealing with crime is a practicality. If you support the death penalty as a deterrent to crime but live in a state where executions are prohibited by law, then you probably believe that your state legislators have taken the easy way out, allowing principles to crowd out practicalities. You may be more conservative than the legislature, but do you have less scholastic aptitude?

For that matter, why not E? Nuclear disarmament is an extremely popular "issue" at the moment. Overcrowded prisons are a tenacious and unpopular "problem." If you invite Teddy Kennedy to speak to your breakfast club next week, which topic do you think he'll be more likely to address? The fact that unglamorous problems like prison reform almost always take a back seat to (important but) nebulous and generally intractable issues like nuclear disarmament is, I would argue, an unfortunate aspect of democratic government. When a politician wants to avoid a problem, there's always an issue to hide behind.

I think a case could even be made for A. The point, though, is that getting this question "correct" depends less on understanding its verbal content than on whether you happen to subscribe to ETS's locker-room idealism about the way things ought to work. If — for cultural, ideological, or practical reasons — you think it's just fine that elected representatives don't spend more time lounging on the steps of the Capitol asking, "And what is Truth, Socrates?," then you're just plain out of luck. Yet ETS contends that through questions like this one, it can rank people with precision on a 600-point scale of "aptitude."

Let's try another. Here's an analogy. In SAT analogy items, students are given a pair of words and asked to select, from among five choices, another pair "that *best* expresses a relationship similar to that expressed in the original pair" (emphasis in original). Number 41 reads as follows:[15]

---

41. THREAT : HOSTILITY : :

    (A) plea : clemency
    (B) promise : benevolence
    (C) lampoon : praise
    (D) capitulation : malice
    (E) compliment : admiration

ETS suggests that students approach analogy questions by forming a sentence using the words in capital letters (referred to as the "stem") and then plugging in the lettered choices to see which fits best. If we form our sentence as "A threat is an expression of hostility," we probably won't have much difficulty in settling on E, which is the desired answer, or "key." A compliment, after all, is an expression of admiration.

But suppose we form our sentence in a slightly different way and say, "A threat produces hostility." Isn't this every bit as true as the other sentence? Working from this statement, however, A now seems like the best choice (with D a nearly elegant and possibly profound runner-up).

When I discussed this and other questions with Pamela Cruise, the ETS official in charge of putting together the verbal SAT, she told me that an analogy is no good "if you have to use 'sometimes' " (even though ETS hides behind a "sometimes" in number 35, the sentence completion discussed first). A plea only *sometimes* produces clemency. But ETS's answer doesn't work without 'sometimes,' either. After all, a compliment is only *sometimes* an expression of admiration. Compliments are uttered for all sorts of reasons, and sincere admiration probably isn't even the most common one. Can ETS honestly argue that a student who understood all of the words in this item, and could formulate the possible relationships between them, might not be justified in selecting A as the answer?

When I talked to Lewis Pike, the former head of verbal test development at ETS, he told me that he had sometimes received letters and phone calls from the parents of test-takers who disagreed with the way ETS had keyed some analogy items. "It really helped my thinking, it made me a better researcher," Pike said, "to have to answer letters from mothers." In one case, he said, a mother told him that her son's choice on one such item seemed just as good as ETS's and that she couldn't understand why his answer had been counted as wrong. She then explained her son's rationale in answering as he had.

"I thought, Well, that's fascinating," Pike told me. "I never even thought of it that way." The woman seemed to have a point, so Pike went back to the item and looked at it closely. Much to his surprise, he found quite a few relationships — some of them better than others — between various possible answers and the stem of the analogy. He tallied up these relationships, producing a sort of scorecard for the possible answers. When he had finished, he discovered with great satisfaction that ETS's answer had more of these relationships than the unhappy student's did, and he concluded that ETS's answer was thus the better one. His investigation had taken him about half an hour, and it had renewed his confidence in the verbal SAT.

But this little experiment really ought to have shaken Pike's confidence. A student is only supposed to spend a few seconds answering an analogy item. If he spent half an hour, he'd use up all the time allowed for an entire *section* of the test. Should students be penalized because they take the test exactly as they are told to, by answering each item as quickly as possible after forming a sentence that accommodates both the stem and the presumed key?

Let's try another. Here are the first two paragraphs of a three-paragraph reading comprehension passage, along with one of the questions that follow it:[16]

Suppose that a rod is moving at very high speed. At first it is oriented perpendicular to its line of motion. Then it is turned through a right angle so that it is along the line of motion. The rod contracts. This contraction, known as the FitzGerald contraction, is exceedingly small under ordinary circumstances. The size of the contraction does not depend at all on the material of the rod, but only on its speed.

It may seem surprising that the dimensions of a moving rod can be altered merely by pointing it different ways. But what rod is being considered? If the rod is thought of as continuous substance, extending in space because it is the nature of substance to occupy space, then there seems to be no valid cause for a change of dimensions. But the rod is really a swarm of electrical particles moving about and widely separated from one another. The marvel is that such a swarm should tend to preserve any definite extension. The particles, however, exert electrical forces on one another, and the volume they fill corresponds to a balance between the forces drawing them together and the diverse motions tending to spread them apart. When the rod is set in motion, these electrical forces change.

30. When the author refers to the idea that a solid rod is "continuous substance," he implies that this idea is which of the following?
  I. A common conception of the nature of solid matter
  II. A concept that is not particularly useful for explaining the Fitz-Gerald contraction
  III. An accurate description of some kinds of matter

  (A) I only   (B) III only   (C) I and II only
  (D) II and III only   (E) I, II, and III

We have no trouble agreeing with I and eliminating III. But what about II? We could agree with it immediately if it were worded differently: "A concept that does not explain the Fitz-Gerald contraction." But this isn't the way it is worded. Is ETS getting at something?

We have already determined, in answering item 26 (not shown), that "The major purpose of the author is to describe a phenomenon." Given that this is his purpose, what does he imply when he begins the second paragraph with a reference to the "continuous substance" idea? Surely he implies that he finds this idea useful, if only in a negative way, for achieving his major purpose. (If he didn't think it was useful, why did he bring it up?) He is telling us what the FitzGerald contraction is by telling us first what it is not. Writers, orators, and advertisers do this all the time. It's a run-of-the-mill rhetorical device.

When I administered this test to myself, I pondered item 30 for a very long time and finally settled on A as my answer. I knew that the author of the passage didn't think the "continuous substance" idea *explained* the FitzGerald contraction. But that wasn't what the item asked. The item asked whether *referring* to the "continuous substance" idea helped *the author* to explain the FitzGerald contraction. I decided that ETS had had a purpose in choosing to say "not particularly useful for explaining" instead of "does not explain."

As you must have guessed already, this line of thinking didn't win me any points with ETS. The "correct" response is C. I am left to conclude that ETS didn't realize how sloppily the item was written. Perhaps ETS ought to be required to print, on the cover of every SAT, the names and SAT scores of all the people who contributed to it.

Here's one last item:[17]

---

42. MAGNET:IRON::   (A) tank:fluid
    (B) hook:net   (C) sunlight:plant
    (D) spray:tree   (E) flame:bird

You probably didn't have any trouble in selecting C, the answer ETS wants. But if you thought harder (a mistake, of course), you might have noticed that the analogy is stated incorrectly: magnet-*ism* is to iron as sunlight is to plant — or magnet is to iron as *sun* is to plant.

In an ETS pamphlet called *Preparing for Tests*, students who are about to take the SAT are told, "Be careful to eliminate those relationships that are not exactly parallel to the relationship of the original pair."[18]

If we follow this advice we'll be in trouble, but let's do it anyway. Even though this item may not have struck you as the least bit confusing, it reveals quite a bit about the ETS mentality. And the ETS mentality is what the SAT *really* tests.

First, the rationale for selecting C: a magnet attracts iron, just as sunlight attracts a plant. It seems simple. But there are problems. For one thing, the "stem" is true even if you read it backward, while C is not; you can attract a magnet with a piece of iron, but you can't attract sunlight with a plant. Furthermore, while any piece of iron can be attracted with a magnet, some plants don't respond to sunlight. If you separate a magnet and a piece of iron for, say, a year, the relationship between them will still be the same when you bring them back together; not so with sunlight and the plant (the plant will be dead). A magnet and a piece of iron are both inanimate and made of matter; not so with C. Sunlight brings about a visible physical change in a plant; not so with a magnet and iron.

Is there a better answer? How about B? You can pick up a net with a hook, just as you can pick up a piece of iron with a magnet. You can also pick up a hook with a net, as you can a magnet with a piece of iron. Any net can be picked up with a hook, any hook can be picked up with a net; likewise with magnet and iron. You may have a net too big to pick up with a particular hook, or a hook to big to pick up with a particular net, but the same is true of magnet and iron. The relationship between hook and net remains true no matter how long you keep them apart. Hook and net are both inanimate and both are made of matter. And so on and so on.

We could even choose D as the answer. After all, you can make a magnet out of a piece of iron (by banging it with a hammer), just as you can make a spray (as in bough) from a piece of a tree. For that matter, why not choose E?

When I said all this to Pamela Cruise at ETS, she said, "It doesn't really strike me as an analogy. I mean, there's a reason for pairing magnet and iron. I mean, that's the kind of thing that seems to go together. You've done it yourself, you've picked up pieces of iron or pins or something with a magnet. God, I've done it millions of times. But you don't really think of hook and net in that same kind of sense. I mean, if you had suggested that as a stem and key for an analogy, I would say that doesn't really strike me as an analogy."

Let's consider what I take to be Cruise's major point: In approaching an SAT analogy problem, the most important consideration is the primary relationship, the obvious connection, between the elements of the stem and between the elements of the key. Magnetic attraction is certainly the primary relationship between a magnet and a piece of iron; but is photokinesis really the primary relationship between sunlight and a plant? Isn't it instead photosynthesis? Doesn't the most obvious relationship between a sunlight and a plant have to do with the conversion of light into chemical energy and not with physical movement in response to light?

"Yeah," said Cruise, "that would be one thing you would think of, but in the context of this item, this seems like a perfectly good relationship."

This is a fascinating point, because if it is "the context of the item" (the test? ETS?) that is most important, we're left to say something like, "It's the right answer because it's the sort of answer that ETS always picks." Number of correspondences doesn't matter, direction of correspondence doesn't matter, precision of correspondence doesn't matter (despite what Lewis Pike told me about the analogy items *he* had wrestled with). Even having to say "sometimes" doesn't matter. Cruise's response is finally one of exasperation: yeah, but it's so *obvious* what the answer is. This isn't a useful basis for making intelligent decisions. After all, in precisely the same sense it is "obvious" that the sun revolves around the earth.

I'm not saying that I think B is a *good* answer. All I'm saying is that according to the analogy rules laid down by ETS itself, B could reasonably be regarded as the *best* answer — which is all ETS tells students to look for. Can ETS prove "objectively" that it is not?

To see the inherent flaw in questions like this, all you have to do is put them in a different context. Suppose I typed out the magnet item on a piece of paper, handed it to you, and said, "Here's an analogy problem that's got everybody up at MIT bamboozled. See what you can make of it." Wouldn't you hesitate before selecting C as your answer? Might you not discover that you could make a case for one of the other choices? Might you not begin to lean toward this new answer if you thought the tester was looking for something more than an ability to think the way ETS does? And what is an item like this doing in a test of verbal skills in the first place? All you need to answer it is a little first-grade physics (magnets) and a little fourth-grade biology (plants). Is that what ETS is testing? Surely it isn't trying to determine whether high school juniors and seniors know the meanings of magnet, iron, sunlight, and plant — although it does call the analogy section a "vocabulary" test. If students of even moderate ability miss this item,* they

---

*According to ETS's statistics, this item is very difficult. Only about 20 percent of the students who try it get it "correct" — exactly the same percentage you would expect if all students selected their answers entirely at random.

probably do so not because they don't understand the words or the relationships between them but because their ability to read the mind of Pamela Cruise has momentarily faltered and they have read more into the item than was intended.

It may be interesting to look at an earlier version of this same item:[19]

---

iron — magnet :: moth — (1 dust, 2 myth, 3 fur, 4 insect, 5 light)

This is the item as it appeared in the analogy section of the first SAT ever, published in 1926. Notice that in this form, with the first half of the key provided, the possibility for ambiguity is greatly reduced. That's because in 1926 the SAT didn't need ambiguity to make students miss items they understood. Instead, it used time. The analogy section contained forty items, and students were given six minutes to complete them all.

When I first wrote in *Harper's* about these four items (and remember, all four are from a single thirty-minute section of a single verbal SAT), I expected ETS to respond immediately. I had impugned the quality of its best-selling test, if not the verbal aptitude of its staff, and ETS had occasionally responded to similar challenges in the past. In the early 1960s, ETS had replied to Banesh Hoffmann when he objected, also in *Harper's,* to its scoring of a question on its Achievement Test in chemistry. The question:[20]

The burning of gasoline in an automobile cylinder involves all of the following *except*

(A) reduction
(B) decomposition
(C) an exothermic reaction
(D) oxidation
(E) conversion of matter to energy

Hoffmann wrote, "The average chemistry student quickly picks the wanted answer E, doubtless arguing that conversion of matter into energy refers to nuclear reactions and is thus inappropriate here.

"But the student who is unfortunate enough to understand, even if only in an elementary way, what $E = mc^2$ is really about finds himself at a distinct disadvantage. He knows that . . . here, just as in nuclear reactions there is 'conversion of matter into energy.' So the superior student correctly concludes that none of the given answers is correct."[21]

This is quite straightforward. Although forgetting about Einstein in the early 1960s is perhaps a bit more understandable than forgetting about negative numbers in the early 1980s, ETS had nonetheless clearly made an embarrassing blunder. Einstein's equation, after all, was half a century old.

ETS didn't see it that way. "The superior student is as aware of the *classical* concepts of matter and chemical change as he is aware of the model of *modern* physics," the company's experts wrote in their published, official response to Hoffmann. "He is likely to be more aware than is the average student that the 'conversion of matter into energy' has been demonstrated only for nuclear changes. Perhaps he realizes that if the energy freed by the burning of gasoline comes from the conversion of mass to energy, the loss in mass is only about a ten-billionth of the mass of the gasoline burned, a loss too small to be measured by available methods."[22]

As Hoffmann pointed out in his counterresponse, this was quite an extraordinary statement. "The remark that the loss of mass is 'too small to be measured by available methods' may well impress the non-specialist," he wrote, "yet it is incorrect as stated. The mass can be measured by measuring the amount of energy released and using Einstein's formula, $E = mc^2$." And although ETS was correct when it pointed out that the loss in mass is extremely tiny, this minuscule loss accounts for absolutely *all* of the energy released in the reaction. "If ALL released energy comes from this conversion," Hoffmann continued, "the process is certainly not a negligible one here, though ETS would have us think otherwise."[23]

ETS smugly ignored Hoffmann's response and has not, to this day, admitted it was wrong. Its only acknowledgment of Hoffmann's argument was to stop responding publicly to such challenges.

Even so, I expected ETS to respond to mine. The company had never thrown out a verbal item before, and I felt that I had found four bad ones (actually, I believe there are more than four) in a single section of a single verbal SAT. Furthermore, in ETS's 1982 annual report, President Anrig had made much of ETS's "commitments to public accountability" and its willingness to "hold itself accountable" to broad guidelines governing its programs. "After 26 years in public positions," he wrote, ". . . I am no stranger to spotlights or controversy, and I don't shy away from either.* Rather than wait for a renewal of debates over testing, we took the initiative . . . to demonstrate that openness was good for, and attainable by, a private, not-for-profit educational organization."[24] The report also asserted that complaints about tests, "regardless of which ETS testing program is involved," would be "replied to within ten working days."[25] Reading about Hoffmann's experience made me especially eager to hear what ETS would have to say.

But the only response I got was a very brief letter to the editor from Anrig pointing out an embarrassing factual error in my article (I'd given his first name as George).[†] I waited a month for a further response and, receiving none, wrote to Anrig. I told him that I thought ETS had "an obligation either to defend or to rescore the four verbal items I challenged in my article" and pointed out that many more than ten working days had passed. I told him that I thought ETS was "stonewalling." I also said that I was going to expand my article into a book, and that "in the interest of providing as fair a picture as possible, I will gladly make

---

*Actually, he shies away from both where I'm concerned. He turned down an invitation to appear on a panel with me, explaining to the event's organizer that he had already given me my "due" by permitting himself to be interviewed.

†As the months went by, in the minds of the Information Division, this unfortunate mistake was transmogrified into a blunder of Himalayan dimensions. About a year after the article was published, I twice called Information to ask two or three simple questions regarding ETS policies or programs. On both occasions, a cheerful employee wrote down my questions, read them back to me to make sure she had transcribed them accurately, asked me for my phone number, promised to call me back directly, and was never heard from again. When I later asked the division for an explanation, I was told that because of my error with Anrig's name, "we prefer not to deal with you on the phone."[26] ETS had also notified me of two errors (one serious, both acknowledged immediately) that I had made during a radio interview, but both of these had occurred some months after the precaution of not calling me back had been instituted.

myself available to any and all ETS representatives who take issue with my article."[27]

Anrig's response, I later learned, was to send a confidential memo to all his executives, instructing them not to talk to me and asking them to report me to the Information Division if I tried to make contact with the company.[28] I tried to call Anrig three times, but he didn't return my calls. Finally I received a call from Joy McIntyre of the Information Division, who said, "I am calling you as a courtesy to tell you that Mr. Anrig isn't going to return your call. . . . That should be about it from us." ETS's bold new commitment to accountability, it seemed, did not apply to anyone who disagreed with ETS. A few days later, I received a letter from Anrig in which he professed to be "surprised" and "amazed" at the letter I had written to him.

"It is obvious from the article that you rejected outright anything we had to say," he wrote. "It seems that you or *Harper's* had decided at the beginning what kind of article this would be. What you now describe as 'complaints' indeed were responded to during your visit to ETS but you did not accept any of our explanations. It therefore is not surprising that we disagree with most of the assertions and characterizations in your article." He ended by saying that "your actions make clear that no constructive purpose can be served by further communication with you."[29]

As it happened, none of this was correct. Although incapable of seeing bias in its tests, ETS can conceive of no other explanation for the opinions of its critics. But I came to my opinions about ETS slowly, over the course of several months and as the result of considerable research. I had no prior gripe against ETS. If Anrig thought I was an irresponsible researcher, he gave quite a different impression when I was with him. "You've been impressing the hell out of a lot of people around here by being well prepared," he told me when we began. When we finished, he asked me, "Do you always spend this much time on stories?" Our conversation was friendly on both sides, although it was clear that we had substantially different views of standardized testing and of the proper business of his company. My interview with him was my last at ETS. He had been receiving regular reports on my conversations with his employees. His professed surprise at my opinions is disingenuous.

Anrig implied in his letter that ETS had already defended the items I had challenged. But of the four mentioned in my article, Pamela Cruise and I had discussed just two — the magnet item and the threat/hostility item — and those only superficially, as ought to be obvious from the caliber of Cruise's comments, quoted earlier ("I mean, that's the kind of thing that seems to go together"). Even in the context of these two items, ETS had not responded to all my questions. In the course of my interview with Cruise, I had asked for a copy of a statistical item analysis that she had shown me. Cruise and a representative of the Information Division said they would look into the matter. When, after hearing nothing from ETS, I tried to follow up my request by telephone, Joy McIntyre told me that ETS had decided to refuse further communication with me on this and all other matters.* (This was several months before my article was published; if anyone had "decided at the beginning what kind of article this would be," it was ETS.) She told me that I had interviewed "umpteen skillion people" at ETS (I had talked to thirteen) and that she and the rest of her media relations staff had better things to do than answer questions from the media.†

More than sixty days had now passed since ETS had learned of

---

*I tried several times to obtain a copy of this item analysis, but ETS wouldn't let me have one. McIntyre once told me in a letter, "We know of no instance in which a researcher has been denied access to data." When I pointed out that *I* had been denied access to data, she responded: "As for you considering yourself a researcher denied access to data, we just don't see it that way. For one thing, you had three days of interviews here at ETS and we certainly have provided you with quantities of printed information. This is more time than we've ever given any other reporter which is what you are — not a researcher. Our responsibility to be responsive surely doesn't require us to be *your* researcher!"[30]

†Though dangerously overworked by me, the Information Division later found time to send the editor of *Harper's* a letter urging him to consider assigning an article about ETS: "As fall approaches, students will be opening new books, returning to familiar settings and experiencing anxieties once again. . . . What are the tests for? What does the score reflect? What skills do various test items measure? . . . . Although these questions are frequently asked in homes and schools, they are just as frequently answered incorrectly or not at all. A feature demystifying the subject of standardized tests and allaying some of the concerns students, teachers and parents have would catch the interest of a diversity of readers. . . . Please feel free to contact me if you'd like to prepare a story on expert advice about standardized tests."[31]

my objections to four of its SAT verbal items. I wrote another letter to Anrig, restating my challenge and citing the relevant passages in ETS's annual report. "If . . . you are genuinely concerned about 'product accuracy' and 'test quality,' " I wrote, "then you should be overjoyed to be given an opportunity to improve both. . . . Since ETS's status as a nonprofit institution effectively protects it from the scrutiny of anyone it decides it doesn't like, you have an added responsibility to answer your critics." Since Anrig had told me he and ETS would have nothing more to do with me, I also wrote to ETS's trustees and to George Hanford, president of the College Board. "I look forward to learning from you," I wrote, "why it is no longer the policy of the Educational Testing Service to respond to challenges of published test items." I enclosed copies of my article, my letter to Anrig, and our previous correspondence.[32]

At ETS's 1983 Invitational Conference on Testing Problems,* held at the Plaza in New York City, Anrig made many references to the "openness" of ETS and to its eagerness to hear the views of "critics" and "independent researchers." He mentioned the company's published *Standards for Quality and Fairness,* which formalize ETS's commitment to public accountability, and said, "If we don't live up to those standards, then we are not doing our job." Anrig is a round, jovial, red-faced man who shares Ronald Reagan's knack for setting an audience at ease. In one of his favorite stories, he explains that he accepted his job at ETS on one condition: "That I wouldn't have to take a test!" At the end of the conference, he urged the members of his audience to get in touch with him if we had any questions at all about testing or ETS. "I'm easy to reach," he assured us, beaming from the podium. "Write me. I promise a response."

But Anrig did not respond to my letter. George Hanford of the College Board wrote only to say that "the disagreement about which you have written me is between you and ETS, and I prefer not to complicate the exchange."[33] Of ETS's sixteen trustees, I heard from only two: Donald M. Stewart, president of Spelman

---

*ETS holds these conferences annually and publishes the proceedings. My written request for a copy of the 1983 proceedings was denied.

College and chairman of the ETS board, and Ernest L. Boyer, president of the Carnegie Foundation for the Advancement of Teaching. (Boyer had missed the trustees meeting at which my letter was discussed and thus hadn't gotten the message that he wasn't supposed to answer it.)

In his letter, Donald Stewart wrote, "Those items are going through the review process that is normally followed when a test candidate challenges a test item."[34] This normal process apparently consists of (1) claiming that the challenge has already been answered, (2) asserting that the challenge will never be answered, and (3) stating that the answer is now being formulated, and what's all the fuss about, anyway? Although suggesting that I had no right to expect such treatment, Stewart said that "in this case Mr. Anrig asked his staff to continue the process and to send the items to a group of independent external subject matter experts who are not employees of ETS. . . . The outcome of this review process will be shared with you when it is completed." (He was apparently unaware that Anrig had asked his employees not to communicate with me.) "The Board of Trustees," he concluded, "is fully satisfied that actions have been taken in an appropriate manner to respond to your questioning of the four SAT items."[35]

A little more than a month later, I received a letter from Ernest W. Kimmel, ETS's director of test development. He described the review process ETS had undertaken:

> Six scholars in the humanities, not employed by ETS, were contacted and asked to review a set of items. Then each received a set of 20 items to review and answer; the four items you challenged were embedded within this set. After reviewing the items and writing down his answers, each reviewer then checked his answers against the ETS answer key provided in a separate envelope. The reviewers returned the twenty items and their answers, along with any comments, to ETS. For the two analogy items, each of the six reviewers chose the response scored by ETS; five chose the ETS key for the sentence completion item, the sixth chose neither the ETS key nor your preferred answer. Five of the six reviewers chose the ETS key for the reading comprehension item. One reviewer chose the key for which you have argued. We went over his comments carefully but discovered nothing to persuade us that the other five reviewers were wrong in choosing (C) as the *best* answer.[36]

ETS's review process is indeed extraordinary, although not for the reasons Donald Stewart and Ernest Kimmel think it is. Even though I had given ETS quite detailed explanations of why I thought the four items were flawed, ETS chose to ignore them. ETS wasn't taking any chances. It stacked the odds in its favor by burying the challenged items in a large group of other items, thus making it less rather than more likely that the anonymous reviewers would detect any flaws that happened to exist. Indeed, ETS gave the six reviewers no reason to believe that there was anything unusual about any of the items they were sent. And in case these reviewers had any doubts about which responses ETS wanted, an answer key was provided.

ETS would never have treated a challenged math item solely in this manner. It would not have based its reassessment of the pyramid problem or the negative-integer problem on the opinions of experts who had been given the items "blind" and asked to compare their answers with an ETS key.* The reason is obvious. The flawed math items had made it through ETS's standard review process in the first place because the errors in them weren't obvious, at least to ETS personnel. Likewise with my four items. I wasn't arguing that they contained spelling errors or some other glaring defect. I was arguing that they were ambiguously worded and subtly flawed and that someone who viewed them differently from ETS would be justified in choosing other answers as the "best" answer. An honest response to my challenge would have been to ask the six reviewers to go over my arguments point by point and explain why I was wrong.

But even though ETS went to a great deal of trouble to determine the results of its review, the anonymous experts were not unanimous in their responses. On the sentence completion question about "certain aspects of democratic government," one of the six reviewers failed to select the ETS key. Ernest Kimmel tries to make this discrepancy sound trivial by saying that the answer this reviewer chose was neither ETS's nor mine. Since I said in my challenge that I thought A, D, and E were no worse than ETS's

---

*When ETS sent the pyramid problem out for review, none of its experts caught the error, although "they all agreed that Daniel Lowen was correct when we gave them his reasoning," according to an ETS vice president.[37] Why didn't ETS give its reviewers my reasoning?

choice, which was B, this can only mean that the reviewer thought that C was the best answer. In other words, ETS, the reviewer, and I among us think that any of the five choices on this item could pass as the "best" answer. (Kimmel's prose is vague here. He says that five of the reviewers were "not wrong," but he doesn't say that the sixth was "not right." We could all take lessons in ambiguity from ETS.) Another of the reviewers also disagreed with ETS, and agreed with me, on the reading comprehension item about "the FitzGerald contraction."

I wrote back to Kimmel to ask if ETS would identify the "six scholars in the humanities" who had participated in the review. I also asked him which answer the sixth reviewer had chosen on the "certain aspects" item, and whether I could have copies of the reviewers' comments.[38] When Kimmel responded, he (1) told me he couldn't give me the names of the "scholars," although he didn't say why; (2) didn't answer (or even acknowledge) my question about the reviewer's choice on the "certain aspects" item; (3) didn't answer (or acknowledge) my question about the reviewers' comments.[39]

Although he wouldn't tell me who the reviewers were, he did provide me with "a thumbnail sketch of each." One was the "chief academic officer of an Ivy League university." Another was "the Head Master of one of the most distinguished preparatory schools in the country." A third was "an associate professor of English at a selective women's college in New England." Altogether, the six had 120 years' experience in teaching. "It should be obvious from these descriptions," Kimmel concluded, "that we sought out highly qualified reviewers familiar with the variety of students, schools, and colleges that participate in the Admissions Testing Program."*

I was very impressed. I wondered why Kimmel was not. After all, he had gathered six of the most distinguished educators he could find — and then decided to ignore the opinions of 16 percent of them, even after stacking the experiment in his favor. If I had

---

*Kimmel described the six reviewers as "independent" and "external." But all six, as Kimmel notes, were from institutions directly involved in the ETS/College Board Admissions Testing Program.

been in his position, my faith in two of the items would have been shaken, not confirmed. The SAT is a test designed for eleventh- and twelfth-graders. The vocabulary and "reasoning" skills it is supposed to measure ought to be well within the reach of six of the nation's most experienced scholars. If two of these pedagogical paragons were fooled by questions from a test for teenagers, doesn't that suggest that something might be wrong with the questions? But Kimmel's letter makes it clear that there was never even the slightest possibility that ETS would reconsider its scoring of the four items I challenged or of any other verbal items. The whole "review" process does nothing more than enable ETS to conduct its business undisturbed.

Since ETS wouldn't tell me the names of its "independent external subject matter experts" or even tell me their comments, I decided to assemble six independent external subject matter experts of my own. My experts, unlike ETS's, didn't mind signing their names to their opinions.

My first expert was Nicholas von Hoffman, a highly respected political writer in one of the nation's most prestigious eastern cities (Washington). I didn't have to ask von Hoffman; he volunteered, by writing an article about my article. In one of his syndicated columns, he wrote that the "certain aspects of democratic government" item was "so poorly constructed" that it couldn't be answered. "How can there possibly be one right answer?" he continued. "Any of those four pairs [A, B, C, and E] can plausibly be dropped into that sentence. The 'right' answer is supposed to be item B, but that is based more on the predilections of the test writers than it is on any demonstrable objective truth. With tests made up of questions like that, the incredulous and cynical conclude that examinations test the ability of the test taker to please the test writer. Tests test test-taking."[40]

Von Hoffman is quite liberal. He used to debate James J. Kilpatrick on the "Point-Counterpoint" segment of *60 Minutes*. I didn't want ETS to accuse me of having a left-wing bias, so I asked William F. Buckley, Jr., to join my panel. Buckley is the editor of the conservative journal *National Review*. He's an elegant prose stylist and a man justly renowned for his verbal skills. Von Hoffman had focused on the "certain aspects" item, so I asked Buckley to do the same.

"Thirty-four years ago," Buckley wrote,

> I took the law school aptitude test, vaguely thinking I intended to study law. It was six hours long, and if memory serves, two hours were devoted to giving the "correct" answer to such questions as you describe. I can honestly say that I spent most of the time wondering which was the answer the examiners probably desired me to give. I.e., something quite different from: Which was "the" correct answer. As often as not, no answer was "correct" in any exclusive way. Preemptively correct answers were scarce. What level of sophistication did the examiners want? Were they trying to establish whether the mind of the advocate was slyly at work? That kind of thing.
>
> You have succeeded not only in demonstrating that another answer is plausible in the example you treat, but that more than one other answer is plausible. And indeed the probe is of the ethos of the student, inquiring (most pruriently) into his own sense of personal or even social hierarchy. I further agree that stylistically many of the questions are objectionable on the grounds that the language affronts a sensitive user. You exactly explain why "immediacies . . . ultimates" is an awful case of Sunday-suited English. In short, you establish that the authors of the test questions are not equipped to ascertain exactly what they exactly insist they are ascertaining.

Von Hoffman and Buckley are both journalists. To add a more academic tone to my panel, I called upon Stephen R. Graubard. Graubard was a professor of history at Harvard for many years. Today he teaches at Brown and edits *Daedalus,* the journal of the American Academy of Arts and Sciences. Although acknowledging that he was "not an expert on the subject," Graubard wrote that the "certain aspects" item is "an example of a choice that in effect gives no choice at all. I would say that a really intelligent student might have chosen the answer that ETS wanted, but the chances just as good that he or she might have chosen at least two of the others. They would also be 'correct.' I don't think that questions of this sort ought to be asked."

I next called on John Simons, associate professor of English at Colorado College. I know that ETS values Simons's judgment, because for the last half-dozen years, ETS has flown him to Lawrence Township every summer to grade essay examinations. Simons was reluctant to join my panel; he enjoys his free trip east each year and I had warned him that ETS probably wouldn't invite him back if he dared to contradict its anonymous scholars. But after reading my critique of the "certain aspects" item, he felt obliged to risk his vacation. His analysis:

> At least three of the possible answers, (A), (B), and (E), are so closely related, and so clearly based on certain definite assumptions about democratic governments, that it seems impossible to argue that there is *one* right answer to the question. The answers are ambiguously worded in order to tantalize students into believing they *may* be right. But if argued in certain ways, why wouldn't they be right? This must certainly lead to confusion and consternation on the part of students who are asked to arrive at *one* correct answer.

I next called upon Elizabeth Hardwick, a novelist and a critic and advisory editor of the *New York Review of Books.* Her most recent book is *Bartleby in Manhattan,* a collection of literary essays. She didn't find the "certain aspects" item unambiguously ambiguous, but she did end up with a different answer from ETS's. "I agree that this is not a well conceived question," she wrote. "The only thing that makes B the best answer is that it is the only one with a sensible word order. The best answer, I think, would be D if the order were reversed to practicalities . . . principles. *Immediacies* and *ultimates* are not good English usage here, or at least not a felicitous usage. By way of certain thought patterns and a close examination, any of the alternatives could be described as reasonable, with the exception of perhaps C. Everything considered, I think I would have answered D."

The content of the "certain aspects" item is political, so I invited Andrew Hacker, professor of political science at Queens College in New York, to join my panel. Hacker teaches American politics and political theory. He is also a distinguished essayist who has written widely about education and other topics. "After examining the question, and fitting each pair of words into the blanks," he wrote,

> I concluded that the "correct" answer could be *either* (B) *or* (E). I was rather puzzled by the terms "immediacies" and "ultimates" in

(B), if only because they are not ones political scientists (or other students of politics) ordinarily use.

Still, I put myself in the shoes of a student taking the test, which meant I could only choose one answer. Well, truth to tell, I couldn't. I kept going back and forth between (B) and (E), with no resolution. Like Burden's Ass, who starved to death when faced with two piles of oats, I would have wasted so much time on this question, that my final score would be quite dismal.

By my count, five and a half of my six experts think ETS is out of its depth on the "certain aspects" question. Remember that this item passed every single test, both ordinary and extraordinary, subjective and statistical, that ETS could think to give it. Remember also that ETS has never once rescored a verbal item; as far as ETS is concerned, there has *never* been a flawed verbal question on a scored SAT. I think my experts have proved that ETS is incapable of detecting the real flaws in its test questions. And I think that such questions abound in ETS tests. (See Appendix A.)

Will ETS agree? Of course not. If past experience is any indication, ETS will arrogantly remain silent on this matter, despite its alleged eagerness to answer the questions of its customers and improve the quality of its tests. The company's test-makers will go about their business, confident that the objections of ignorant outsiders are too trivial to be taken seriously. The SAT, after all, is an objective test. Its assessment of "verbal aptitude" is arrived at with scientific precision. No question in it could possibly have more than one "best" answer.

I hereby challenge ETS to publish a written defense of its scoring of the "certain aspects" item and a point-by-point explanation of why Nicholas von Hoffman, William F. Buckley, Jr., Stephen Graubard, John Simons, Elizabeth Hardwick, Andrew Hacker, its own anonymous expert, and I are wrong. Bogus reviews by nameless "scholars" don't fulfill ETS's responsibility to back up its tests.

4

Numbers

IF ETS COULD SOMEHOW be persuaded to respond to the challenge at the end of the previous chapter, it would respond first with statistics. When I talked to Pamela Cruise about some SAT items I thought were flawed, she began by showing me a piece of paper called an item analysis on which several rows of numbers had been printed by a computer. These numbers, she said, proved me wrong. Looking at the item itself wouldn't really be necessary. The numbers would tell us everything we needed to know.

ETS almost always makes this sort of response to criticisms of its test items. Even in cases where it has acknowledged that its answers were incorrect, it has frequently also maintained that, on the strength of the statistics, the questions were really fine.

That the numbers say it all is the single great tenet on which the cult of mental measurement is founded. Statistics provide not only the justification for the scoring of individual items but also the blueprint by which tests are put together and the rubric according to which their results are interpreted. Understanding ETS requires first an understanding of the numbers that are its soul.

The most familiar ETS numbers are test scores. For the SAT and several other tests, these scores are reported on a scale that runs from 200 to 800. The scale was created by the College Board in the 1920s in an effort, according to Arthur Kroll, an ETS vice president, "to come up with a scale that was so different from any others that people wouldn't in fact start relating performance on it to other kinds of performance that's been distorted over time." The Board wanted a scale for the SAT that wouldn't look like the 0–100 scale used in schools. A score on the SAT shouldn't look like just some ordinary *grade*.

The Board also wanted a scoring method that wasn't subject to large yearly fluctuations. In 1926, 52.8 percent of the students who took the Board's physics examination earned the passing grade of 60 percent; in 1928, 81.9 percent passed. The difference was caused not by a sharp increase in knowledge of physics but by changes in the test. Some educators wondered aloud whether the College Board knew what it was doing. By switching to the 200–800 scale — which had no recognizable "passing score" — and by adjusting the scoring formula annually to reflect the shifting difficulty of the tests, the Board was able to solve, in the words of ETS, one of its "oldest and most embarrassing problems."[1]

Actually, the ETS scoring scale could just as easily run from 20 to 80; for more than a decade now, the third digit has always been a zero.* "The meaningful third digit was dropped some time ago," Kroll told me, "because it was clear that people were drawing too fine distinctions among scores on the SAT than what was warranted." In other words, the third digit ceased to be meaningful as soon as people began to ascribe meaning to it.

Kroll told me that the meaning*less* third digit had been adopted "because there was a long tradition" of having three-digit scores. Of course, back in the old days, the College Board had decided *not* to use the 0–100 scale partly for this same reason: there was a long tradition of using it. But nowadays the power of the SAT is inextricably linked with the numbers that represent it. Using two- instead of three-digit scores on the SAT would be like using simple percentages instead of batting averages in baseball: the numbers wouldn't seem quite so numinous anymore. Any change, Kroll said, "would in fact create discontinuities in the way the scale has been viewed all the time."

ETS puts an enormous emphasis on the continuity of scores. A 500 on this month's SAT is supposed to mean the same thing as a

---

*Even though every reported SAT score has only two meaningful digits, ETS initially computes each score to four decimal places (e.g., 591.2024). Every two-digit SAT score thus starts out as a seven-digit parody of precision.[2]

500 on last month's SAT, which is supposed to mean the same thing as a 500 on the SAT given in 1969. The process by which this uniformity is accomplished is called equating. Each edition of the test is equated, or linked statistically, with two that have preceded it. An SAT given this month might contain a section from an SAT given last year; if this month's students do better or worse than last year's, the scoring formula for this month's test will be adjusted accordingly. ETS maintains elaborate genealogical charts on which it is possible to trace each test's pedigree. The math SAT administered in December 1965, for example, was linked back to the ones in May 1963 and December 1960. It in turn provided one of two benchmarks for the tests given in January 1966 and May 1968.[3]

Every SAT administered in the last forty-five years can be traced back to the great-granddaddy of all equated SATs, the test given in April 1941. Until 1941, the SAT's 200–800 scale had been readjusted every year so that the mean grade was always 500. (ETS's Achievement Tests are still scored this way.) But in 1940 the College Board decided that because the scoring scale was constantly being redefined, "it was obviously not possible to make precise comparisons between candidates tested in one administration and candidates tested at another administration."[4] In order that such "precise comparisons" might be made, the mean score was set adrift, and the equating of tests began.

The great significance of equating is that it makes certain characteristics of the SAT quite uniform and predictable from year to year. Change in the test comes only very slowly. One advantage of this uniformity, in the eyes of ETS, is that it gives SAT scores a sort of indestructibility. Whatever else has changed in the world, the numbers are still the same. But this uniformity also has disadvantages. One of them is that the SAT's ultimate frame of reference is the spring of 1941, when, as it were, the test's DNA was encoded. To be sure, the SAT has evolved since then. For one thing, the hardest vocabulary words on the test are now considerably easier than they once were (ETS discovered that students just didn't know the tough words anymore). But innovations have been incorporated only if their performance on the test has been statistically indistinguishable from whatever it was they replaced.

ETS's faith in uniformity determines the process by which the SAT is built. Each form of the test is assembled according to a set of content and statistical specifications that stipulate exactly how individual items will be arranged, what their difficulty will be, and, in a more general way, what kind of material they will cover.

The verbal SAT's content specifications are extremely broad, leaving ETS's test development office a great deal of latitude. Antonyms, analogies, and sentence completions are divided into just four general content areas: (1) aesthetic/philosophical; (2) practical affairs; (3) science-related; (4) human relations. Sentence completion items are further classified according to whether they contain one blank or two. Analogies are classified according to whether the words represent real things or not and according to whether the words in the stem are related to the words in the options. For example, the specification 312 defines the content of the following SAT analogy:

SNAKE:PYTHON::
(A) bird:starling   (B) flower:blossom   (C) mammal:reptile
(D) lion:tiger   (E) rat:mouse

The first digit of the specification describes the content area (science-related); the second digit says the words are concrete (if they had not been concrete, this digit would have been 2); the third digit says meanings overlap (if there had been no animals among the choices, this digit would have been 1). That's all there is to it.*[6]

Vastly more important than the content specifications, in terms of assembling the test, are the statistical specifications. These are strict numerical guidelines that determine exactly how each test will be constructed. To find out whether newly written questions conform to these requirements, ETS "pretests" all new items. One thirty-minute section of the SAT consists of untried questions that

---

*ETS, in response to published criticism, has said that its items are "written according to very rigorous detailed specifications in terms of content, skills, and level of difficulty." With regard to content and "skills," anyway, this claim strikes me as being, at the very least, exaggerated.[5]

don't count toward students' scores. How students respond to these items determines whether they will ever be used on real SATs and, if so, how they will be arranged. This "experimental" section, as ETS calls it, is also used to equate current forms of the test with forms that have been used before.

Once the results of the pretest have been calculated, a new test can be assembled very quickly. The test assembler simply selects items with the proper statistics from a large pool of pretested ones and plugs them into the appropriate slots on the new test. Each new form also contains room for new pretests, ensuring that the SAT's genetic inheritance can be passed along to the next generation.

The equating and assembling of SATs both depend primarily on two statistics derived from pretests. The first is called the biserial coefficient of correlation. When I talked with Pamela Cruise, this was the first number she showed me. It was the number that proved, she said, that the items I had complained about were not ambiguous. ETS always refers first to this number in defending its test items. In the ETS canon, the biserial correlation is the holiest of holies.

Biserial correlation coefficients are used to express the statistical relationship between students' performance on a single item and their performance on the entire test. If the students who select ETS's answer to an SAT item score higher on the test as a whole than students who select the several incorrect answers, then the item has a high biserial correlation and is said to be working properly. In Cruise's words, it is distinguishing the "more able" from the "less able."

In a booklet for students published in 1962, ETS described in general terms how biserial correlations are used: "A question is considered effective to the extent that good students, as judged by their total score on the test, answer the questions correctly and poor students do not. If as many poor students as good students answer a question correctly, obviously such a question will add nothing to the effectiveness of the test, and it is discarded."[7]

But this definition is entirely circular. If ETS's only standard of "ability" is performance on the test (as it is), and if performance on the test is measured by individual items (as it is), then we end up back where we started: students who do well on individual items tend to do better on the test than students who do poorly. This would be hard to argue with, since it's true by definition. And yet this is the standard by which ETS assures its critics (and itself) of the quality of all its test items.

ETS's other favorite statistic is called delta. Like virtually all ETS statistics, delta sounds more sophisticated than it is. It's really just a fancy way of expressing the percentage of students who consider a particular item but either omit it or get it wrong. (Or, as ETS inimitably describes it, delta "is the normal deviate of the point above which lies the proportion of the area under the curve equal to the proportion of correct responses to the item.")[8] These percentages are converted to a different scale and tinkered with slightly to reflect the ability (as measured by performance on the test as a whole) of the students in the sample (as compared with the students who took the test back in 1941). For all practical purposes, the SAT delta scale runs from about 5.0 to about 19.0. An item that very few students get right might have a delta of 16.8; one that many get right might have a delta of 6.3.

Once again, ETS's logic is circular. Its only measure of "difficulty" is entirely internal. A question is hard if few people answer it correctly, easy if many do. But since delta refers to no standard beyond the item itself, it makes no distinction between difficulty and ambiguity or between one body of subject matter and another. Nor does it distinguish between knowledge and good luck. Delta can say only that a question was answered correctly by the exact percentage of people who answered it correctly. It takes a simple piece of known information and restates it in a way that makes it seem pregnant with new significance.

To see the effects of this circularity, we can do a little experiment. Suppose that Pamela Cruise has created a test with which she intends to rank you, me, and Gregory Anrig in terms of scholastic aptitude. The test has three questions, 1, 2, and 3. All three of us choose the correct answer to question 1. You and Anrig choose the correct answer to question 2. Anrig alone chooses the correct answer to question 3. According to Cruise's test, Anrig is the most able, you are second most able, and I am the least able. She runs her statistical analysis and is happy to discover that the test is working exactly as it should. Question 3 has the highest delta, because only one of us got it right. Therefore it's the hardest question. It also performed exactly as it was supposed to — that is, it had a perfect biserial correlation — because the one who got it right was also the one who scored the highest on the entire test. And the same is true for you and me and questions 1 and 2. Cruise happily reports to her boss that he's the smartest of the three of us and says she has the statistics to back it up.

But suppose we go back and administer the test again — with a different question 3. This time *you* get 3 right while Anrig and I get it wrong. Question 3 still has the same delta (because only one person got it right), and it still has a perfect biserial correlation (because you also had the highest score). But it has ranked the three of us in a different order. Our "aptitude," apparently, has changed.

Cruise could keep rewriting her test so that it would rank us in any order she desired. The test's results would depend only on which of the three of us happened to be familiar with whatever subject matter she selected for the particular items, or which of us happened to be tuned to her wavelength, or which of us happened to be lucky at guessing. Because of the circularity of the statistical standard by which she judged her results, Cruise would never be able to state with certainty that one of her tests was better than another or that one ranking was accurate and the others were not. As long as the items produced acceptable biserial correlations, the different outcomes would be statistically indistinguishable. The statistics can't tell us anything about the content of the items, or about ambiguity masked as difficulty, or about Cruise's point of view, or about the nature of whatever it is she thinks she's measuring.*

---

*Cruise told me that ETS relies on biserial correlations to help it eliminate ambiguous questions from the SAT, but ETS routinely uses items that must be considered ambiguous even by its own inadequate standard. SAT items with the highest deltas typically also have the lowest biserials. Indeed, the very "hardest" items on an SAT frequently have biserials that fall below ETS's arbitrary level of acceptability (.30). This must mean that in ETS's eyes, these items are the worst on the test at discriminating the "more able" from the "less able." And yet they are also the items that provide virtually all of the "selectivity" between students scoring in the top third of the scale. In 1971, in a technical publication prepared

ETS's statistical method is further weakened by flaws in its pretest procedure. Since the pretest sample for an individual edition of the SAT typically contains fewer than 1,500 students, tiny variations in these students' responses can have a huge impact on the way the final test is constructed. For example, only about 3 percent of the students who take the verbal SAT each year score in the upper third of the scoring scale — 600 or above. In a pretest sample precisely representative of this national testing population, only 45 of the 1,500 students would be expected to score in the same range. But this tiny subgroup would largely have the power to determine which "difficult" questions would be included on future SATs and which would be rejected. Lucky guesses by even two or three of these students could cause highly ambiguous questions to be approved for use on real SATs. ETS has no way of detecting this flaw. (Nor does it have any way of detecting the *intentional* sabotage of SAT pretests. For more on this, see Chapter 7.)

ETS uses a routine statistical formula to calculate the "measurement error" of its tests. Based on this calculation and others derived from it, it advises admissions officers to exercise caution in comparing test scores. "Our recommendation to colleges is that differences of less than 60 points should not be considered significant," said William H. Angoff, ETS's director of developmental research, in 1977.[10] Actually, Angoff's figure understates ETS's estimate of the SAT's measurement error. According to the 1983–84 *ATP Guide for High Schools and Colleges,* "Only when scores [on the verbal SAT] differ by more than 64 points . . . can there be reasonable certainty that there is a genuine difference in abilities being measured."[11] The *ATP Guide* for some reason doesn't mention it, but the comparable cushion for the math SAT is around 73 points. (For more on this very confusing subject, see Chapter 10.) Since SAT scores are reported only in 10-point increments, it follows that, according to ETS, admissions officers

---

for the College Board, ETS said that the "relationship between difficulty level and biserial coefficient may surprise readers" but noted that "it is not easy to write unambiguous difficult items."[9] Just so. One reason for the low biserials on hard items is that more students guess on these items and guessing throws off the correlation between correct answers and overall scores. But there is no way to distinguish a low biserial caused by guessing from one caused by bad writing or ambiguity.

should actually ignore differences of less than 70 points on the verbal and 80 points on the math — not 60, as Angoff stated.* Why doesn't ETS tell this to admissions officers?

Even after correcting for ETS's forgiving approximations, these calculations do not fully express the "error" of the SAT. Because of the narrowness of the statistical formulas by which they are derived, they fail to account for many factors that produce meaningless variations in scores. They do not, for example, "take into account day-to-day differences in examinee behavior or differences in administration environment," as ETS acknowledges.[13] Nor do they account for differences in test-taking skills. Nor do they account for the structural flaws in ETS's pretest procedure. Nor do they account for the sort of item ambiguity that doesn't show up in biserial correlations. Because they assume that speed is not a factor on the SAT, they understate the measurement error for students who have to hurry or don't have time to finish.[14] Since ETS's calculations of measurement error are based on single tests, they also fail to account for many of the blind spots in ETS's statistical model. Two editions of the SAT can conform to this model while producing substantially different results. Tests that seem to be working correctly for a group can nonetheless be highly variable in the scoring and ranking of individuals.

The "error" in an SAT score is thus far larger than ETS says it is. Should differences of even 100 points be considered significant? Should SAT scores perhaps be reported as a *single* digit (or not at all)?

In Chapter 3, I described four SAT items from a single section of a single SAT verbal test that I thought were flawed. Let's suspend reason for a moment and pretend that ETS has just conceded that

---

* If there is an admissions officer alive today who doesn't treat 60- and 70-point differences as though they were significant, I have yet to meet him. Characteristically, ETS likes to play both sides on this point. James Braswell, ETS's senior examiner in mathematics, told me that he thought 50-point differences were significant. Furthermore, ETS has said that although 60-point differences are statistically insignificant, "all things being equal, the student with an SAT verbal score about 60 points higher than another student is likely to have superior verbal ability. However, ETS emphasizes the statistical fallibility of scores to *discourage* overreliance on scores alone generally and on small score differences in particular."[12] But why then does it also *de*-emphasize this statistical fallibility? In order to *encourage* overreliance on scores?

all four items are indeed ambiguous and misleading. Would ETS believe these flaws to be significant? Would it think they cast doubt on the results of the test from which they were taken?

Certainly not. ETS believes — largely because of biserial correlations and other statistics — that a test is better than the sum of its flaws and that imperfections in individual items, assuming they could be proven to exist, don't have a significant impact on overall results. If a test contains enough questions, the theory goes, mistakes will take care of themselves.* This line of thinking is central to the standardized testing industry, but it isn't necessarily logical. "It is reminiscent," Banesh Hoffmann wrote, "of the manufacturer who said he lost money on each item he sold but made up for it by enormous volume of sales."[16]

Taking the SAT is an ordeal of mythic proportions, but the test is actually quite modest. The scored portions last just two hours. There are only eighty-five verbal questions and sixty math questions, all of them multiple-choice. With the exception of a few difficult math and reading comprehension items, students are expected to spend just a few seconds on each. There's nothing particularly daunting about the item types; antonyms, sentence completions, and analogies could as easily be called opposites, fill-in-the-blanks, and words-of-a-feather. If they appeared in a Sunday supplement, they would attract a loyal following.

A multiple-choice test is quite a crude device. One of the inescapable facts about it is that you can't use a single item to measure a *range* of performance. Each question is like a bit in a computer's memory: yes-no, true-false, right-wrong. Every question you add to your test increases the *test's* range of measurement (assuming each new question asks something different from what the previous one did), but each *question* adds only a single piece of information to the total picture.

Suppose that you want to find out how high a group of test-takers can count, up to a limit of, say, eighty-five. In a free-

---

* "Multiple-choice tests with as many as 100 questions permit wide sampling of subject matter and qualities of student thinking," wrote Henry Chauncey, the president of ETS, in 1961. "If a student should misinterpret one question or even several, his over-all score would not be seriously affected."[15] Note Chauncey's emphasis: questions aren't ambiguous; they are *misinterpreted*. This has always been the ETS position.

response test you could simply say, "Write out all the whole numbers between 0 and 86 in order." But in a multiple-choice test (i.e., in a test that can be graded by a machine) you'll need eighty-five items ("The first whole number larger than 0 is (A) 5 (B) 44 (C) 1 (D) 20 (E) 13; the second whole number is. . . ." And so on). Assuming you remember not to number your questions, you'll end up with a similar picture of your group's counting ability. But you'll have needed eighty-five questions to discover what you could have discovered with one. Furthermore, the quality of your results will depend on how well you wrote all your questions; if "85" is not among the choices on the eighty-fifth item, you won't be able to distinguish a person who can count up to eighty-five from one who can only count up to eighty-four. In addition, your results will be somewhat distorted because some of your multiple-choice test-takers will have been more successful than others in guessing the answers to items they didn't know.

A verbal SAT, as it happens, consists of eighty-five items. Since each item has its own delta, you can take all eighty-five items and line them up, from 1 to 85, in order of their "difficulty," the same way we arranged the items in our counting test. In fact, ETS does essentially this in building its exams. Every test, section, and subsection is arranged so that it tends to increase in difficulty from beginning to end.* Thus, the last item in an antonym subsection will be more difficult than the first one, and all the other items will be arranged along a rough scale in between. Test-takers who understand this know that, for instance, it is foolish to spend a lot of time puzzling over the last few items in a given subsection if the *first* few items in the *next* subsection have not yet been attempted, since they will certainly be easier. The only sensible strategy is to save all puzzling items for the very end, after the easy points have been scored. (It also makes sense to save reading comprehension questions till the end, since, compared with the rest of the test, these cumbersome items offer a very small return in possible points on a very large investment in time.)

---

*The only exceptions to this rule are the items that follow reading comprehension passages. The arrangement of these items is based on the organization of the passages to which they refer. A question about the first paragraph comes ahead of a question about the last paragraph. The passages themselves, however, appear in ascending order of difficulty.

It undoubtedly seems simplistic to compare an SAT to the multiple-choice counting test I described earlier, but the two tests are *intended* to perform in exactly the same way. There's nothing remarkable about this; it follows necessarily from the way the tests are built. If the SAT is functioning exactly as it is supposed to, each student will climb the delta ladder, answering questions correctly precisely up to the limit of his "aptitude," and then he will be able to answer no more.

ETS will say that no one would ever expect a real test to behave in this ideal manner. But by ETS's own criteria, an SAT must be viewed as *flawed* precisely to the extent that it fails to do so. Suppose that you and I take an SAT verbal exam and that we each miss five items. We'll both receive the same score — on a recent test, it would have been 720. But suppose that the five items you missed were the five "easiest" items on the test, while I missed the five "most difficult." In my case, the test behaved exactly as it was supposed to. I missed the items that a person who scores 720 is supposed to miss. But in your case, something went wrong. Our performances on the test don't mean the same thing. In the test's own terms, my score is more accurate than yours, because the errors I made — once again in the test's own terms — were more meaningful than yours. But of course there's no way to tell us apart by looking at our scores.

On any single SAT that is functioning *exactly* as it should, there is only one important item: the last one on the delta ladder that the student gets correct. For a student who scores 720 on an ideal SAT, the first seventy-nine items on the delta scale are superfluous, because 100 percent of the information his score conveys about him is conveyed exclusively by his performance on the eightieth item. We can now think of a verbal SAT not as a single eighty-five-item exam but as a large number of very much smaller exams, all of which have been lumped together in a single booklet in order to make it more convenient for ETS to measure, at one sitting, more than a million people of widely disparate backgrounds, abilities, and levels of education. All those easy "tests" at the bottom of the scale don't add any accuracy to the score of someone who performs at the very top; all they can do is subtract from it, by failing to convey the information that the logic of the test says they should. And for someone who scores at the bottom of the scale, the questions at the top can affect his score (and hence its accuracy) only to the extent that he beats or doesn't beat chance in guessing at the answers.

For any given SAT-taker, the true "test" that determines ETS's assessment of his "scholastic aptitude" is actually very much smaller than the entire eighty-five-item sample. If the real business of determining your score (and thus your attractiveness in relation to other people applying to the college you want to attend) is actually being done by five or ten difficult questions, the quality and content of individual items begin to take on an immense significance. No college would ever consider creating a ten-minute, ten-item multiple-choice test (with, say, two sentence completions, two analogies, two antonyms, and two reading comprehension passages with two questions each) and using it to determine anything at all about its applicants, much less their "scholastic aptitude." The idea is ridiculous. Yet all selective schools do essentially this very thing every time they allow an admissions decision to be affected by an SAT score.

Let's return to the four items I discussed earlier, still assuming that they really are flawed and ambiguous. Choosing the answers I argued for instead of ETS's answers would lower a student's verbal SAT score by about 50 points.* If we assume that the other three sections of the test contain an equal number of ambiguous items (and I think they contain at least as many), the penalty is 200 points over the test as a whole.

But let's assume that the four bad items I found in one section are the only bad items on the entire test, and that the penalty is just 50 points. Fifty points on the verbal, according to the 1984–85

---

*Missing four questions on a verbal SAT could lower a student's score by as many as 70 points or as few as 10, depending on how he did on the rest of the test.[17] Although, according to ETS, no item on an SAT is worth more points than any other, items actually become more valuable as a student answers more of them. On a recent verbal SAT, the difference between getting no questions right and getting six of them right was 20 points — the same as the difference between getting eighty-four and getting eighty-five.[18] The rungs on the delta ladder, as it were, are much closer together on the lower reaches than they are near the top. A 50-point difference in scores near the top end of the scale thus means much less, in terms of actual performance on the test, than a 50-point difference near the bottom. But admissions officers aren't told this.

edition of the *Selective Guide to Colleges,* is the difference between Princeton and Pomona, or Williams and Wake Forest, or Stanford and Occidental, or Smith and Agnes Scott.[19] Not a desperate predicament, perhaps. But should the outcome be determined, even in part, by how a student decides — over the course of perhaps a minute — to answer a handful of badly written multiple-choice questions? And remember that we haven't even looked at the rest of the verbal test, or at any of the math test, or at the sort of flaws that *can* be detected by statistics, or at anything besides sloppy writing and ambiguity.

Fifty points, wherever they come from, can make a very big difference on the SAT. Dropping from 600 to 550 on the verbal test would have lowered a student from the ninety-third to the eighty-sixth percentile of college-bound seniors in 1982, a difference of approximately 70,000 students. If you divide the number of students who take the SAT each year by the number of questions on the verbal test, you find that each question is responsible for "selecting," on average, 14,000 students. Assuming that the test makes a difference in admissions decisions, item quality is not a trivial matter.[20]

The impact of badly written items is felt throughout the test, but it is probably felt more in the upper third of the scoring scale. Like virtually any standardized multiple-choice test, each SAT contains a disproportionate number of items with intermediate delta values, since most students who take the test score nearer the mean than either extreme. In other words, because many more students score 450 than 750, many more items are geared to the former than to the latter. According to ETS, this makes the test more "discriminating" in the middle range. This is desirable, ETS says, because the middle range is where most of the students who take the test end up. As two ETS researchers wrote in 1971, "The requirement that the SAT be useful for many colleges and candidates sets a distinct limit on its scope, for in order for the test to be efficient it should contain only test materials that are suitable for measuring the abilities of the majority of students who are asked to take it. This makes sense, for it would not be efficient to widen the scope of the content . . . at the expense of requiring most students to be examined on material that has little relevance to their particular college admissions situation."[21]

But loading up the middle of the SAT also makes the test *less* discriminating in the upper range — from, say, 600 to the top. Fewer students score in this range than in the middle or below, and fewer items are aimed directly at them. But these high-scoring students are precisely the ones for whom test scores presumably make the most difference in admissions decisions. When highly selective colleges — the colleges that make the most use of SAT scores — select their freshman classes, they do so from applicant pools that typically abound in attractive candidates — good grades, good scores, lots of activities, nice recommendations, well-written essays. Small score differences between otherwise similar candidates in these groups can presumably have a decisive impact. But the part of the SAT that determines these score differences — the last few widely spaced rungs of the delta ladder — is the least meaningful part of the entire test, even by ETS's standards. The questions that constitute it are the worst at distinguishing, in ETS's terms, the "more able" from the "less able" (because they have the lowest biserial correlations). They are the items most subject to sampling error (because there are so few of them). They are the items most likely to be ambiguous (because, as ETS says, "it is not easy to write unambiguous difficult items").[22] They are the items most likely to be ambiguous in ways that ETS can't even begin to detect (because they are the items most likely to contain flaws that are invisible to ETS's statistical model).

All of this is not meant to suggest that the SAT is accurate at the bottom end of the scoring scale. Down in the dreary region between 200 and 350 or so, the SAT has virtually no discriminating power at all. Perhaps 4 percent of all test-takers (and as many as 15 percent of black test-takers) would score higher on the math SAT if they answered *none* of the questions and simply left their answer sheets blank.* So many students score below the chance level on the math SAT that ETS has to calculate negative raw

---

*Actually, they should fill out their answer sheets at random. ETS doesn't score sections left entirely blank. If a student doesn't respond to at least three items, he receives the minimum score of 200. An even better strategy would be to spend the entire thirty minutes allotted for each of the two math sections on the first three problems in each section. Answering just these six problems correctly (and leaving all fifty-four others blank) would produce a score of about 320 — better than more than a third of blacks and roughly 10 percent of all students.

scores in order to achieve a "normal" (bell-shaped) distribution of scaled scores.* If ETS didn't do this, there would be a huge black bulge at the bottom of the scoring graph. A raw score of zero — which a student would earn by leaving his answer sheet blank — translates into a scaled score of anywhere from 250 to 280. This is a scoring level that perhaps 40,000 students failed to achieve in 1983.[23]

To get an idea of what ETS *really* thinks about the "accuracy" of SATs, all you have to do is look at its principal method of detecting cheating. ETS's scoring machines are programmed to set aside the answer sheets of students who, in taking the SAT for the second time, score suspiciously higher or lower than they did before. In order to set off the machines in this way, there has to be a 250-point difference between the first verbal or math score and the second. (The computer will also kick out a test on which the *combined* score is 350 points higher or lower than it was the first time.)[24]

If you take the verbal SAT and score 500, and then you take it again and score either 260 or 740 — scores that encompass all but 120 points of the total scale — ETS's computers won't bat an eye. (If the difference is more than 250 points, ETS will look for irregularities in your signature or similarities to the answer sheets of students who sat near you. In most cases, ETS says, no damaging evidence is found and the scores are allowed to stand.) If a 250-point difference in scores on two versions of the same test isn't cheating, what is it? Does ETS think that "scholastic aptitude" is so volatile that it can grow or shrink by 50 percent during the summer between a student's junior and senior years?

---

*On the verbal SAT, by contrast, a student can answer two or three questions correctly and still receive a 200. There is only one subsection on the verbal SAT on which significant subgroups perform below the chance level, the analogy subsection. The problem would disappear if ETS were better at explaining to students exactly what sort of analogy it counts as correct. Many students are confused on this point, and several SAT preparation books compound the problem. For more on this, see Chapter 7.

5

Tempting the Medicine Freaks

ETS USES NUMBERS to build its tests, but it needs people to write the items. Understanding how these people think is one of the keys both to doing well on their tests and to penetrating the mystique in which they cloak their work. Despite ETS's claims of "science" and "objectivity," the company's tests are written by subjective human beings who tend to think in certain predictable ways.

The easiest way to see this is to look at the tests themselves. Which test doesn't really matter. How about the Achievement Test in French? Here's an item from a recent edition:[1]

---

2. Un client est assis dans un restaurant chic. Le garçon maladroit lui renverse le potage sur les genoux. Le client s'exclame:

    (A) Vous ne pourriez pas faire attention, non?
    (B) La soupe est délicieuse!
    (C) Quel beau service de table!
    (D) Je voudrais une cuiller!

My French is vestigial at best. But with the help of my wife I made this out as follows:

---

2. A customer is seated in a fancy restaurant. The clumsy waiter spills soup in his lap. The customer exclaims:

    (A) You could not pay attention, no?
    (B) The soup is delicious!

(C) What good service!
(D) I would like a spoon!

Now, B, C, and D strike me as nice, funny, sarcastic responses that come very close to being the sort of remark I would make in the situation described. A spoon, waiter, for the soup in my lap! But, of course, in taking a test like this, the student has to suppress his sometimes powerful urge to respond according to his own sense of what is right. He has to remember that the "best" answer — which is what ETS always asks for, even on math and science tests — isn't necessarily a good answer or even a correct one. He has to realize that the ETS answer will be something drab, humorless, and plodding — something very like A, as indeed it is (even though, of the four choices, the only genuine exclamation — which is what the question seems to ask for — is C). Bright students sometimes have trouble on ETS tests, because they tend to see possibilities that the question writers missed. The advice traditionally given to such students is to take the test quickly and without thinking too hard.

Another way to learn about the ETS mentality is to investigate how ETS writes and assembles examinations. This is difficult to do, because most of the information that is publicly available is cursory, scattered, and misleading. But with some determined digging around, even an outsider can get an idea of what goes on inside ETS's test development office.

ETS likes to imply that most of its questions are written by eminent professors and carefully trained experts in whatever fields it is testing. In fact, most test items, and virtually all "aptitude" items, are written by ordinary company employees, or even their children. Frances Brodsky, the daughter of ETS executive vice president David J. Brodsky, spent the summer after she graduated from high school writing questions for ETS tests. Writing questions requires no special academic training. Aileen L. Cramer went to ETS in 1963 after working as a juvenile probation officer and as an elementary school teacher. Her first job at ETS was writing and reviewing questions for the Multistate Bar Examination (MBE), the Graduate Record Examinations (GRE), the National Teacher Examinations (NTE), and the California Basic Educational Skills

Test (CBEST). ETS occasionally runs advertisements in the company newspaper, telling secretaries and other employees that writing test items is a good way to earn extra money. Other item writers are brought in on a freelance basis. Former employees sometimes earn pocket money by writing questions part-time. "Student interns" from nearby colleges and graduate schools are also hired.

Frances Brodsky and Aileen L. Cramer, for all I know, are excellent question writers. But they aren't the sort of people outsiders think of as the people who write ETS's tests. Many people, for example, assume that the questions for the Law School Admission Test (LSAT) are written by law school professors or prominent attorneys. But this is not the case.

"We would sit around and discuss," I was told by a young man who, on the invitation of a friend at ETS, wrote questions for the LSAT while a graduate student in English at Princeton. "Say I had written a question. I would say, 'Well, it seems to me that I was looking for answer A to be the right answer, for these reasons.' But then in fact people would say, 'Most of us chose answer B,' and then what we would try to do was revise the passage or the stem in some way to lead people more directly to what seemed to be the reasonable answer. It was all pretty pragmatic. It wasn't very theoretical or anything.

"I had always known this to be true, but it had never been presented to me with such force: that there is no Platonic correct answer to any of these questions; it's all determined by the statistical performance of the question as it relates to other questions. And if students who tend to do well on the exam generally tend to pick the same answer, then the question must be pretty good."

This item writer had never actually taken — or even seen — the test he helped to create, but he became fairly adept at writing questions for it. "I did quite a few," he told me. "It's pretty tedious. The first time it took a week or two to do ten. By the end I could do ten or twenty a day. I think we were paid fifteen dollars a question whether or not it appeared on a test."

Every test is built by a single assembler, who arranges individual items in strict accordance with the statistical specifications described in Chapter 4. When the test has been put together, the assembler gives it to two or three colleagues for a review. ETS's test reviews aren't meant to be seen by the public. The words SECURE and E.T.S. CONFIDENTIAL are stamped in red ink at the top of every page. But the review materials for the SAT administered in May of 1982 were used as evidence in a court case, and I obtained a copy.[2] (The test itself can be found in *6 SATs,* beginning on page 79.)

An ETS test review doesn't take very long. The reviewer simply answers each item, marking his choices on ordinary lined paper and making handwritten comments on any items that seem to require improvement. For example, the fourth item in the first section was an antonym problem:

---

4. BYPASS: (A) enlarge   (B) advance   (C) copy
   (D) throw away   (E) go through

The first reviewer, identified only as "JW," suggested substituting the word "clog" for one of the distractors, because "Perhaps clog would tempt the medicine freaks." In other words, JW said, if the item were worded a little differently, more future physicians might be tempted to answer it incorrectly. The assembler, Ed Curley, decided not to follow JW's suggestion, but the comment is revealing of the level at which ETS analyzes its tests.

In ETS test reviews, the emphasis is not always on whether keyed answers are good or absolutely correct but on whether they can be defended in the event that someone later complains. When the second test reviewer, Pamela Cruise, wondered whether answering one difficult item required "outside knowledge," Ed Curley responded, "We must draw the line somewhere but I gave item to Sandy; she could not key — none of the terms were familiar to her. She feels that if sentence is from a legit. source, we could defend." ETS test reviewers alternate between an *American Heritage* and a Webster's dictionary, depending on which supports the answer ETS has selected. (See Appendix A.) In reviewing item 44, JW wrote, "Looked fine to me but AH Dict. would suggest that *matriarchy* is a social system & *matriarchate* a state (& a gov't system). Check Webster." Curley did this and responded, "1st meaning of 'matriarchy' in Webs. is 'matriarchate' so item is fine."

I'd always thought that ETS item writers must depend heavily on dictionaries. ("I had some pause over this too, but tight by dictionary," Curley wrote in response to a criticism of item 10 in the first section.) The diction in SAT questions is sometimes slightly off in a way that suggests the item writers are testing words they don't actually use. ("It ain't often you see CON-VOKE!" noted JW of a word tested in one item.) SAT items also often test the third, fourth, or fifth meanings of otherwise common words, which can create confusion. In the following item from the same test, the word *decline* is used peculiarly:

---

17. He is an unbeliever, but he is broad-minded enough to decline the mysteries of religion without —— them.

     (A) denouncing (B) understanding (C) praising
     (D) doubting (E) studying

My *Webster's Seventh New Collegiate Dictionary* gives the fourth meaning of *decline* as "to refuse to accept." This is more or less what ETS wants to say. But the dictionary goes on to explain that *decline* in this sense "implies courteous refusal esp. of offers and invitations." This usage, and not ETS's, is the proper one. What ETS really wants here is a word like *reject*. Pamela Cruise made a similar comment in her review, but the item was not changed. ("Sounds fine to me and is supported by dictionary," wrote Curley.)

It may simply be that ETS item writers don't write very well. Here's a sentence from a reading passage in the same test: "Yet if Anne Bradstreet is remembered today in America, it is not, correctly, as the American colonies' first poet, but as a 'Puritan poet,' even though her 1650 edition is an essentially secular volume — not only not 'Puritan,' but not particularly Christian." Yet if . . . it is not . . . but . . . even though . . . not only not . . . but not. JW pointed out that this sentence was "*very* confusing." And Cruise noted that the first question following the passage was "unnecessarily confusing cause of the negative in the stem & in the options." Curley agreed with JW and apologized to Cruise (with a "sorry" in the margin), but neither the passage nor the question was rewritten.

ETS is almost always reluctant to change the wording of test items, or even the order of distractors, because small changes can make big differences in statistics. Substituting *reject* for *decline* could make an item easier to answer, thus lowering its delta and throwing off the test specifications.* Making even a slight alteration in an item can necessitate a new pretest, which is expensive. Revisions are made only grudgingly, even if assembler and reviewer agree that something is wrong. "Key a bit off, but ok," Cruise wrote in regard to one item. JW commented on another: "At pretest I would have urged another compound word or unusual distractor. However its tough enuf as is."

Test assemblers don't like being criticized by test reviewers. When Cruise described item 26 as a "weak question — trivial," Curley responded in the margin, "Poop on you!" The question stayed in the test. Curley's most frequent remark is a mildly petulant "but OK as is," which is scribbled after most criticisms. Assemblers invest a great deal of ego in their tests, and they don't like to be challenged. Reviewers often try to soften their comments so the assembler won't take umbrage. "I keyed only by elimination, but I think that was my problem," JW wrote about item 10 in the first section. Sometimes the reviewer is nearly apologetic. "Strictly speaking (too strictly probably), doesn't the phoenix symbolize death & rebirth rather than immortality. Item's OK, really. It needs Scotch tape." JW concluded this comment by drawing a little smiling face. (The item was not changed.)

The phoenix item also drew a comment from Pamela Cruise. "Well — item ok — but this reminds me of the kind of thing we used to test but don't do much now — relates to outside knowledge — myth, lit., etc. . . . . This might be an item that critics pick on." The item:

---

42. PHOENIX:IMMORTALITY::

    (A) unicorn:cowardice (B) sphinx:mystery
    (C) salamander:speed (D) ogre:wisdom
    (E) chimera:stability

---

*ETS doesn't pursue the implications. If correcting the wording of a question changes the way it performs on the test, then some of the people now getting it wrong (or right, as the case may be) are doing so *only because* it is badly written.

Cruise said she would "be more inclined to defend item if it were a delta fifteen." The item had been rated somewhat lower, at delta 13.2. What Cruise *thought* she was saying was that if the item had been more "difficult," and thus intended for "abler" students, the ambiguity in it would have been less objectionable. But all she was really saying was that she would have been more inclined to defend the item if fewer people had answered it correctly. (Or, to put it another way, she would have thought it less ambiguous if it had been more ambiguous.) This, of course, doesn't make any sense. Cruise had forgotten the real meaning of delta and fallen victim to her own circular logic. ETS's scientific hocus-pocus ends up deceiving not only us but also ETS.

Curley didn't share Cruise's peculiar concern. "Think we can defend," he wrote. "Words are in dictionary, they have modern usage, and we test more specialized *science* vocab than this. Aren't we willing to say that knowledge of these terms is related to success in college?"

Some items, including the following one, provide especially revealing glimpses into the ETS mentality. The intended answer is E.

---

15. Games and athletic contests are so intimately a part of life that they are valuable ———— the intensity and vitality of a given culture at any one time.

    (A) modifiers of   (B) antidotes to   (C) exceptions to
    (D) obstacles to   (E) indices of

"What does intensity of culture mean?" asked JW, answering, "Nothing, I suspect." This strikes me as a comment worth pursuing, but Curley made no response. Cruise also paused at number 15: "Odd to say that games are indices of the intensity & vitality of a culture — more like intensity & mood or intensity & special interests. When I think of the vitality of a culture, I want to take a lot more than games into account." (The "special interests" of a culture?) Curley, in a marginal note, explained that the word "vitality" was "needed to make B wrong." He also explained why A was not a suitable answer: "Cuz why would you want to *lessen* the vitality? And if by 'modifier' you mean 'changer' or 'qualifier' then the word still has negative connotations."

Ed Curley, believing that to modify something is to "lessen" it and that change has only "negative connotations," found this item okay-as-is and moved on to other matters. But he ought to have thrown it out. Number 15 is badly written ("given" and "at any one time" are meaningless padding; most of the other words are vague; what does it mean to be "intimately a part of life"?), and ETS's answer is not obviously the "best" choice. "Intensity" of culture, as JW points out, is meaningless; to say that one culture is more intense than another is like saying that one animal's biology is more intense than another's. Curley says that the purpose of the word "vitality" is "to make B wrong," which implies that in his mind cultural intensity is a negative quality, something for which an antidote would be desirable. If this is true, ETS's sentence is nonsensical: vitality and intensity are terms in opposition to each other.

Chess and basketball, two games played avidly in both the United States and the Soviet Union, are not, in and of themselves, indices of anything at all about the "intensity and vitality" of these two very different cultures. Games and athletic contests are more nearly *modifiers* of culture than *indices* of it: they are part of culture (along with literature, painting, government, music, and so on), and by being part of it they change it. Whether this is "valuable" or not is a matter of opinion and surely ought not to be the basis for scoring a question on a vocabulary test. Answer A strikes me as the "best" choice among five very unappealing possible responses to a badly written and ill-conceived question.

In a defense of this item, Ed Curley and his colleagues might haughtily imply that they had delved more deeply into its nuances than any layman could ever hope to. But the confidential test reviews prove that ETS's test-makers are hardly the sophisticated scientists they pretend to be. Their trademarks are flabby writing, sloppy thinking, and a disturbing uncertainty about the meanings of shortish words.

A committee of "prominent specialists in educational and psychological measurement,"[3] appointed by the College Board, reviews each SAT before it is administered. ETS and the Board talk publicly about the SAT Committee as though it were a sort of psychometric Supreme Court sitting in thoughtful judgment on every question on the SAT. According to the official mythology, the SAT Committee ensures the integrity of the test by subjecting it to rigorous, independent, expert scrutiny. But in fact committee members are largely undistinguished in the measurement field. They seem to have no real power.[4]

"They always hate to see my comments," says Margaret Fleming, one of the committee's ten members and a deputy superintendent in Cleveland's public school system. "Now, we have had some showdowns about it. Sometimes they change, but I find that item writers are very pompous about their work, and they don't like you to say anything. I am saying something, though, because I feel that maybe forty people are responsible for writing items, let's say, for the verbal area, and why should forty people govern by chance what thousands of youngsters' opportunities might be?"

Far fewer than forty people are involved in writing an SAT, but no matter. I asked Fleming if she thought ETS resisted her criticisms.

"I *do* find resistance," she said. "It's different in mathematics, for example, where there is a hierarchy of subject matter rather agreed that one ought to know some geometrical principles or know equations and the way to handle them, and then the processes of addition, subtraction, etc. In the reading areas, the verbal area, there's not that, you know, well-defined hierarchy of what we think it is. We do feel, though, that a person with an extensive vocabulary base, a person who is well read, generally does better in a college situation. But how one samples this preparation is what is at issue. You know, which words. Theoretically, any word that is in the English language that you could arrange in an antonym or an analogy or a sentence completion or a reading comprehension format could be tested. And I just want to make sure that youngsters have had an access to that in some way. Oh, for example, occasionally something will creep in that is not just through information in that test item; it is something based upon past experience which may be related to your social class or your ethnic group, and that's what I'm always on the lookout for. I think you ought to try to get some universal items rather than something like, say, the rules of polo. Well, who knows the rules? I don't. Do you?"

I think she meant that good verbal tests are harder to write than good math tests, although, as she told me later, "they make more goofs on mathematics than they do on the verbal, because the verbal you can always come up with a reason." Perhaps she meant only that language is less precise than mathematics — an opinion that would be hard to argue with under the circumstances. I asked her again how ETS responded to her criticisms.

"They generally many times try to dismiss it," she said. "Sometimes they're very stubborn. Now, the one I got back recently was about a word that my dictionary said is a noun. Now, I'm using *American Heritage Dictionary,* which I feel is common access across the country. I haven't got the Oxford English unabridged thirty-volume thing. All I've got is what most people would have. And I said, the options here are verbs, and it appears that this is the only item with different parts of speech for the stem and the options. And they said, 'Well, this word is also a verb, and it's tested as such in this item.' You see, they are going around my complaint."

I called Hammett Worthington-Smith, an associate professor of English at Albright College in Reading, Pennsylvania, and asked him to describe his duties on the SAT Committee.

"We review exams," he said, "we prepare questions, we take the tests, and that type of thing."

"You prepare questions in addition to reviewing tests?" I asked.

"Yes, we have that opportunity."

"And do you do that?"

"Yes."

But committee members *don't* write questions for the SAT. Willie M. May, chairman of the committee and assistant principal for personnel and programming at Wendell Phillips High School in Chicago, told me in no uncertain terms that preparing questions was *not* one of his committee's duties. "We are in an advisory capacity," he said. "We don't do any tinkering at all."

When I asked Worthington-Smith what test reviewing involved, he said, "You know, normally what anyone else would do with this one particular test. Now, I don't want to spend much more time on this, because we do exactly what the College Board statement says, so I don't know what you're out fishing for."

"I'm not fishing for anything," I said.

"Okay, so that's enough for today." And he hung up on me. Our phone conversation had lasted exactly two and a half minutes.

According to the College Board's one-paragraph "Charge to SAT Committee," each member reviews, by mail, two tests a year.[5] An ETS answer key is included with each test. I asked committee member William Controvillas, a guidance counselor at Farmington High School in Farmington, Connecticut, what these reviews entailed. "Reviewing involves both verbal as well as the math," he said. "You review the questions to make sure that the question is legible and that there aren't any trick language aspects to it, and that it's clear, and that you come up with the answer that you think should be gotten. You get an answer sheet and some statistics with it. If you happen to be less competent in math, you still review it for language. I tend to be more verbal."

In the course of our conversation, Controvillas used the word *criteria* twice as a singular noun and told me that the committee reviews each test "physically" (he also seemed to be uncertain about the meaning of *legible*). In general, he said, he found the SAT impressive. "These are tests, of course, that are made up by professional test-makers, so in a sense what you're doing is applying some kind of quality control. A quality control function."

Another of the official duties of the SAT Committee (the College Board's "Charge" lists eight altogether) is "to become thoroughly familiar" with the test's "psychometric properties." To make this possible, ETS encloses a package of statistics with every SAT it sends out for review. Committee members — even those whose strengths, like Margaret Fleming's and William Controvillas's, are primarily verbal — are supposed to consult these numbers in making their reviews. The computerized "item analysis" for a single SAT runs to roughly fifty pages and contains thousands of very daunting calculations, including observed deltas, equated deltas, response frequencies, P-totals, M-totals, mean criterion scores, scaled criterion scores, and biserial correlation coefficients. What committee members make of these numbers is hard to say. "Math is not my forte," said Jeanette B. Hersey, dean of admissions at Connecticut College and a recent member of the committee. But she learned a lot about psychometrics during her term. "I was really very innocent when I went on the committee about what was involved in testing," she told me. "So that's why I say I learned a great deal about the orderly development of tests, the kind of fieldwork that's done, and the resources that are used."

The SAT Committee's *real* duties have more to do with public relations than with test development. Committee members tiptoe through questions and statistics they don't understand, flattered to have been asked to look at them in the first place, and then help spread the good word about ETS. ETS has little interest in their opinions. By the time the committee receives a test, changing it is virtually impossible. "Minor revisions can be made in questions at this stage," says an ETS document, referring to a test development stage *prior* to the one in which the committee is consulted, "but a major revision in a question makes it necessary to repretest the question in order to determine the effect of the changes on the statistical characteristics of a question."[6] Such revisions are almost never made. As soon as committee members have completed their busywork, the test is sent to the printer.

6

Coaching

ETS AND THE COLLEGE BOARD have consistently held that coaching for the SAT and similar examinations doesn't work. "The [SAT] is not built around any particular course normally offered in secondary school," the two organizations argued in 1955, suggesting that success on the test was the "product of two things: the student's native ability — 'the brains he was born with' — and the opportunities for mental exercise that he finds in his school, his home, and his community. Thus the only 'preparation' for the SAT that might have an effect on the score is, in a sense, a lifetime of intellectual challenge."[1]

In order to discourage students from attempting to improve their scores by doing much beyond remaining alive, ETS and the Board have made similar pronouncements many times over the years. "The magnitude of the gains resulting from coaching vary [sic] slightly," said the Board in 1965 (in a booklet that has come to be known, even in some circles at ETS, as "The Little Green Book That Lies"), "but they are always small regardless of the coaching method used or the differences in the students coached."[2] In 1970, the Board's Commission on Tests gravely pondered the coaching question and concluded that "if verbal and mathematical aptitude, especially verbal aptitude, can be developed within the length of, say, a school year, no one has yet demonstrated a way to do it."[3]

Coaching was of great concern to the Board even before the SAT was introduced. In the early 1900s, some high school teachers developed a knack for predicting which passage from Virgil, or which scene from Shakespeare, would be selected for the next year's College Boards. Hoping to eliminate this problem, the Board in 1916 made a partial shift away from examinations that were directly linked to identifiable curricula. The new College Boards were called "comprehensives," and their content was designed to be as broad as possible.

"The comprehensive examinations were a symbol of a shift in educational thought," wrote the Board's historian in 1950, "— an evolution from rigidity to flexibility, from narrowness to breadth, from emphasis on content to emphasis on choice. Under the new system the English teacher, instead of being shackled year after year to specified 'classics,' some of them repugnant to youthful minds, could wander as he pleased in the 'realms of gold,' even using contemporary essays and biographies to interest his pupils. . . . For many schools it seemed like the opening of a marvelous era."[4]

This was the first stage of what might be called the Birth of Aptitude, or the College Board's flight from subject matter. Skeptics argued that the new tests "would place a premium on superficial cleverness at the expense of scholarship."[5] But change was in the air, and from comprehensives it was but a small step to SATs. In 1919, Thomas S. Fiske, a professor of mathematics at Columbia and secretary of the Board, spoke of a need for tests that would measure "certain important intellectual qualities which are sometimes described as alertness, power, and endurance. . . ."[6] The new emphasis was not on knowledge but on a sort of vaguely defined intellectual vigor. The comprehensive examinations, and the SATs that followed them, would enable the Board to measure the raw aptitude lurking beyond a fog of facts and figures. The specific content of these aptitude tests, according to the new theory, was largely incidental; the real object of measurement was the vitality of the human mind.

Because the Board thought in these terms — envisioning an opposition between knowledge and "mental power" — it simply assumed that the new tests would not be coachable. How could a student prepare for a test that, by design, was based on no particular course of study? Indeed, a test that *could* be coached could not be thought of as an *aptitude* test at all.

Actually, the early SATs were extremely coachable, certainly more so than the essay examinations they at first supplemented and later replaced. The first SAT was highly speeded and heavily dependent on complicated item types, two features that made it susceptible to the sort of special preparation that the College Board had intended to eradicate. It's improbable that coaching of this sort went on to any significant extent, but students with a knack for rapid puzzle-solving would have had a tremendous advantage, particularly because "objective" tests had not yet become a familiar part of the educational landscape. The College Board recognized this problem and, from 1926 to 1944, required candidates to present a completed practice test when they showed up for their exams in order to prove that they had made themselves familiar with the novel construction of the test. The Board also slowed down the breakneck pace of the exams and eliminated the trickier item types, soon settling on a format not vastly different from the one students see today.[7]

Since coaching is so intimately bound up with their assumptions about aptitude, the College Board and ETS have always been touchy on this subject. "If the Board's tests can be regularly beaten through coaching," declared the Board in 1955, "then the Board is itself discredited."[8] In 1962, Dean K. Whitla, director of testing at Harvard and sometime beneficiary of ETS research grants, wrote that if SAT scores could be improved through coaching, then "the validity and essential purposes for which the test was constructed" would be challenged.[9] In 1971, in an imposing "technical report" prepared for the College Board by ETS, a pair of researchers wrote, "One of the principal aims in constructing the SAT is to make it resistant to attempts to increase scores by means of short-term cram courses. Indeed, the usefulness of the SAT as an indicator of a student's potential for college work depends in large measure on the fact that the SAT measures general ability as it has developed over the full range of experiences in a person's life."[10] Coaching was a threat to the very sanctity of the tests.

In the early 1970s, ETS and the College Board decided to add a new section, the Test of Standard Written English (TSWE), to the SAT. The TSWE is a proofreading test very similar to the multiple-choice versions of the English Composition Achievement Test

(ECT). Colleges are supposed to use the scores in placing admitted students in appropriate classes. The TSWE is a sort of bonus — like a dishtowel in a box of laundry soap — that is used to encourage even schools that aren't selective to require the SAT.

Because ETS didn't want to increase the time required for the entire test in order to accommodate the TSWE, it needed to shorten the SAT. One way to do this, ETS realized, might be to use a different kind of question in part of the SAT.

ETS researchers at that time had been experimenting with a new mathematical item type called the quantitative comparison. The new item required students to look at two values (x-y and $2x$-$3y$, for example) and determine whether the first was greater than the second, the second was greater than the first, the two were the same, or the relationship could not be determined. Quantitative comparisons had the advantage of being, in test-making parlance, extremely "efficient": students could answer a great many of them in a short period of time with overall results statistically comparable to those produced by more time-consuming items. It might be possible, ETS believed, to replace the SAT's entire math section, which at that time lasted seventy-five minutes, with a sixty- or even a thirty-minute section of quantitative comparisons.

Before ETS could use the new items, though, it had to determine whether they were coachable, as some people in the company feared. ETS researcher Frank Evans was asked to design a study to find out, and he invited a colleague named Lewis Pike to join him. Pike said that as long as they were studying the coachability of one item type, they might as well study the coachability of the entire math section. They rewrote Evans's original research proposal and submitted it to a joint ETS–College Board committee.

"They said, well, okay," Pike says today. "I think they figured, well, it's been several years since we did the last summarization of coaching research, and these two guys are a couple of Young Turks who are going to knock themselves out, and we'll still be able to say to everybody that coaching doesn't work. They really believed their own rhetoric. So they gave us the green light."

ETS in those days published a small booklet for test-takers that contained practice SAT questions. Pike and Evans sat down with this booklet and blocked out the sort of coaching course that they thought an intelligent high school math teacher might put together if he had only the practice questions to go on. Algebraic inequalities seemed to be important, so they prepared a section on inequalities. Likewise with certain geometric principles and with what might be called peculiarities of multiple-choice testing. "Mathematicians love elegance," Pike explains, "and they love things to come out simply, so you know you're going to have a lot of items where finding the correct answer has substantially less to do with computation than with understanding some special properties of zero and one, or with understanding the strange things that happen with inequalities when you change from plus to minus." Pike and Evans also decided to make their students memorize the test's instructions, leaving them more time to work on problems.

The course Pike and Evans developed emphasized mathematical content rather than test-taking skills. But when instruction began, the researchers discovered that many of the students were confused about how to take standardized tests. For example, even though SAT-takers are supposed to use their test booklets as scratch paper, a number of students in the study were reluctant to do so. They had to be persuaded that the booklets were just going to be thrown away at the end of the test and that it was all right to make sketches of geometric figures, cross out answers that were obviously wrong, or circle problems that required further study.

Most of the students were also hesitant to guess when they weren't certain of an answer. They felt that guessing was not only risky but even immoral, equating it with cheating. Some of the instructors were also uncomfortable with the idea. When Pike visited one of the coaching classrooms, he found "The Ten Commandments of Mathematics" written on the blackboard. One was: "Thou shalt not guess." But in fact, for most test-takers, intelligent guessing is one of the keys to doing well on the SAT.

When ETS grades the SAT, it first calculates a "raw" score. This is simply the number of right answers minus a fraction of the number of wrong ones. Students receive one raw-score point for every question they answer correctly and no raw-score points for every question they leave blank. For every incorrect answer, ETS subtracts either a quarter of a point (if the question has five answer choices) or a third of a point (if the question has four). Total raw scores are then converted into the "scaled" scores that are reported to students and colleges.

ETS refers to the subtracted fraction as a "guessing penalty" and says that it is intended to discourage students from guessing indiscriminately. Students will hesitate to guess, an ETS researcher told me, if they know they'll lose points when they're wrong. But this is quite misleading. The guessing penalty isn't actually a penalty for guessing; it's only a penalty for being wrong. If a student guesses blindly on five five-choice items, the laws of probability say that on average he'll be wrong four times and right once. ETS will give him one raw point for the right answer and subtract a quarter of a raw point for each wrong one, giving him a net raw score of zero — exactly what he would have earned if he'd left all five items blank. There's no *guessing* penalty at all. In fact, a student is just as likely to raise his score by guessing as he is to lower it.

Now that the "meaningful third digit" has been eliminated from reported SAT scores, there's sometimes actually a slight guessing *reward* in the ETS scoring system. In the old days, a quarter-point raw-score penalty might have translated into two or three points on the reported score scale. Guessing the wrong answer on a single question would have lowered a student's score from, say, 515 to 512. But nowadays, because the last digit of an SAT score is always zero, scores can rise or fall only in ten-point increments. ETS now rounds raw scores to the nearest whole number, which means that a student has to miss at least *two* answers before losing any scaled points. It also means that there's no difference, in terms of the "guessing penalty," between two wrong answers and five wrong answers. Thus, to extend the example in the paragraph above, a student who guessed blindly on six five-choice items would only have to be right once in order to keep his score from being lowered.

Of course, if a student can eliminate one obviously wrong answer from among the five choices, the laws of probability state that he will now be most likely to *improve* his score by guessing blindly among the remaining choices. The more answers he can eliminate, the better the odds become. A student who knows how to take advantage of probability in selecting answers to difficult questions can raise his score substantially. (Good poker players make good SAT-takers; they know how to figure odds and take calculated risks.) "Guessing is at the heart of it, in some ways," Pike says today.

Most test-takers would score higher if they guessed more. Students who don't guess put themselves at a great disadvantage. ETS knows this. In 1981, the company did something it had never done before: it analyzed, item by item, an entire school's performance on a PSAT (Preliminary Scholastic Aptitude Test, given to high school juniors) and compared the results with the national average. One unexpected discovery was that students at this particular school weren't guessing the answers to items they didn't know. It turned out that the administrator of their exam had told them not to. Their scores were generally lower as a result.[11]

Thousands of students across the country receive similar misinformation. My wife's mother teaches high school English at a private school in upstate New York. The school's guidance counselor instructs students not to guess on an SAT item unless they have eliminated three of the five possible answers. This is terrible advice that, if followed, hurts students' scores. A great many other counselors and teachers tell their students not to guess at all. These are people who, quite simply, don't know what they're talking about.

The source of their confusion is probably ETS, which has never been entirely forthcoming on this subject. In the "Test-Taking Tips" section of the current edition of *Taking the SAT,* for example, ETS says, "You *can* guess. If you know that some of the choices for a question are definitely wrong, then it's to your advantage to guess from the remaining choices."[12] This is very misleading. If ETS were honest, the passage would read, "You *should* guess. If you know that even one of the choices for a question is wrong, then guessing randomly among the remaining choices will probably raise your score." (And increase your aptitude?)

Pike and Evans taught their students to overcome their reluctance to guess by telling them that guessing would enable them to receive "partial credit for partial information." If a student knew enough about a problem to eliminate one of the choices but not enough to be absolutely certain about the answer, shouldn't he receive some credit? Guessing intelligently, Pike told the students, would enable them to do this.

The Pike and Evans study involved about four hundred juniors and seniors from twelve high schools. The students were randomly sorted into three experimental groups and one control group. Each of the experimental groups received twenty-one hours of classroom instruction in one of three item types: "regular math," which, then as now, made up the bulk of the SAT; "data sufficiency," a complex item type later abandoned; and quantitative comparisons. The instructors, who were trained in a two-day workshop, were math teachers from the students' schools.

Even before Pike and Evans had finished their experiment, several ETS executives began to worry. One circulated a memo asking, in effect, "What are we going to do if these guys get results?" Another responded with a memo saying that there wouldn't be a problem because getting results would be impossible. Just a year before, the College Board had published a book, written by ETS personnel, that stated the two organizations' official position on coaching. "Studies of coaching have produced quite consistent results," the book said. "The score gains directly attributable to coaching generally amount to fewer than 10 points."[13] ETS was generally confident that the new experiment would buttress the official position. But there was still uneasiness.

All the students in the Pike and Evans study were tested before and after instruction. According to the published report, students in the quantitative comparison group registered average score increases that would be equivalent to gains of roughly 100 points on SATs made up solely of such items. (The scores of controls given the same test rose the equivalent of about 25 points.) Boys in the data sufficiency group also had gains equivalent to 100 points; girls had gains of about 75 points. (The controls' scores rose the equivalent of about 33 points.) Students in the regular math group improved their scores by the equivalent of roughly 50 points. (The controls' scores rose the equivalent of about 20 points.) Pike and Evans estimated that a course of the same length covering both regular math and data sufficiency items — which together constituted the SAT in those days — might be expected to yield gains of about 33 points above and beyond increases attributable to other causes, such as "practice and growth."[14]

When the results of the study were tabulated, Pike began making tentative recommendations within the company. First of all, he said, ETS had to abandon its plan to build the math SAT out of quantitative comparisons, which had proved to be especially coachable. Second, he said, the College Board needed to give students and teachers vastly better information about how to take the SAT. Third, ETS and the College Board needed to inaugurate a public relations campaign to let people know that coaching actually was effective and that previous statements to the contrary had been incorrect.

All these proposals got a very chilly reception. ETS went ahead with the quantitative comparisons, although it decided to limit them to a single section. (They now constitute a third of the items on the math SAT.) Far from making an effort to give students more information about taking the test, ETS went ahead with an existing plan to *stop* publishing the booklet to help students prepare for the SAT. When ETS resumed publishing such material, no mention was made of the instructional methods Pike and Evans had found to be most effective. The only public relations campaign that ETS undertook was intended to dispel the notion that coaching might work. Indeed, some executives at ETS and the College Board believed that Pike and Evans shouldn't even be allowed to publish their results.

The College Board eventually did publish the study, but under several restrictions. "We had to agree to an innocuous title and that sort of thing," Pike told me. "The study was called *Effects of Special Instruction for Three Kinds of Mathematics Aptitude Items*. It didn't say SAT, and it didn't say coaching, and it didn't say it works. And there were other pressures — namely, that this certainly wasn't supposed to be talked about beyond publication. And those pressures also prevailed." One ETS executive accused Pike of being a traitor to the company — although he later asked discreetly whether Pike would be willing to give his daughter a little help in preparing for the SAT.

"One of my main concerns," Pike says, "was what happens to real people out there. When people who have money debate whether to pay for coaching, they say, 'Well, it can't hurt and it might help, so we might as well shell out the bucks.' But if you're poor, and you don't have the money, and someone quotes ETS or the College Board saying that coaching doesn't work, then you kind of breathe a sigh of relief and say, 'Well, it doesn't work anyway, and thank God, because where would we get the three hundred bucks?' These people get what I call double jeopardy; that is, they're getting shafted in the schooling they receive *and* getting shafted by the SAT. You're never going to eradicate all of that, but if you pretend that coaching doesn't help, you're being irresponsible and you're adding to the problem instead of helping it."

ETS was extremely nervous on the issues of income and race. Having billed the SAT for years as a test that put rich and poor, black and white, on an equal footing, it had no desire to announce that people who could afford coaching had an advantage over people who couldn't. According to Pike, a top executive at ETS tried to persuade him that acknowledging the effects of coaching would actually hurt blacks rather than help them. The executive said that the SAT helped blacks by proving that they weren't being educated, and that if the test were discredited by Pike, it could no longer perform this function. He also said that straightforward information about coaching would help only those blacks who would probably succeed anyway and that the blacks "in the back of the class falling asleep" would just fall further behind.

There were also some positive reactions at both organizations. S. A. Kendrick, head of the College Board's Division of Research Studies and Services, wrote a generally favorable preface for the study, praising it for its "complex but very neat" design and concluding that "the report of the study is . . . the best summary now available on the subject of coaching for mathematics tests, and should be widely read for that reason alone." But Kendrick also hinted that the Board's patience was not unlimited. "The coaching materials developed and used in the course of the study are extraordinarily attractive," he wrote, "— this is probably as far as anyone is likely to go in coaching for tests."[15] It was certainly as far as the College Board was going to go.

At ETS, William Angoff, a senior researcher who also had

strong connections at the Board, concluded reluctantly that the time had now come to revise the official line on coaching. He argued that the logical course of action would be to have Pike do a similar study on the coachability of the verbal SAT, with a view toward publishing a comprehensive statement on coaching sometime in the future. Research studies had to be approved by a joint ETS–College Board committee, and Angoff urged it to commission another study from Pike.

"God, they put me through it," Pike says today. "They knew I wanted to work on it. I was in charge of the verbal section, and I knew the verbal much better than I knew the math. They kept inviting me to do a sort of pre-proposal, explaining what my study would be like. Then they would squirm and say, 'Well, we want you to redefine coaching, we want you to do this, we want you to do that.' And this went on for two or three years. Finally I drew the line and said, 'I'm not going through this anymore; either fish or cut bait.' I got some pretest data and put in some very solid ideas — especially about verbal analogies, which I knew I could help people with — and I put it all into a proposal to show them that it could really be coached. Which was dumb, of course. The main statement I got back from one of the high-echelon College Board people — they were told to bring the message to me orally — was, essentially, 'We paid Pike to study the math coaching, and he showed it worked, which has made no end of problems for us; I'll be damned if we're going to pay him to go out and do the same thing with the verbal.' "

In the end, Pike says, "they sort of bought me off." He was given a research grant — not to study the verbal test but to do a "literature review" of previous coaching studies. The grant was fairly small, but Pike had been keeping up with the coaching literature in the course of his other work. His original plan was to distribute his report only inside the company, but a colleague suggested jokingly that he might release it instead as a semiformal ETS publication called a research bulletin. Pike found this idea attractive — a research bulletin carried more prestige than an internal memo — although other colleagues urged him to reconsider, warning that he was pushing his luck.

Pike's study, called *Short-term Instruction, Testwiseness, and the Scholastic Aptitude Test,* was published in 1978.[16] He summarized the results of previous coaching studies (including several that ETS had neglected to cite in its earlier summaries) and concluded that the math SAT was clearly coachable and that the verbal SAT probably was, but that no comprehensive study of the latter had been attempted. He made several suggestions for future research.

"There are three ultimate objectives toward which the research would be directed," he wrote. "The first is to maximize the fairness and validity of the SAT with regard to its short-term and intermediate-term instruction (STI and ITI) score components. The second is not to discourage concern and activity regarding test-preparedness, but rather to foster realistic understanding and expectations regarding possible outcomes of STI and ITI. The third, which would derive from the pursuit of the first two, is the emergence of a more basic understanding of the processes involved in test taking and contributing to aptitude test scores."[17]

A few weeks later, Lewis Pike was fired. The following year, the College Board issued a new official statement on coaching, published under this headline: "Board reaffirms its position that 'coaching' for SAT is not likely to improve students' scores."*[18]

Nervousness over the original Pike and Evans study had contributed to a growing and very general distrust of outsiders at both ETS and the College Board. "Outside review of the tests, supposedly encouraged, was not welcome," Steven Levy wrote in an article in *New Jersey Monthly* called "E.T.S. and the 'Coaching' Cover-Up." "One government researcher who tried to get some SAT data for a study was told that the data for the year requested were not available. Could I have *any* year's data? he asked. He was told that all data had been destroyed. If true, this meant that E.T.S.

---

*ETS and the College Board maintain strenuously that Pike's dismissal had nothing to do with his coaching studies and that he was fired in a cost-cutting reduction of the research staff. The research department was indeed undergoing a cutback, but the people dismissed tended to be recent appointees or inveterate troublemakers. It seems clear that if Pike hadn't stuck his neck out over coaching, he wouldn't have had it lopped off. For more on research department firings, see Chapter 11.

researchers had been conducting experiments with data that did not exist."[19]

Pike's second report on coaching made ETS even more uncomfortable, and the company did its best to keep it under wraps. When Steven Levy said as much in his article, ETS issued a prompt and angry denial. In an internal memorandum that later provided the basis for a letter to the editor of the *New Jersey Monthly*, ETS president William Turnbull wrote: "While the attack in the article is extensive, the main thrust is that ETS does not tell the truth, and did suppress research on the effectiveness of coaching. There is absolutely neither substance nor truth to either allegation. . . . Far from being suppressed, Pike's latest published work was requested and supported by the College Board, and has been published by them as a Research and Development Report. . . . It is routinely available, and over a thousand copies have been distributed by ETS and the College Board to date."[20]

But ETS had consistently suppressed research about the effectiveness of coaching. Well into the 1970s — years after the Pike and Evans study had been published — ETS continued to cite, as its official position on coaching, the 1965 College Board booklet ("The Little Green Book That Lies"), which stated that "score gains directly attributable to coaching amount, on the average, to fewer than 10 points" and that "the magnitude of the gains . . . are [sic] always small regardless of the coaching method used or the differences in the students coached."*[22] This was simply not true.

As for Pike's second report, a wide distribution was the last thing ETS wanted, and the company did its best to keep the report from being circulated. Still, rumors of its existence began to get around. Warner V. Slack and Douglas Porter, the two Harvard Medical School professors who were preparing a scholarly article on the SAT, heard one of these rumors and tried to obtain a copy from ETS.

---

*ETS has since become somewhat sheepish about this booklet. When I tried to obtain a copy in 1984, ETS told me that it would probably be impossible to locate a document of such antiquity (even though, as I reminded ETS, there is a copy in the ETS library, and despite my offer to "happily pay all Xeroxing and other costs"). A few days later, after a "search" had been conducted, I was told that my request had simply been denied, apparently at the request of Gregory Anrig.[21]

"I got on the phone and called around," Porter told me, "and everyone I talked to said, No, there's no such thing. Finally I got a woman at the College Board who said, Wait a minute, I'll have to let you talk to someone else. And I talked to a very nice lady, and she said, Ye-es, there is a study that's recently been done, but we aren't giving it out. I asked her whether it was a publication, and she said, Yes, but it's an internal one. I said, Well, I'd very much appreciate it if you could make a copy available to me. She said she'd have to check that out. So she talked to someone else, who evidently didn't know what we were writing about, and this person finally said, All right, we'll give you a copy, but we'd prefer that you not cite it and that you not refer it to anyone.

"We knew people who'd tried to get a copy but had been unable to. We just lucked out, I think. It was by virtue of the fact that the College Board tends to hire very nice, cooperative women to meet the public."

Slack and Porter's article, called "The Scholastic Aptitude Test: A Critical Appraisal," was published in the May 1980 *Harvard Educational Review.* "If scores on the SAT reflect preparation," they wrote, "those students who believe the admonishments of the test designers and do not prepare for the test may be needlessly deprived of admission to the college of their choice. More important still, if a student with a low SAT score believes that this score accurately reflects his aptitude, and that no study or preparation could have altered his performance, his mental capacity is disparaged, and his self-esteem is weakened. If the message is untrue, the student has been seriously wronged."*[23]

Slack and Porter reviewed existing research on coaching and concluded that ETS and the College Board, in their numerous public pronouncements on the subject, had systematically failed to cite studies showing that students could increase their scores through special preparation. Two studies in particular — both of which reported large gains in SAT scores — had been repeatedly ignored. ETS and the Board knew of these studies. One of them had been partly funded by the Board. Both had serious flaws, but most coaching studies do, including the ones that ETS had cited

*Slack and Porter's article dealt with more than coaching. For more on it, see Chapter 10.

again and again. Slack and Porter also concluded that ETS had misrepresented the size of gains achieved in the studies it did cite.

"In publications sponsored by ETS or the College Board," they wrote, "we found nine conclusions that studies to date had demonstrated coaching to be ineffective, even though the published experimental evidence indicated the contrary. We also found seven assertions that gains in scores from coaching were not significant, although they were statistically significant. . . . Common sense as well as experimental evidence belies the contention that students cannot effectively study for the SAT. Sample test items that are provided to students who are preparing to take the test reveal nothing to justify the conclusion that the test measures 'insightful reasoning' or 'basic reasoning abilities.' "[24]

ETS responded to Slack and Porter in the next issue of the *Harvard Educational Review* in a statement written by Rex Jackson, a corporate vice president. Jackson began by impugning the professors' integrity, calling their article "a pastiche of familiar charges* . . . characterized by a strident tone and by the use of half-truths, out-of-context quotations, and misinformation — characteristics that will be familiar to those who have closely followed the recent political movement to discredit tests used in admission to institutions of higher education."[25]

One might have thought that ETS would solicit its response from one of the actual scientists whose research Slack and Porter, themselves scientists, had criticized. But ETS typically employs laymen to respond to scientists and scientists to respond to laymen. In this case, it settled on an executive whose duties consisted largely of public relations. The clear suggestion was that Slack and Porter were not careful scientists at all but rather the minions of some treacherous "recent political movement" and not to be taken seriously. (The College Board later tried to discredit the study by pointing out that Slack and Ralph Nader had graduated from Princeton in the same year.)

Jackson asserted that "every one of the studies listed by the authors has been cited in ETS reports, notably in a review of both

*On major testing issues, ETS's responses to critics follow a very predictable evolutionary path: (1) in the first stage, ETS flatly denies all charges; (2) in the second stage, it ignores them; (3) in the final, mature stage, it dismisses them as "familiar."

coaching and longer-term instructional programs by Pike (1978)."[26] This, of course, was the report that had cost Pike his job and whose general circulation ETS and the College Board had tried so hard to prevent. Jackson implied that Slack and Porter had ignored this study. But they had cited it directly, pointing out that it contained ETS's only reference — thirteen years after the fact — to one of the phantom studies.

Although Jackson contended that ETS *had* cited these studies, he also had an explanation for why it had *not*. He said that the successful coaching efforts Slack and Porter had described were not coaching at all but rather "longer-term instructional interventions." No one but Pike had ever bothered to mention them, he alleged, because they had had to do with "score gains by students involved in lengthy educational programs that go well beyond what is ordinarily described by the term 'coaching.' " But both studies clearly fit anyone's — including ETS's — definition of coaching. One of them had even been specifically described by its author and by Pike as "short-term." Indeed, it had lasted only seventeen minutes longer (forty-five hours as opposed to forty-four hours and forty-three minutes) than a study that ETS had cited repeatedly.[27]

Jackson chastised Slack and Porter for paying scant attention to a recent coaching study performed by the Federal Trade Commission. This was a bizarre allegation for a number of reasons: (1) Slack and Porter had indeed cited the FTC report, noting that they had received a copy only after their article had been submitted for publication; (2) the FTC report in its original version (which was prepared in 1978 by the FTC's Boston office) had concluded that, despite denials by ETS and the College Board, "coaching can be the determining factor in deciding who is admitted to undergraduate and graduate colleges and universities"[28] and had recommended that ETS and the Board, among others, be investigated "to alleviate or eliminate the unfair and deceptive acts or practices we have discovered";[29] (3) ETS had refused to supply testing information to the FTC until the FTC had obtained a subpoena ordering it to do so; (4) ETS had privately but directly pressured the FTC both to revise the report and to withhold it from the public; (5) the FTC had not released the report until after Slack and Porter had requested it under the Freedom of Information Act and filed suit in federal court; (6) the FTC had allowed ETS's lawyers to argue the government's case against releasing the information to Slack and Porter.

All this adds up to a kettle defense of classic dimensions. At one point Jackson even said that although ETS had never believed that *coaching* was effective, it had always believed that "training" was.[30]

"On the issue of coaching," Slack and Porter concluded in an accompanying response, "Jackson employs a tautology; 'coaching,' as he uses the word, is preparation for the SAT that doesn't work. Preparation that does work cannot be 'coaching'; it must be 'intensive education.' "[31]

In 1978, ETS began publishing a booklet called *Taking the SAT*. This booklet, ETS said in a subsequent research study, was

> intended primarily to reduce anxiety and to help students meet the tests with greater confidence. The underlying assumption is that if all examinees are to approach test-taking on as nearly equal grounds as possible, they should remain undistracted by such extraneous influences as familiarity with test format or general competence in test-taking. To this end, the booklet presents careful descriptions of the SAT and TSWE, explains the different types of test questions, and suggests strategies for guessing, answering questions, and using time efficiently. It also includes a full-length sample test and answers to its questions. . . .[32]

Having produced this new coaching tool, ETS — with that imperviousness to irony so necessary to an authentic kettle defense — set out to prove that it did no good. An experiment was hastily designed ("We did it in a bit of a hurry," an ETS executive told me). About a thousand high school juniors were mailed prepublication copies of the booklet. Their SAT scores were later compared with those of a group of students who had not received it. Although relatively few of the students who received the booklet bothered to take and score the sample practice test it contained, the comparison was based on the entire group.

When the results were tallied, ETS proudly announced that the students who had not received the booklet had scored slightly higher on their SATs than the students who had. The gentlemanly response to this discovery, certainly, would have been to recall all extant copies of the booklet and burn them. But ETS continues to publish *Taking the SAT*. And ETS officials continue to cite their "study" as evidence that coaching doesn't work.[33]

This experiment was an important milestone in ETS's manful struggle to discredit coaching. No longer dependent on unreliable outsiders, ETS could now produce the very coaching materials it would later prove to be ineffective.

In 1982, the College Board and ETS published a study called *Test Disclosure and Retest Performance on the Scholastic Aptitude Test*. The study had been performed by Lawrence J. Stricker, an ETS psychologist. Its purpose was to determine whether test disclosure, as stipulated by New York's truth-in-testing law, was having an effect on the scores of students who bought copies of their SATs and then took the test a second time.[34]

The study involved 7,500 high school juniors who had taken the SAT in New York State on May 2, 1981. Shortly after they had taken the test, 2,500 of them received a package from ETS.

"Although you may not have requested them," the enclosed letter began, "I am sending the questions and answers, as well as a copy of your own answer sheet, for those parts on the May SAT that counted toward your scores on the test. The College Board is sending these materials, on an experimental basis, to a cross-section of all students who took the test."

The students who received this letter were referred to as the "not encouraged" group.

Students in the second, "encouraged" group — also 2,500 strong — received the same package, but their letter included a second paragraph intended to make them eager to study the test they had just taken: "In the event that you plan to take the SAT again, you may find these materials useful in preparing for the test. They should help you to become more familiar with the instructions and the kind of questions used, and may make it possible for you to take the test with greater confidence."

Having thus inflamed the curiosity of these students, Stricker poised himself to measure the effects. Naturally, he found no difference between receiving the package and not receiving it or between being "encouraged" and being "not encouraged." He also found that the materials had no more effect on the scores of students considered "likely" to have read them — on the basis of their race, parents' education, parents' income, high school type, high school rank, high school grade point average, and a few other factors — than on the scores of students considered "unlikely."

Very few students realize that their test fees are used to finance this sort of mindless exercise, whose real purpose may be simply to keep members of ETS's research staff from twiddling their thumbs all day long. Even Stricker, in his conclusion, sounds a bit sheepish about the whole thing. "The negative results," he wrote, "necessarily raise questions about the efficacy of the experimental operations, particularly the encouraging letter, the variables used to form the subgroups, and the criteria." He also speculated that since copies of old SATs were fairly widely available anyway, "the familiarization and anxiety reduction provided by using the disclosed material may have already been accomplished."[35]

There's a certain dark genius in all of this. ETS makes students pay for the development of "anxiety reduction" materials, then makes them pay for studies to prove that the materials are ineffective, then (in the case of *Taking the SAT*) makes them pay for the continued production and distribution of the same materials whose ineffectiveness they have paid ETS to demonstrate.

But the real master of the ETS coaching study is Samuel Messick, whose title at ETS is vice president and distinguished research scientist. ETS executives refer to Messick in reverent tones, and his scholarly publications are numerous. In 1980 he produced a lengthy study for ETS called *The Effectiveness of Coaching for the SAT: Review and Reanalysis of Research from the Fifties to the FTC*. Messick's study is ETS's most comprehensive statement on the coaching question in recent years (and the only one listed in ETS's catalogue of publications). Outsiders who inquire about the effectiveness of coaching are referred to it.[36]

Messick's analysis consists largely of finding reasons to reduce the size of score gains reported in previous studies. "Sam takes the company line, whatever it is," a former colleague told me. "If he finds a number that's too high, he throws it out." Adjustments are made for "self-selection," "differential growth rates," "demographics," "motivation to earn a higher test score," and other factors presumed to have disguised themselves as coaching effects. Many coaching studies have overstated the gains achieved by students; others have understated them. But ETS's zeal in whittling down results goes far beyond the correction of errors. For example, although ETS claims that "motivation" accounts for some score gains that have been attributed to coaching, it maintains elsewhere that the SAT "does not measure . . . motivation."[37] How can scores be improved by something the SAT does not detect? And while ETS reduces gains presumed to have been caused by this supposedly irrelevant factor, it does not *increase* gains achieved by students not motivated to improve. Nor does it instruct admissions officers to consider "motivation" in interpreting SAT scores. Nor does it address the question it raises indirectly: If students can improve their SAT scores simply by becoming motivated to do so, why does ETS spend so much time and money trying to *un*motivate them?

ETS has been extraordinarily successful in defining the terms in which the Coaching Question is debated. Most psychometricians would probably agree with Messick that score gains attributable to coaching need to be distinguished from those arising from motivation, family wealth, and other factors. But it should be remembered that for a student preparing to take a test, all this semantic hair-splitting is entirely irrelevant. All he wants to know is how he can improve his score significantly in a short time. As long as his score goes up, he doesn't care whether it's because he's been "coached" or because he's been "motivated." ETS pursues these distinctions unrelentingly because it believes (correctly) that if the test can be coached, the justification for using it is weakened if not destroyed. But ETS has never shown a similar avidity for analyzing the effect of these same factors on test scores in general. If favorable "demographics" can cause coached students' SAT scores to rise, then part of what the SAT measures is "demographics." Sam Messick may be able to define coaching out of existence, but in doing so he leaves his employer with some ugly questions it has never been eager to address.

Indeed, the desire to debunk coaching is so powerful that ETS is willing to abandon positions it elsewhere defends to the death.

Messick says that score gains attributed to coaching by the FTC are suspect in part because "the coached students . . . differed significantly from the noncoached students in a number of ways that could have influenced both their decision to attend coaching school and their performance on the SAT (such as having higher rank-in-class and higher parental income). . . ."[38] This presents as a given what ETS usually takes excruciating pains to deny, that rich people have an unfair advantage over poor people on the SAT. (As usual, ETS takes the kettle position on this issue. An ETS researcher once told me that some of the difference in scores between rich and poor was probably simply because rich people had easier access to coaching. Money doesn't help, coaching does; coaching doesn't help, money does.)

In discussing the Pike and Evans study described earlier, Messick bases his analysis on whole-test score changes, even though the study was not directed at the SAT as a whole but rather at three distinct item types. The final number, half the size of Pike's estimate, is averaged in with other numbers.[39] Similar "adjustments" are made throughout the study. Effective and ineffective courses are averaged together. No distinction is made between good materials and bad. Having heard that the Wright brothers have taken off at Kitty Hawk, ETS samples the general state of aviation and announces that man, on average, can't fly.

Messick's method is typical both of ETS and of the psychometric world in general. Rather than confronting the question directly — how could the tests be beaten? — Messick sifts through the old numbers one more time. The procedure is known as meta-analysis, and it's a very popular approach to the coaching question. The old studies, good and bad, in time achieve a sort of scientific equality. They all become "data."

For all his apparent confidence in the ineffectiveness of coaching, however, Messick is cautious enough to hedge his bet. Setting out what I take to be ETS's new and improved position on the subject, he writes that the SAT "was designed to reflect verbal and mathematical abilities that are acquired over an extended period and hence can be expected to be difficult to improve substantially through short-term instructional efforts. However, these reasoning abilities are learned, and if effective learning experiences, including effective coaching programs, facilitate their development, one would expect not only increases in SAT scores but also increases in criterion performance — in this case, performance in college."[40]

The path by which he arrives at this conclusion is circular, beginning with an unproven assumption about what the tests measure. But if ETS really believes this — and not, as it did in 1971, that coaching necessarily has a "subversive effect" on "the goals of education"[41] — then shouldn't ETS stop spending test-takers' fees on make-work projects intended to dissuade students from preparing for the SAT and start spending them to develop new, effective coaching methods, the shorter-term the better? If such a project were successful, and if it were really aimed at whatever ETS means by "abilities," students' scores would rise, their performance in college would improve, and everyone would be happy.

For all their professed skepticism about coaching, however, ETS and the College Board know a good business proposition when they see one. In 1980, as a direct result of New York's truth-in-testing law, they entered the coaching business themselves by publishing a paperback collection of previous test forms. Called *4 SATs*, this book was followed in succeeding years by *5 SATs* and *6 SATs*.[42] Like all great marketing strategies, this one was elegantly simple: ETS took tests that had been developed and published with test-takers' money, duplicated them in booklet form, and sold them to test-takers again.

Not long before *4 SATs* was published, George Hanford, president of the College Board, had urgently warned Board members in Ohio that proposed truth-in-testing legislation could "prove to be educationally unsound by legitimating the use of certain tests as teaching tools, a purpose for which they are not designed."[43] Hanford's fears apparently evaporated shortly after this note was sent. In order to make it easier for teachers to use the tests for precisely the purpose for which Hanford said they had not been designed, the Board offered substantial discounts for bulk classroom orders of *4 SATs*.

Having taken a giant step down this fatal road, ETS and the College Board decided to go all the way in 1983. They joined with the Scribner Book Company, a major New York publishing house, and produced a glossy paperback called *10 SATs*. This book, unlike its predecessors, is sold in bookstores, where it is shelved alongside *How to Take the SAT, How to Beat the S.A.T., How to Ace the SAT, Inside Strategies for the S.A.T.,* and a dozen others. It contains not only "10 ACTUAL SATs!" — to quote a tease from the back cover — but also the entire contents of *Taking the SAT,* the booklet that ETS once went to so much trouble to discredit but now describes as "the College Board's official advice to students planning to take the test." *10 SATs* is, in short, a coaching book. Whether it's worth $8.95 or not depends on which ETS statement you believe.[44]

ETS does quite a lively business in test preparation materials. One package, a 20-minute slide presentation called *A Little Anxiety: Test-Taking Skills,* contains "specific strategies for actually taking the test," including "strategies for guessing, how to approach multiple-choice questions, and ways to improve performance on reading comprehension, word problems, verbal analogies, and other kinds of questions," according to ETS's promotional flier. The slide show contains some good advice. "Sometimes, after going back and reviewing the test," says the flier, "a student may want to change an answer — and should not be afraid to do so. Contrary to popular belief, on most standardized tests, when students change their answers this way, it is more likely that they are changing incorrect answers to correct ones rather than the other way around." Contrary to popular belief, ETS does not mention this fact in *Taking the SAT* or in any of the other materials it gives to students. To find out about it you have to pay $94.75, shipping not included.[45]

ETS also offers "A Testing Preparation Program for Elementary School Students!" (according to another promotional flier) called *It's Good to Know.* The kit, which costs $190, is intended to raise students' test scores. It is especially designed for public school students, many of whom, the flier says, "do not get enough practice" with standardized tests (something ETS is otherwise strenuous in denying). According to ETS, the real problem is anxiety. "Sometimes fear in children keeps them from doing as well as they can on a test," the flier explains. "When this happens, test scores don't give the teacher much help in figuring out each child's strengths and weaknesses. . . ."[46]

This is indeed good to know. But if ETS believes that anxiety produces inaccurate test scores, why doesn't it make this information available to students who can't afford expensive coaching materials? And if the SAT scores of anxious students don't give admissions officers much help in figuring out each applicant's strengths and weaknesses, why doesn't ETS ever mention this problem in the information it gives to high schools and colleges? The official guide to the Admission Testing Program, intended to help admissions officers interpret SAT scores, says nothing about the anxiety problem (or about public school students' lack of exposure to test-taking skills). The information on anxiety in *Taking the SAT* is simply deceptive. This booklet says that "drill and practice on sample test questions" may help students "reduce anxiety about what to expect" but asserts that this will "generally result in little effect on test scores."[47] ETS tells a very different story to those who can afford to pay.

7

Beating the Test

LEWIS PIKE'S EXPERIMENTS with math coaching are extremely interesting, but they are flawed. His results, though significant, were limited by several assumptions he made about the nature of coaching and about the nature of the SAT. Most methods of preparing for the SAT suffer from these same defects.

Pike's first error was his emphasis on "education." In hopes of making his study palatable to his employers, who had always held that coaching was subversive, he tried to make his courses as much like *math* courses as possible. To be sure, he taught multiple-choice guessing strategies and other skills that had little or nothing to do with mathematics; but he also wanted his methods to seem legitimate in the eyes of ETS. He tacitly accepted the company dogma that the SAT measures what ETS and the College Board used to call "aptitude" but have lately taken to describing as "higher-order reasoning abilities." He accepted, in effect, ETS's untested assumption that the SAT cannot be beaten. Pike told me with a good deal of pride that the students in his experiment had improved their performance in their regular math courses as a result of what they had learned from him. This is laudable. But in terms of raising SAT scores, it's beside the point. Teaching math isn't the same as teaching the math SAT.

Lewis Pike was handicapped as an SAT coach by his yearning for legitimacy. This yearning is powerful, and most testing coaches succumb to it. Stanley H. Kaplan, who prepares more people for more tests than anyone else in the United States, refers to his coaching schools as "educational centers." Kaplan's brochure says that his SAT course teaches "the mathematical and verbal skills needed not only for this examination, but for success at the college level itself."[1] It's not coaching, by God, it's longer-term instructional intervention. Kaplan is now so respectable that the College Board invited him to appear on a panel at its annual meeting in 1983. Like Lewis Pike, Stanley Kaplan sees the SAT through ETS's eyes. He'd get better results if he didn't.

Pike's second error was in failing to consider the possibility that genuinely *short* short-term coaching might be just as effective as longer-term "instruction." ETS has always assumed that coaching produces results only to the extent that it approaches ordinary schooling in terms of the time devoted to it. But this doesn't necessarily make sense. The "abilities" measured by the SAT are quite finite. There's no reason to assume that acquiring an understanding of them — given that the instruction is properly designed — wouldn't follow a steep learning curve, with most of the gain coming relatively quickly. Ineffective coaching courses tend to be so not because they are too short but because their curricula are cluttered up with "educational" materials that have little or nothing to do with the "abilities" measured by ETS. The Pike and Evans study would have been more interesting if the students in it had been tested every week or two and if Pike had been less concerned with making his course look like something ETS might one day be inclined to endorse.

Pike's third error was in assuming that coaching would be ineffective for students who were already "sophisticated in mathematics." Students who had A averages in math or were enrolled in accelerated courses were automatically excluded. The mean pretest math score for students in the study was around 400, close to a full standard deviation below the national average. Virtually all of the students had initial scores below 500.[2]

Pike's results would almost certainly have been better if he had let "sophisticated" students participate. Indeed, it's a shame that he didn't create a fourth experimental section limited to students in accelerated math courses or students with math scores that were already fairly high. Once again, Pike had accepted an ETS assumption, which is that if math coaching helps anybody, it helps only students who aren't currently enrolled in math courses or who are a little rusty on their basic algebra and geometry. These students can be helped enormously by coaching, but they aren't the only ones. Advanced students often have trouble on the SAT because they aren't adept at recognizing the tricks ETS uses to make familiar problems look unfamiliar. All they need to do, in effect, is learn to translate the test out of the peculiar form ETS uses in order to make the SAT seem like an "aptitude" test instead of an "achievement" test. The only aptitude they need to increase in order to score higher is their aptitude for detecting the ETS mentality.

The errors I have described probably don't sound like errors at all. What do tricks and strategies have to do with education? Nothing, of course. But they have everything to do with the SAT.

Most commercial coaching materials have very little to do with either education or the SAT. Many are written by people who clearly know very little about the tests they purport to explain. Some probably even lower the scores of the students who use them.

One of the very worst coaching books is Harcourt Brace's *How to Prepare for the SAT*, by Morton Selub and Doris Selub. Many of the Selubs' test items bear no resemblance whatsoever to items on a real SAT. Here's one of their analogies:[3]

---

34. ROOSEVELT : TRUMAN : :

  (A) Washington : Adams
  (B) Eisenhower : Kennedy
  (C) Johnson : Nixon
  (D) Lincoln : Johnson
  (E) Ford : Rockefeller

Ignoring for the moment that this question is ridiculously ambiguous (anyone who can't come up with half a dozen justifications for any of the answers isn't trying), the simple fact is that ETS never writes analogies using proper nouns, much less ones based on American history.

Here's one of the Selubs' sentence completions:[4]

30. Augustus John is ——— for his work as a portraitist, but ——— for his bohemian life style.

    (A) famous..infamous
    (B) renowned..revered
    (C) known..famous
    (D) renowned..notorious
    (E) reviled..despised

Choice E comes fairly close to expressing my own feelings about Augustus John. Other readers will have other preferences. The Selubs' answer is D. They eliminate A on the grounds that "infamous" is "too harsh a word to apply to a bohemian (unconventional) lifestyle."[5] Questions like this make ETS's tests look almost good.

Another book not to buy is *Barron's How to Prepare for the Scholastic Aptitude Test*, by Samuel C. Brownstein and Mitchel Weiner. This is one of the most popular coaching books around. One of its main features is a vocabulary list that contains, I would judge, every word in the English language. A line on the cover says that these are the "3,000 words you need to know for the SAT." Most of them have no more chance of turning up in an SAT item than your mother's name does. (If *termagant, thaumaturgist, tocsin,* or *triolet* ever appears in an SAT, I'll eat my copy of the book.) Brownstein and Weiner don't quite have the Selubs' flair for utterly inappropriate items, but they come close, in one case requiring students to identify an imported dog breed:[6]

2. SPITZ:DOG::   (A) philosopher:stone (B) whale:fish
  (C) growth:cancer (D) whale:mammal
  (E) reptile:crocodile

They even quiz students on *synonyms,* an item type that hasn't been used on the SAT since 1929.

Arco's *Preparation for the College Entrance Examination SAT* is also popular, and also horrible. Its word list is shorter than the one in *Barron's,* but it's also full of words that will never, never, never appear on the SAT. *Aconite, agnomen, aigrette, alienist, aliquot, ambergris* (actually, I know that one; it's the stuff in sperm whales), *amentia, anadromous* ("going up river to spawn"; *sperm* and *spawn*, incidentally, are two words you won't see very often on a test for adolescents), *anchorite, anserine, ataxia.* These are just the best ones. The list goes on and on. The Arco book was supposedly "prepared by SAT experts." Some other SAT, perhaps.

Arco's experts are also ignorant of the way SAT items are constructed. Their advice on analogies, for example, will certainly reduce the scores of students who follow it. They tell students to prepare for half a dozen analogy types that are never used on the SAT, including anagrams, rhymes, proper nouns, non sequiturs, titles and authors of literary works, and historical events. They also recommend a strategy based on a very common misconception about SAT analogies, a misconception that accounts for many of the errors on these items. In fact, students who follow the Arco strategy will *invariably* select wrong answers on the SAT. Here's an Arco example:

KEY:DOOR::

(A) lox:glass
(B) stack:book
(C) main:subordinate
(D) wine:steward
(E) skeleton:trap

"This is an easy one," the Arco experts say. "A *skeleton* is a kind of *key*; a *trap* is a kind of *door.*"[7] But ETS analogies simply do not work this way. If this were an SAT item — and it could never be — the only important relationship would be the one between KEY and DOOR. The student's task would be to find another *pair* of words with the same relationship. Any presumed relationship between KEY and some other word or between DOOR and some other word would be strictly irrelevant. The Arco strategy might occasionally be useful to a student, but only as a method for finding obviously incorrect answers.

Sometimes you wonder whether the authors of coaching books have ever seen the tests they're writing about. In *Monarch's Preparation for the SAT,* by Edward C. Gruber and Morris Branson, the

Test of Standard Written English (TSWE) is referred to as the Standard Written English Test (SWET). The authors begin with a list of "Important Tips" about the SAT. Tip 3: "There are Antonyms, Analogies, and Sentence Completions as part of each Verbal Section of the SAT."[8] The practice tests in the book look nothing like the SAT, and the questions aren't arranged as ETS would have arranged them.

Another bad book is *How to Beat the S.A.T.*, by Michael Donner, a former editor of *Games* magazine. His book contains some good advice ("It is unwise to linger over any problem so long as there are still questions available that may be answered more quickly"),[9] but many of his strategies are completely for the birds. Donner shares ETS's infatuation with meaningless statistics. To support his contention that students, when guessing blindly, should avoid answers A, C, and E, he produces a chart showing the "variance between actual count and chance" of these three choices. Donner concludes that a student who has no idea what the answer to a problem is should "guess either *b* or *d* — it doesn't much matter which, in theory — and you gain a slight statistical advantage over not guessing at all. (In this toss-up situation, I myself [Donner] slightly favor *b*, but there is not enough statistical basis for urging this answer on you.)"[10]

"Not enough statistical basis" is right. The data in Donner's chart are taken from a *single* SAT. If he had looked at a different form — say, the first test in *5 SATs,* which was published around the time of his book — he could have proved that students should *avoid* B and D and guess *only* A, C, or E. (In the test just mentioned, A and E are the most frequent keys; D is the least frequent.)

Many coaches advise their students to stick with the same letter when guessing, on the theory that, in the words of one, this "increases the probability of getting some answers right."[11] This is silly. On a randomly keyed test, you can't change the odds by always guessing the same letter, by picking answers with your eyes closed, or by adopting any other "method" that takes no account of the way the test is constructed. There are good guessing strategies that involve letter choices, but they're more complicated.

Computerized coaching courses are becoming quite popular.

Harcourt Brace Jovanovich sells one for $79.95.[12] It consists of a copy of the Selubs' book, a "User's Manual," and two computer diskettes. Students are supposed to read test questions from the book, then enter their answers on the computer. The computer tallies mistakes and keeps track of the time but doesn't do much else. The SAT is a pencil and paper test; what anyone could gain from practicing it on a computer I can't imagine. Barron's sells a similar system, for the same price, based on its own execrable study guides.[13]

The worst (and most expensive, at $299.95) computer SAT course I've tried is *Krell's College Board SAT Preparation Series.** Relatively few of Krell's SAT items are anything at all like ETS's. A great many of Krell's analogies are based on misspellings and anagrams (LOOP:POOL); ETS's never are. And I mean *never.* Krell students also have to draw their own math diagrams, which is both an absurd waste of time and a terrible way to learn about the SAT.

I've seen only five books that would actually help a student prepare for the SAT. Four are by the College Board (*5 SATs, 6 SATs, 10 SATs,* and the new edition of *5 SATs*)[†] and one is by Gary Gruber. Gruber's book is called *Inside Strategies for the S.A.T.* Unlike most of his competitors, Gruber gives evidence of having actually seen an SAT. Students who work through his book carefully — in conjunction with, say, *10 SATs* — will learn quite a bit about the test. He offers sixty-four tips, each with a fairly detailed (though usually clumsily written) explanation.

Many of Gruber's strategies are quite useful: "When a [quantitative] comparison does not contain simple numbers like 0 or 1, and where there are no mathematical manipulations that would simplify the question, then the quantities are probably equal."[14] This works well on the SAT. Here's the example Gruber gives:

*The most expensive I know of is Borg-Warner's *Microsystem 80 College Entrance Examination Preparation*, at $1450. I haven't actually tried this package, but I know that it includes a synonym section.

†There are other books that would be helpful to a serious student of the SAT. The book you are reading is one of them. There are also several revealing technical books and research reports published by ETS or the College Board. Both organizations have annual catalogues listing these publications.

Column A		Column B
	R = 2s + 3q + 5k	
	s = 5, q = 3, R = 49	
k		6

In a quantitative comparison, remember, a student is supposed to select: (A) if the quantity in Column A is greater; (B) if the quantity in Column B is greater; (C) if the quantities are equal; (D) if the relationship cannot be determined from the information given. The information in the middle, between the two columns, is the given.

If you take the first given equation and plug in 5 for s, and 3 for q, and 49 for R, you end up with 49 = 10 + 9 + 5k, or 30 = 5k, or 6 = k. Because k can only be 6, the quantities in Columns A and B are equal, and the only possible answer is C. But on an item like this, there's no need to do all that computation. Gruber's explanation is a little confusing, but the principle is fairly easy to understand. As he says, what a student needs to do is learn to look at all such problems "from the test-maker's point of view."[15]

When ETS looks at this problem, it sees an opportunity to trip up students who are careless in performing simple arithmetic. A student can arrive at the correct answer *only* if he makes no mistakes in plugging in the values for s, q, and R. If he makes a computation error and ends up with any number other than 6 as the value of k, then he'll select A or B and get the item wrong.

This would not be true if ETS had selected some other number than 6 for Column B. Suppose it had selected 5. The value of k would still be 6 because the givens wouldn't have changed, but the correct answer would now be A, because 6 is greater than 5. A student who did the math correctly would arrive at this answer. But so would a great many students who did the math *incorrectly,* because 6 is also greater than 4, 3, 2, 1, and 0. A student who, through various errors, arrived at any of those incorrect answers would also select A and would also be marked correct. "Thus," writes Gruber, "the test-maker would defeat his goal for finding whether the student legitimately got the correct answer."[16] The only way to make this kind of problem work on the test is to make the answer C.

Gruber has discovered the secret of the biserial correlation. Unfortunately for his readers, he doesn't pursue it as far as he could. This is the last strategy in his book. But it's really just the first step in beating the test.

Gruber has a new, Brobdingnagian book called *The Gruber S.A.T. Self-Instruction Course,* but it is extremely disappointing. The strategy described above, for example, isn't in it. Many of its 584 pages are filled with bizarrely superfluous information: the number of pecks in a bushel, esoteric math terms, a logarithm chart, a section on trigonometry. None of this stuff is ever tested on the SAT. Gruber also includes an enormous word list, which, although not quite as awful as the one in *Barron's,* contains many words ETS would never use: *diapason, billingsgate, flagitious,* and the ever-popular *termagant.* The main features of the book are four simulated SATs, but they are poor imitations. (Why buy *anyone's* imitations now that real ones are available?) In Gruber's antonym problems, one of the distractors (usually the first one) is always a synonym of the word being tested. This is never true on the SAT.

Gruber may be exhibiting early symptoms of the deadly yearning for respectability, also known as the Stanley Kaplan Syndrome. His earlier book of strategies is still excellent. But if you really want to learn how to beat the test, you'll have to go to someone like the Princeton Review.

John Katzman graduated from Princeton in 1981 and went to work on Wall Street. "I discovered I didn't like working on Wall Street," he says. Six weeks later, he quit. In college, he had worked for a New Jersey coaching school run by a Wharton graduate named Bob Scheller. Scheller used a computer program to analyze the SAT and develop strategies for beating it. Now, with nothing better to do, Katzman decided to start a school of his own, which he called the Princeton Review.

His first course, which he convened in his parents' Manhattan apartment, had nineteen students. His second had forty-three. His mother, at some point, kicked them out. Soon he had a hundred students, then two hundred. He didn't have to advertise, because former students told their friends about him. ETS says that the average score gain for a student who takes the SAT twice — first as a junior and then as a senior — is about 10 points on the math and 15 points on the verbal. For 40 percent of the students who repeat, scores actually go *down*.[17] Katzman's students' scores went up an average of 140 points, math and verbal combined. He began to boast that he had the best results of any coaching school in New York.

One day he got a phone call from a young man named Adam Robinson, who had set himself up as an SAT tutor after earning a law degree at Oxford. Robinson had worked with Bob Scheller a couple of years before Katzman had, and he had helped Scheller develop many of his coaching techniques. He told Katzman that his results were just as good. "I was tutoring students from a private school in Manhattan," Robinson says. "After ten hours, their average gain was about 140 points." Katzman and Robinson decided to get together for lunch. As they talked, they realized that their approaches to the SAT, though quite different, were complementary. Robinson joined forces with the Princeton Review.*

"When we combined our approaches," Katzman says, "both of our results went up, to about 185 points. That's our average. With kids who are serious, our average is closer to 250 points. Roughly 30 percent of our students this past spring went up over 250."

The tools ETS uses to build the SAT enable the Princeton Review to pick it apart. "The methods we use are aimed at the weaknesses we see in the statistical techniques used by ETS," Katzman says. By poring over old SATs and by analyzing them with computers, Katzman and Robinson have essentially deduced the SAT's specifications. ETS's obsession with consistency makes its tests extremely predictable. Katzman and Robinson don't drill students on item types they'll never see; they teach them how to put themselves inside the minds of the test-makers. One afternoon, Robinson taught me how to answer the hardest ETS analogies without looking at the stems — the words in capital letters — only at the answer choices. With a little practice, I was able to pick nine

---

* Bob Scheller's coaching school is called the Pre-test Review. It and the Princeton Review use exactly the same techniques, many of which were invented by Adam Robinson. For the sake of simplicity, I will generally refer to these techniques as Princeton Review techniques, even though many did not originate with the Princeton Review.

out of ten. Once you know how the test developers think, you don't always need to see the question to find the answer.

ETS and the College Board have never leveled with students about the content of the SAT. In order to put all students on an equal footing, they have claimed, the test is designed to be independent of any particular curriculum. The SAT, writes ETS's James Braswell, is "a broad-gauged predictive measure as opposed to a test of specialized subject matter achievement."[18] A student studying poetry won't have an advantage over a student studying fiction, the theory goes, because the SAT will look beyond superficial content differences and focus on "reasoning." Nor will a student at one school have a necessary advantage over a student at another. The subject matter, in short, doesn't matter. The verbal SAT, Braswell says, "is completely independent of specific course content."[19] On the math SAT, he says, "most of the mathematical content is held to topics generally taught prior to the tenth grade. By including only the subject matter to which most college-bound students have been exposed, the test strives to measure differences in students' ability to think quantitatively."[20]

But all of this is wrong. The SAT tests a very definite body of content that changes very little from test to test. This content, as ETS says, isn't generally taught in classrooms. But it can easily be taught. Math "taught prior to the tenth grade" is much less important, in terms of doing well on the SAT, than the math tested on the SAT — and the two are not the same. The real subject matter of the test, contrary to what Braswell says, is the test itself.

"Right from the start," Katzman says, "I tell our kids, 'I'm not a teacher. This isn't school. I'm not going to teach you English. I'm not going to teach you math. I'm going to teach you the SAT.' I tell the kids that they're not competing with each other, they're competing with ETS. And the mindset is: Let's blow those assholes away."

The key to Katzman, Robinson, and Scheller's method is, in a sense, the biserial correlation. ETS's circular logic is meaningful after all: students who do well on the SAT really *do* do well on the SAT. And because they do, it's possible to beat the test.

In order for a test question to make it onto a real SAT, it has to have certain statistical characteristics, as I described in Chapter 4. A question is used only if high-scoring students tend to get it right and low-scoring students tend to get it wrong. If low-scoring students do as well on it as high-scoring students, then the question — unless it is intended to be easy for all — will have an unacceptably low biserial correlation, and ETS will either have to rewrite it or discard it.

On a multiple-choice test, remember, the correct answer is always right there on the page. If that answer looks right to the wrong people — if low scorers pick it just as often as high scorers — then the question will wash out on the pretest and never make it to a real SAT. Imagine a math problem in which students are asked to find the square root of four. Most of the highest-scoring students know what a square root is, and they get the question right. Most of the middle-scoring students don't know what a square root is, and they get it wrong. But most of the lowest-scoring students think that the square root of any number is that number divided by two. They do exactly as well on this item as the highest-scoring students. There are two ways to arrive at the correct answer, one of them right and one of them wrong. The question fails its biserial correlation test, and it is replaced by a question that asks students to find the square root of nine. This is what Gary Gruber had begun to figure out in the strategy I mentioned earlier.

ETS's test-makers use this principle to help them write "effective" items. They also use it to help them write appealing distractors. In order to lure the average student away from correct answers on difficult items, the test-makers try to anticipate the errors, both of logic and of computation, that he will make. Each time this student strays from the proper path, a distractor will be waiting to tempt him.

Adam Robinson calls this average test-taker Joe Bloggs. When Joe Bloggs takes the SAT, he scores 450. When ETS lays a trap for him, he steps in. Princeton Review students learn how to avoid these traps by learning to understand how Joe Bloggs thinks. When Princeton Review students come to a hard question they don't understand, they ask themselves: What would Joe do here? Then they do something else.

Here's a question from a recent SAT.[21] *Don't actually read it; just glance at the two numbers in it, then look at the answers:*

---

25. In how many different color combinations can 3 balls be painted if each ball is painted one color and there are 3 colors available? (Order is not considered; e.g., red, blue, red is considered the same combination as red, red, blue.)

    (A) 4 (B) 6 (C) 9 (D) 10 (E) 27

This is the twenty-fifth question in a twenty-five-item math section. Therefore, according to its statistics, it's the hardest question in the section. It wouldn't be here if Joe Bloggs had been able to answer it on the pretest. The correct answer, therefore, must be something that Joe didn't think of. All we have to do to find the correct answer is to eliminate everything Joe *did* think of. Doing this doesn't require any real computation.

There are two numbers in this problem, 3 and 3. Joe added them and got 6. That means B is wrong. Then he multiplied them and got 9. That means C is wrong. Then he raised 3 to the third power and got 27. That means E is wrong. Now that we've narrowed it down to A and D, we can actually read the problem. Unless we're careless, we'll realize that we can easily think of more than four color combinations, so the answer can't possibly be A. That means it must be D. It is.

Here's another:[22]

---

35. The price of a shirt, after it was reduced 20 percent, was *P* dollars. What was the price of the shirt before the reduction?

    (A) $1.80 *P*   (B) $1.25 *P*   (C) $1.20 *P*
    (D) $0.80 *P*   (E) $0.75 *P*

The only number here is 20. Joe will add it to and subtract it from everything he can think of, so we can eliminate A, C, and D. Those dollar signs are in there just to confuse Joe, so we can ignore them. Let *P* be 1, just to keep things simple. We don't have to do any arithmetic. The answer is clearly B, since a shirt couldn't have cost *less* than a dollar before its price was reduced to a dollar.

When this question was used on a real SAT, only eight students in one hundred got it right. *Two and a half times as many* would have gotten it right if all had merely guessed at random. Princeton Review students, on the other hand, seldom get it wrong. And questions like this abound on the SAT.

Of course, Joe Bloggs isn't always wrong. On easy items, the obvious or apparent answer is usually the right answer. Fortunately for Princeton Review students, ETS clearly labels these items. It always puts them in the same place on every test. Because every section and subsection on the SAT increases in difficulty — in delta, rather — from beginning to end, Joe's problems are always in the first part of each section. Princeton Review students learn different strategies for different parts of the test. Sometimes they can answer a question without looking at much more than its number.

Princeton Review students love geometry items. Here's an example from a recent test:[23]

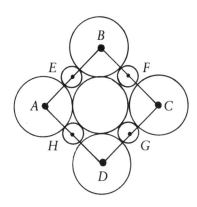

24. Four circles of radius 2 with centers A, B, C, and D are arranged symmetrically around another circle of radius 2, and four smaller equal circles with centers E, F, G, and H each touch three of the larger circles as shown in the figure above. What is the radius of one of the small circles?

(A) $\sqrt{2} - 2$ (B) $\sqrt{2} - 1$ (C) $2\sqrt{2} - 2$
(D) 1 (E) $3\sqrt{2} - 1$

Even for a good math student, this is a very imposing problem. But not for a Princeton Review student.

To solve this problem in math class, a student would have to realize that the distance from *A* to *C* or *B* to *D* is 8 (four large-circle radii). Then, using the Pythagorean theorem, he would calculate the length of one side of the square by taking the square root of half of the square of the diagonal ($4\sqrt{2}$). Subtracting 4 from this length would give him the diameter of the small circle ($4\sqrt{2} - 4$). Dividing that by 2 would give him the radius ($2\sqrt{2} - 2$), which is the right answer. Using this method, the path to the answer is long, uncertain, and filled with traps. Very few students realize that they're supposed to calculate the length of the diagonal of the square, much less that they can do so from the information provided.

To solve this problem the Princeton Review way, you don't need your pencil. The student simply eyeballs the diagram and thinks: the diameter of the little circle looks a little smaller than the radius of the big circle, which is 2. Therefore, the *radius* of the little circle — which is what the problem asks for — must be a little bit less than 1. He knows he can trust the proportions of the drawing, because ETS says right in the instructions that every diagram is drawn exactly to scale unless it says otherwise. Now he looks at the answer choices. He knows (because it's one of the few facts the Princeton Review has told him to memorize) that $\sqrt{2}$ equals 1.4. Answer A is thus out of the question, because $1.4 - 2$ is negative, and a length can't be negative; B equals .4, which is less than 1, but a lot less, and so probably not the answer; C equals .8, which is much better; D is 1, which is out, because we already know that the answer is *less* than 1; E is out for the same reason, because it works out to 3.2. The answer is thus C. The Princeton Review student hasn't come within hailing distance of the traps ETS laid not only for Joe Bloggs but also for good math students.

On some geometry problems, eyeballing isn't enough. In these situations, the Princeton Review student uses the edge of his test booklet as a ruler. It's an especially useful ruler, too, because it can bend around curves. If he needs to measure an angle, he uses one of the protractors that ETS kindly (though unknowingly) provides on every answer sheet and every page of the test booklet for the

exclusive use of Princeton Review students: any page corner is a
perfect 90-degree angle; carefully folding on the diagonal produces a perfect 45-degree angle; folding again produces a 22.5-
degree angle.

Sometimes Princeton Review students can answer questions that
ETS says can't be solved. This doesn't happen very often; when it
does, it costs the Princeton Review students a few points. This is
just one of the occupational hazards of knowing more about the
SAT than ETS does. Here's an example from a recent SAT:[24]

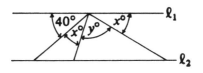

16. In the figure above, if lines ℓ_1 and ℓ_2 are parallel, what is the value of
    y?
    (A) 30
    (B) 40
    (C) 70
    (D) 80
    (E) It cannot be determined from the information given.

ETS says that the answer to this problem is E. We can tell from the
diagram (because we know that a straight line is a 180-degree
angle) that $y + 2x = 140$; if we treat this as an algebra problem,
as ETS apparently intends, we can't go any further, because we
aren't told what either x or y is. We have two unknowns and no
other information, so we can't solve the equation.

But if we treat this as a geometry problem — which seems more
logical, under the circumstances — we can go a great deal further.
We know from the instructions that this diagram is drawn "as
accurately as possible." We also know, again from the instructions, that all such diagrams "are intended to provide information
useful in solving the problems." Part of the useful information
provided by this very accurate diagram, therefore, is the exact
value of y. This value can be measured exactly. One way to do it,
of course, is to use a protractor. Another is to use the test booklet
first to measure and then to double the distance between the arms

of the given 40-degree angle at points equidistant from the vertex. A student who does this (or who accurately eyeballs the drawing or uses any of several other possible methods) will discover that the value of *y*, which is what the question asks for, is exactly 80, which is choice D. ETS tells students to select "the best of the choices given." Isn't exactly the right answer, D, a *better* answer than a demonstrably wrong one, E? This item is really quite unfair. It isn't a test of "insightful reasoning," as ETS claims. It's a test of familiarity with the ETS mentality. The student has to know that this problem, although it can be answered precisely, is the sort of problem that ETS claims has no solution.

I challenge ETS to defend or rescore this item.

Quantitative comparison items are just as coachable as geometry problems and much more coachable than Lewis Pike ever dreamed. There are twenty of these problems on every SAT. A Princeton Review student has a great advantage over them; he can usually solve at least two and sometimes half a dozen *without reading them*. John Katzman calls this technique "the Force," after the cosmic power that enabled Luke Skywalker to wield his laser sword blindfolded in *Star Wars*. The student simply looks at the page through Joe Bloggs's eyes and *knows* the answers to several of the questions.

Using the Force is quite exhilarating. The technique is intended for the five or so hardest quantitative comparison items, numbers 23 through 27 in section 5. Put somewhat simplistically, the Force says that if one of these items looks hard, then it's easy; if it looks easy, then it's hard.

Column A	Column B
23. The sum of two different odd positive integers each less than 10	The sum of three different even positive integers each less than 10
25. Area of the triangular region bounded by the X-axis, Y-axis, and the graph of the line x + y = 6	18

Number 23 looks simple and straightforward; therefore, it's not, and the answer is D, the relationship cannot be determined from the information given. Number 25 looks absolutely impossible; therefore, it's not, and the answer is C, the two quantities are equal.

"Using the Force can give an incredible boost to a kid's confidence," says Katzman. "Most of the students who take the SAT are terrified. But it's hard to be intimidated by a test when you can answer the questions on it without reading them."

When Princeton Review students have to do math-class math, they do it in a simplified form tailored precisely to the SAT. In "Taking the SAT," ETS tells students that they need to know that when two parallel lines are cut by a third line, the alternate interior and corresponding angles are equal.[26] Princeton Review students instead learn Fred's Theorem (named after Fred Bernstein, a teacher in the school's Long Island branch): When two parallel lines are cut by a third line, angles that *look* equal *are* equal.

"A safecracker knows more about safes than the people who make them," says Adam Robinson. One thing the Princeton Review knows that ETS doesn't is that many items on the math SAT are more nearly verbal items than math items. (This may be why math SAT scores tend to correlate fairly strongly — around .70 — with verbal SAT scores.) These are items that students miss not because they don't know the math but because they don't understand ETS's ambiguous wording. Here, for example, are two math items from two recent SATs.[27] The first is a regular math item, the second is a quantitative comparison:

---

14. Points A, B, X, and Y lie on the same line but not necessarily in that order. Given the lengths $AB = 12$, $BX = 2$, and $XY = 8$, what is length AY?

    (A)   2
    (B)   6
    (C) 18
    (D) 22
    (E) It cannot be determined from the information given.

24. Along a certain highway, City R is 12 kilometers from City P and 25 kilometers from City Q.

Column A	Column B
The distance in kilometers from City P to City Q along this highway	13 kilometers

(A) the quantity in Column A is greater
(B) the quantity in Column B is greater
(C) the two quantities are equal
(D) the relationship cannot be determined from the information given.

This is the same problem presented in two different ways. The answer in each is "cannot be determined." But notice that the first version explicitly states the key to its solution — the points don't necessarily lie in the order given — while the second one doesn't. ETS's statistics show the second version to be considerably more "difficult" than the first. Surely the only reason for this difference is the ambiguous wording of the second version. These are verbal problems, not mathematical ones. Students who know that ETS loves the points-on-a-line trick, and who understand the gimmick it turns on, have a tremendous advantage over students who don't. (On the other hand, students who know this problem type, but think there's a reason for the absence of the "not necessarily" disclaimer in the second one, get screwed.)

Fred of Fred's Theorem told me about another such math problem, one that his students had found extremely difficult. He realized from talking with them that they simply didn't understand what ETS meant by the word *nonoverlapping*, which appeared in it. He explained, and the difficulty disappeared. If ETS paid half as much attention to the SAT as the Princeton Review, the test wouldn't be so incredibly unfair.

In the spring of 1984, I was interviewed by a Princeton Review student who was writing a paper about ETS for one of his classes. I asked him what he thought of the SAT. "I used to like the verbal a lot better than the math," he told me. "Now I really like the math." Five weeks into the seven-week course, his score had risen from 560 to 780.

The verbal SAT is harder to coach than the math SAT, mostly because it is, to a very great extent, a vocabulary test. This is not to say, however, that it can't be coached or even that it can't be beaten. The Princeton Review gets excellent results on the verbal SAT. Most students improve their scores substantially.

One of the great misconceptions about the SAT is that the words on it are drawn from a pool very nearly as large as the English language. ETS promotes this misconception every time it says that an SAT score reflects a lifetime of learning and that preparing for the test over subgeologic time periods is impossible. A College Board representative once said that a student who understood every word used in the *New York Times* in a year would understand every word on the SAT. But reading the *Times* for a year would be a terribly inefficient way to prepare for the SAT. The *Times*, after all, isn't written by ETS. Why waste time studying it?

Princeton Review students learn their vocabulary from a short word list, compiled by Adam Robinson, called the Hit Parade. Conspicuously absent from it are the words that *Barron's* favors — aptitudinous tongue-twisters, like *sequacious* and *tergiversation*, that ETS's item writers never heard of. Instead, the Hit Parade contains words that tend to crop up regularly on the SAT. Discovering what these words are is easy. High school vocabularies aren't all that large. ETS can't use words that no one's heard of, because items based on such words would have terrible biserial correlations (Joe Bloggs would be as likely to get them right as anyone else). If you read enough SATs, you get a very accurate feel for the sort of words ETS likes to test. Robinson uses a computer. (The most frequently tested words on the SAT are appropriately gloomy: *enigma, apathy, indifferent*.)

Sometimes students don't even need to know what the words on the Hit Parade mean; all they need to know is that they are there. A student who is stumped for an answer looks for words from the list and limits his selection to those.

Princeton Review students also learn how to guess answers when they have little or no knowledge (as Robinson taught me to do with analogies), how to spot the traps that ETS lays over and over, how to avoid the answers that fool Joe Bloggs ("I tell my students to look for stupid answers to stupid questions written by stupid people," a Princeton Review teacher named Rick Lyon told me), and how to manage time. This last is especially important on the verbal SAT. Because reading comprehension items take so long to answer, students who don't know exactly how the test is put together are at a terrible disadvantage. Princeton Review students save reading comprehensions till last, when all the fast points have been scored. Students aiming for scores below 700 or so don't even read the final comprehension passage, the hardest one on the test. They simply cross it out in their test books. This gives them five or ten extra minutes to spend on the rest of the exam.

ETS claims, somewhat incredibly, that the SAT is "relatively unspeeded,"[28] based on the fact that virtually everyone "finishes" at least three quarters of the exam. But a student who answered the last question and no other would be said to have "finished" the test. Although it is true that low-scoring students often find themselves with time on their hands when they take the SAT, because they don't even attempt the harder questions, higher-scoring students know that test-taking speed can make an enormous difference.

Anyone who has spent any time studying ETS tests (except, of course, anyone at ETS) knows that what is tested is primarily the ability to take ETS tests. In order to prove this to the readers of *Harper's* in 1983, I composed a short Scholastic Aptitude Test Aptitude Test (SATAT). The test, which I reproduce here, contains five items taken from a reading comprehension portion of an actual SAT. In answering them, reach back in your mind to the days when you took your own SATs and then look for the kinds of answers you think would appeal to a test writer at ETS.

Oh, yes; I've left out the reading passage that the items refer to. I've also changed the order of the items and eliminated all references to the actual novelist the reading passage discusses. And I've left out titles of any of the novelist's books. You need to know only that the novelist, though dead, has a name you would recognize, and that "the author" referred to in several of the items is the author of the reading passage, not the author of the novels.

So that you will approach this test in a properly anxious frame of mind, I will tell you that when I administered it to myself, after many hours spent reading SATs, I had no trouble getting all of them right. And I *still* haven't read the passage. When I administered the SATAT to four people at a *Harper's* editorial meeting, the youngest member of the staff, who had just emerged from the world of ETS exams, also got all the answers. The editor got three correct, a very respectable score, as did the political editor. The worst score — one out of five — was that of an editor from England who had never taken, or even seen, an SAT. (You'll find the answers on page 307.)

---

1. The main idea of the passage is that

   (A) a constricted view of [this novel] is natural and acceptable
   (B) a novel should not depict a vanished society
   (C) a good novel is an intellectual rather than an emotional experience
   (D) many readers have seen only the comedy [in this novel]
   (E) [this novel] should be read with sensitivity and an open mind

2. The author's attitude toward someone who "enjoys [this novel] and then remarks 'but of course it has no relevance today' " (lines 21–22) can best be described as one of

   (A) amusement
   (B) astonishment
   (C) disapproval
   (D) resignation
   (E) ambivalence

3. The author [of the passage] implies that a work of art is properly judged on the basis of its

   (A) universality of human experience truthfully recorded
   (B) popularity and critical acclaim in its own age
   (C) openness to varied interpretations, including seemingly contradictory ones
   (D) avoidance of political and social issues of minor importance
   (E) continued popularity through different eras and with different societies

4. It can be inferred that the author [of the passage] considers the question stated and restated in lines 8–13 to be unsatisfactory because it

   (A) fails to assume that society and its standards are the proper concern of a novel
   (B) neglects to assume that the novel is a definable art form

(C) suggests that our society and [this novelist's] are quite different
(D) fails to emphasize [this novelist's] influence on modern writers
(E) wrongly states the criteria for judging a novel's worth

5. The author [of the passage] would probably disagree with those critics or readers who find that the society in [this novelist's] novels is

(A) unsympathetic
(B) uninteresting
(C) crude
(D) authoritarian
(E) provincial[29]

Princeton Review students learn similar strategies for dealing with reading comprehension problems. Because they know what to look for, they don't have to read the passages very carefully. Sometimes they scarcely read them at all. As a result, they have ten or fifteen more minutes to spend on verbal sections than other students do.

The Princeton Review uses ETS's statistics to beat the SAT. It also uses the SAT to beat ETS's statistics.

Every SAT contains six sections. One of these, the "experimental" section, doesn't count toward students' scores. It's used by ETS to pretest items for future SATs and to equate current forms of the test with past ones, as noted in Chapter 4. Students aren't told which section is the experimental one, because ETS wants them to work just as hard on it as they do on the sections that count. If they didn't work just as hard, ETS's deltas, biserial correlations, and raw-score conversion formulas would be thrown out of whack. In order to keep students from figuring out where the experimental section is, ETS moves it around. In December of 1983 it was section 3; in May of 1984 it was section 6.

Because hard items are harder to write than easy items, the experimental section is usually quite a bit tougher than the other sections of the SAT. It's also more likely to contain miskeyed, flawed, badly written, and ambiguous items, because the pretest is the screen ETS uses to filter out defective questions (roughly 40 percent of the items in any pretest are eliminated).[30] Encountering the experimental section unawares can throw a good test-taker

completely off his stride. Some students come unglued when they
hit it. Half an hour ago they were calm and doing fine; now
suddenly the sun is rising in the west and setting in the east. If the
experimental section comes early enough — in section 2, for instance, where it's sometimes placed — a student can lose
confidence in his judgment and decimate his score on the rest of
the test.

Warner Slack and Douglas Porter, the Harvard Medical School
professors critical of the SAT, think the experimental section is
unethical. "There are very strict guidelines about the use of human
subjects in research," Slack told me. "If we want patients to take
part in a research project, we have to have their informed consent,
and the volunteers have to be told that they can withdraw from the
study at any time, and they have to be told that their refusal to
participate will not hinder the medical care or any other care that
they receive. It's been Doug's and my position that to coerce students to participate, as ETS's research 'volunteers,' is unfair. If you
want to go to Yale, you have no choice but to be their research
participant — and at your own expense. As a member of the
human studies committee of the Harvard Medical School, I would
disapprove that project."

John Katzman has a simple solution to this problem. He teaches
his students how to find the experimental section. When they find
it, they fill it out at random, thereby saving thirty minutes of
anxiety and frustration. They simply put their heads down on their
desks and rest until it's time to start on the next section. (Or, if
they don't mind doing a little cheating, they use their extra half-
hour to work on other sections of the test. Katzman tells them
explicitly not to do this.)

The Princeton Review's sabotage of the experimental section has
a significant impact on ETS's statistics. The bigger the school becomes, the bigger this impact will be. ETS's pretest statistics are
usually based on samples of fewer than 1,500 students. Depending
on how the test booklets are distributed, Princeton Review students can make up a substantial percentage of the students in
particular samples. When they answer the questions at random,
they actually *reduce the difficulty of future SATs* by making the

pretest questions look harder, statistically, than they are. (See Chapter 4.)

Katzman very graciously told ETS what he was doing. By May of 1984, ETS seemed to have returned to an earlier method of arranging its SAT booklets in hopes of making the experimental section impossible to detect. But Princeton Review students found it anyway, and with ease. As long as ETS doesn't radically change the specifications for the SAT, Princeton Review students will *always* be able to find it. And even if ETS does alter the test dramatically, the Princeton Review will only be fooled for a month at most. The section simply can't be hidden from students who know what to look for.

Nor can ETS make the SAT uncoachable. *Any multiple-choice test built according to a statistical model can be beaten.* The GRE, the LSAT, the GMAT — all are susceptible to methods like the ones used by Adam Robinson and the Princeton Review. ETS can't make its tests harder for Princeton Review students without making them either impossible or entirely meaningless for *non–*Princeton Review students. It's Joe Bloggs who ultimately determines the content of the SAT.

In their latest official coaching statement for students, ETS and the College Board say that under certain unspecified but apparently extraordinary conditions, "particular groups of students or particular programs" have achieved average score gains "*as high as 25–30 points*"[31] (emphasis added). This statement misrepresents even the coaching studies ETS and the College Board have published. It bears no relation whatsoever to the results achieved by the Princeton Review and a number of other SAT coaches. On a radio show in New York in 1984, I told George Hanford of the College Board that I thought this statement was false and that I could raise his SAT score 25 to 30 points in fifteen minutes. He didn't take me up on the offer.

A few days later, I wrote a letter to Hanford suggesting that he invite Katzman and me to give a coaching demonstration at the Board's 1984 annual meeting. He responded that this would not be possible. "As you will see from the enclosed flier," he wrote, "plans for next fall's National Forum are already in place." But the meeting was still six months away, and the flier provided only the very most general description of events that might take place, saying that panels would discuss "such issues as . . ." and that certain "nationally known" but unnamed speakers would be present. It also said that "details on . . . program, speakers, and related activities" for the three-day meeting would not be available until August.[32] I had written to Hanford in April. I called Carol M. Barker, deputy secretary of the College Board and the person in charge of planning the conference. I asked her secretary if the program for the meeting was "in place." She said it was not. I asked her if it was still possible to make changes in the program. She said emphatically, "Oh, yes."

Why didn't Hanford tell me the truth? If you had been saying for more than half a century that dogs couldn't fly, and then someone offered to give you a flying dog, wouldn't you be the teeniest bit interested? But the College Board has nothing to gain from learning that coaching works. Katzman has repeatedly invited the Board to examine his records and conduct any sort of study it wants to. The Board has declined.

"Sometimes I think about suing the College Board for libel," Katzman told me. "Every time they publish a pamphlet that says the SAT can't be coached, they're calling me a liar."

The College Board and ETS are hoping that if they just keep their eyes closed long enough, the Princeton Review will go away. Meanwhile, Princeton Review students are being admitted to colleges that wouldn't have considered them before. And the effect of the course goes far beyond college admissions. "When you raise a kid's score 200 or 300 points," Katzman says, "you change his whole outlook about himself."

If I were a high school student in a city where a school like the Princeton Review was not available* or if my parents couldn't spare $500 for my tuition, I would be terribly upset. "Most of our kids are wealthy," Katzman says. "Those are the kids who have an advantage to begin with. And we're moving them up another

---

*At the moment, there are Princeton Review schools in New York, Westchester, Long Island, Chicago, and in Los Angeles. The Pre-test Review in New Jersey and Philadelphia teaches the same course with the same materials. Many more schools are planned. Adam Robinson teaches in New York and is listed in the Manhattan phone book.

level." I would be even more upset every time I heard ETS and the College Board tell the world that coaching doesn't work. Princeton Review students simply don't take the same test that most other students take. The effect would be the same if ETS randomly selected a thousand white, wealthy students each year, gave them the answers to the SAT in advance, and then denied that it had done so.

Most college admissions officers I've talked to (and virtually all high school guidance counselors) have seemed reasonably certain that, despite ETS's denials, coaching does work. But they are confused about the implications. Should they deduct points from the scores of students they suspect of having been coached? Some do, although they have no idea what they're doing. (James McMenamin, director of admissions at Columbia, told me that "any experienced reader of applications at a selective college is going to be suspicious, at this point, about any big jump in scores." The lesson: get your coaching before you take the PSAT.) Should admissions officers add points to the scores of students who have clearly had only limited exposure, by whatever means, to the ETS mentality? Should they require ETS's Achievement Tests instead of the SAT? ("That would be fine with me," says Katzman. "I can prepare a kid for the math Achievement, English Achievement — three weeks, 200 points." For more on ETS's Achievement Tests as an alternative to the SAT, see Chapter 13.) Some colleges are thinking of asking students to declare on their applications whether they were coached.

All of this is misguided and unfair, if only because admissions officers make no distinction between coaching that produces big gains and coaching that doesn't — between, say, the Princeton Review and *Barron's* or between Gary Gruber and *Krell's* or between Adam Robinson and Arco. Nor do they distinguish between students who take coaching seriously and students who don't. They look at numbers they don't understand and make moral judgments they have no basis for making. Students are caught in a double bind: the College Board swears to them that coaching doesn't work, then college admissions officers punish them if their scores go up.

Admissions officers who penalize students for trying to improve their scores on the SAT are doing what ETS always accuses its critics of doing: blaming the messenger for the message. The message in this case is that the SAT is not the test that ETS and the College Board have always claimed it to be. It's not neutral and objective. It's not curriculum-free. It's not uncoachable. It's not the same test for everyone who takes it. It's not a measure of preparation for college. Admissions officers shouldn't be upset with the Princeton Review. They should be upset with ETS and upset with the SAT.

The advantage Princeton Review students have is no different from the advantage that certain privileged students — students who are testwise, students who share the social and cultural values of the test-writers at ETS, students who have no compunction about guessing — have *always* had on the SAT. The odds have *always* been stacked against kids who aren't tuned to the ETS wavelength or who haven't spent their lives in schools where ETS tests are a way of life. Admissions officers, guidance counselors, teachers, parents, and students should stop listening to ETS and the College Board and start listening to someone who actually understands the SAT.

"The SAT," says John Katzman, "is bullshit."

8

Test Security

You will *not* be admitted to the test center without positive ID," say the instructions ETS and the College Board give to students when they sign up to take the SAT. Test scores would be meaningless if college admissions officers couldn't be certain they had been obtained under secure conditions. Students who lack driver's licenses, passports, school identification cards, or other official documents with photographs are told to provide "a brief physical description of yourself on school stationery. It must be signed by you in the presence of your school principal or guidance counselor, who must also sign it." Social Security cards, birth certificates, and parents' driver's licenses "are *not* acceptable."[1] In order to make certain all these instructions sink in, ETS repeats them when it sends students their test center admission tickets.

When I took the SAT at Julia Richman High School in December of 1983, no one asked for my identification. Indeed, when I took out my wallet to get my driver's license, the proctor told me to put it away. She told all the students to put their identification away. "I just need to see your tickets," she said. Proctors don't have to check the identification of students they know personally, but this woman couldn't have known more than a few of the students in the room, because they were from different schools. She certainly didn't know me. Nor did she seem to notice that I was ten years older than any of the other test-takers. *I* certainly would have asked for my ID.

Our proctor, who was wearing a jaunty scarf made of blue

plastic netting, talked to herself as she waited for students to arrive. She said she was going to give us our test booklets ahead of time but asked that we not open them "in case Dennis walks in." Of course, several students opened their booklets immediately. Someone asked if we were allowed to use the booklets as scratch paper. The proctor said she didn't know. It seemed to her that people had been allowed to the year before but that no one had said anything about it this year. We could probably "use the back," she said.

This is crazy, of course. Students can use any part of the booklet as scratch paper. They are *supposed* to use the booklets as scratch paper. Our proctor would have realized this if she had looked at her instruction book, but she never did. Proctors are required to read several pages of fairly complicated instructions aloud to the students, asking them periodically whether they understand. But our proctor didn't read a word.

Shortly after she gave us our booklets, she told us to begin. We would have thirty minutes to complete the first section, she said, starting now. Then, after we had started, she told us to be certain to fill in the identifying information on both sides of the answer sheet and on the back of the test booklet. Students have to provide quite a lot of information: name, address, birth date, two signatures, sex, test form number, registration number, form code, test book serial number, test site location, test site code. Students fill in much of this information by writing it in little squares and then darkening boxes on the answer sheet that correspond to individual letters and numbers. Doing so takes a long time. Students are supposed to do it *before* the test begins, with the proctor leading them through every step and checking to make certain the test and booklet numbers are entered correctly. The students in my room were cheated out of at least a third of the time allowed for the first section of the test. Even students who ignored the proctor and began working on the test were penalized, because she talked continually. One thing she talked about was the serial number: she wasn't sure if there was one or, if there was, where in the world it might be.

There was no clock in our room, so the proctor periodically marked the time on the blackboard. Her timing was very approximate, according to my watch. She shaved off a few minutes on some sections, added a few minutes on others. My desk was so covered with graffiti that the ink from the tabletop sometimes rubbed off on my answer sheet. Erasing these marks was difficult. All the desks had been carved and gouged. It was possible to tear an answer sheet simply by marking an answer.

Proctors are explicitly required to give students a five-to-ten-minute break at the end of each hour. Our proctor gave us only one break, very late in the test, only because a student complained. Several students continued working during the break. This, of course, is against the rules. It is cheating. The proctor said nothing, although she was clearly able to see what was going on. Other students worked on sections other than the one they were supposed to be working on. This, too, is cheating.

Students who finished the last section early were allowed to leave. This is absolutely forbidden. It's also extremely distracting to the students still working. The students who left early rustled their coats and papers and talked in normal voices. The proctor talked, too. She stood in the doorway and talked to a woman in the hall. I was working on the last few problems in my second math section at the time. Every time the proctor or one of the students started talking, I lost track of what I was doing and had to begin again. When time was finally called, the proctor allowed the remaining students to continue working on the test. Several were still working when I left.

I was appalled. In January I wrote a letter to ETS describing what I had observed at Julia Richman High School.[2] I assumed that ETS would cancel the scores of all the students in the room, if not in the entire test center, and schedule a retest. At the very least, I thought, ETS would contact the other students in the room to let them know they had been given the test improperly and to offer them an opportunity to take it again.

For nearly two months I heard nothing. Finally I received a letter from Patricia A. Goccia in the Candidate Relations Office of ETS's Admissions Testing Program.[*] Goccia said she was sorry I

---

[*]Goccia's stationery is headed "Admissions Testing Program of the College Board," but her office is at ETS. ETS wouldn't tell me which organization she works for.

had found the testing conditions "unfavorable." She said, however, that there was "no indication on the Supervisor's Irregularity Report informing us of the situations described in your letter." She said she had called the supervisor just to make sure. This supervisor, she said, "confirmed" that the identification of all the students had been checked and that all the other rules had been followed.[3]

"In concluding my investigation," Goccia wrote, "the supervisor assured me that all procedures were followed as outlined in the Supervisor's Manual,* and feels that the instructions were in no way breached." As for the cheating I had seen, the failure of the proctor to read the instructions, the misinformation given to students, the failure of the proctor to time the test properly, and the many flagrant violations of official testing procedure I had described, Goccia had no comment. She simply did not acknowledge the substance of my letter. "Had you felt that you did not test to your utmost ability under optimum conditions," she reminded me, "you did have the option to cancel your scores by Wednesday following the test date."

I called Goccia the next day. She was very nice. She sounded young. She was trying to be helpful.

"The supervisor checked with the proctor," she said, "and to her recollection, she said the administration went perfect." Goccia said that my proctor had been "doing the test for six to eight years, so the supervisor felt that she was competent enough. She had never brought any concerns to his attention as far as instructions or pre-admission procedures." She said that the supervisor himself had been giving the tests for half a dozen years, and that "he has never had complaints such as this."

All this apparently reassured ETS. But it made me wonder what had been going on at Julia Richman for the last "six to eight years." The infractions I had observed were apparently standard operating procedure.

I asked Goccia if it was a violation of the rules to make students fill in their names and other information when they were supposed

---

*When I later asked ETS if I could see a copy of a Supervisor's Manual, my request was denied.

to be taking the test. "It's not really a violation," she said, "as long as it's not included in the testing time." But it had been included in the testing time, I said. "Then it would be a violation."

I asked her if students were allowed to work during breaks. She said no. I asked her if students were allowed to continue working after the end of the testing period. She said no. I asked her if students were allowed to work on any section they wanted to. She said no. I asked her if students were allowed to leave before the end of the test. She said no, that was also definitely a violation of the rules. She also said that reading instructions aloud and checking identification were both "mandatory." Failure to do either would be a violation of the rules. Hourly breaks are also mandatory, according to the rules, although Goccia said this requirement wasn't strictly adhered to. "I remember one case," she said, "where the supervisor just said he will not give breaks anymore, because he had windows broken and supervisors beat up, and he just didn't want to have kids go out of the classroom."

For all of this, Goccia seemed uninterested in what I told her. Indeed, she was confused as to why I had called. She told me once again that if I had really thought the testing conditions were inadequate, I should have canceled my scores. I told her I didn't want to cancel *my* scores; I wanted her to cancel *everybody else's* scores. After all, every student in the room had been cheating, or being cheated, or both.

ETS knows that cheating is a problem. "Many types of cheating are currently not detected," said an internal ETS "briefing paper" in 1980. But the document also noted that the cost of detecting cheating had been rising in recent years (from $136,000 in 1978 to roughly $300,000 in 1980) and that "this substantial increase in expense calls into question again the cost/benefit ratio of the test security function." One possible solution would be "discontinuing the test security function altogether" — an attractive option because "test security functions at ETS result in substantial amounts of negative publicity."[4]

Consistent with this concern for its publicity, ETS had referred my letter not to its Test Security Office, the department charged with detecting cheating, but to Candidate Relations. Goccia's job was to calm me down, not to correct an injustice. I asked her what ETS was supposed to do in cases where it "knows that procedures have been violated and that cheating has taken place."

"Well, see," she said, "we have a specific department that deals directly with the supervisors. My job is just basically to handle the candidate inquiries. After I did my investigation, I passed it on to our Supervisor Relations Department, who will take any further action if necessary. I mean, it's going to take the supervisor coming out and saying, 'Yes, this did happen, we didn't do this right.' And he's not doing that."

When I persisted, Goccia said that she would check with Supervisor Relations and see if anything should be done. She called me back to say that ETS had consented to send an observer to Julia Richman the next time a test was administered there, which would be in May 1984. Since this was clearly being done only because I had continued to press my case, I decided to be there, too.

It was shortly after my conversation with Patricia Goccia that I first met John Katzman and Adam Robinson of the Princeton Review. I asked them if their students had ever had experiences similar to mine.

"We hear war stories from the kids all the time," Katzman told me. "It is *unbelievable* how bad some of ETS's test centers are. There was a proctor at Stuyvesant who didn't even bring a watch. So, at some point in the middle of the first section of the test, he asked the students, 'Does anybody know what time it is?' And one of the kids said, 'Nobody has a watch; why don't you go look at the clock down the hall?' And he *did*. Every time he went to see what time it was, he left the kids all alone in the room and they could do whatever they wanted."

I asked Katzman why there was such a problem.

"What you have to understand," he said, "is that these proctors get paid $30. When you figure out all the time they're supposed to spend, that works out to just about the minimum wage. And yet if they lose a test booklet, ETS is after them for the rest of their lives. If they turn in someone for cheating, they have to do a lot of paperwork, and then the kid threatens to kill them, and all for thirty bucks. The proctors just don't take it seriously. They're in a coma. The SAT is an unproctored exam. You take it on the honor system. I would bet that 70 percent of the kids in New York cheat on at least one question on the SAT. And ETS doesn't do anything about it, because they'd rather spend money on their goose pond than on running the tests well."

Princeton Review students know the rules better than the proctors do, so incompetent supervision usually doesn't bother them. Katzman also tries to keep them out of the worst test centers. But ETS and the College Board make this difficult. Several New York test centers have been closed; others are just about to close. Princeton Review students often have to take the test with the hoi polloi. "One time," Adam Robinson told me, "the proctor interrupted them in the middle of a section. He said, 'Oh, excuse me, I forgot to have you fill out these cards.' "

Some proctors turn the other way while students consult pocket dictionaries or work math problems on wristwatch calculators. Students too timid to cheat in the testing room wait for a break and then use their dictionaries and calculators in the bathroom. (ETS's security budget doesn't provide for bathroom supervision.) I've heard stories of testing centers where students flipped through the pages of their test booklets before the test, calling out words they didn't know while students with dictionaries looked up definitions. I've heard about centers where students actually walked around the room during the test, comparing their answer sheets with those of other students. I've talked to six people who told me they'd been paid to take the SAT for other students; four of these imposters were paid directly by the parents of the other students. I heard about one girl who, after doing very well on the PSAT, became the object of a bidding war among classmates willing to pay for the privilege of sitting next to her during the SAT.

One recent fad in cheating is taking the test untimed. ETS permits students with "diagnosed visual, physical, or perceptual handicaps of a temporary or permanent nature" to take the test over periods as long as two days.[5] Many students legitimately need this service. But others see it as a golden opportunity to improve their scores, and there are doctors willing to say that almost anyone has a "perceptual handicap." I heard about two friends (one with a legitimate handicap) who took the SAT untimed about ten days apart. ETS used the same test form both times. The first student to take the test consulted a dictionary during breaks. The second learned many of the questions in advance from his friend.

Do proctors and supervisors ever complain to ETS about security violations and inadequate testing conditions? Some do, but ETS typically responds to them the way Patricia Goccia responded to me. A few months after my *Harper's* article was published, I received a letter from Ralph Lowrance, a faculty member at Sacred Heart College in Belmont, North Carolina, and a supervisor for ETS's Test of English as a Foreign Language (TOEFL). For five years, Lowrance wrote, he had been notifying ETS of security violations and trying to persuade the company to improve its test administration procedures; for five years he had received nothing but "frustrating resistance" from ETS.

Lowrance first wrote to ETS in the fall of 1978. He reported that he had witnessed a number of serious security violations at a TOEFL test center. He received the sort of response the White House sends to people who write to the President to complain about his foreign policy. Willem C. Spits, associate program director for TOEFL, thanked Lowrance for informing ETS of "the disturbing situation you discovered" and said that ETS would "certainly look into the matter further," but he didn't ask Lowrance to provide more information or even to explain exactly what the "disturbing situation" had been. Lowrance wrote back anyway, detailing five specific security violations of the sort I observed at Julia Richman. He never received a reply.

Lowrance wrote more letters to ETS regarding TOEFL during the next five years. In March 1982, he wrote to say that he had double-checked ETS's scoring of his students' tests and discovered an error in one of them. (ETS acknowledged and corrected the error. The student had marked multiple answers on several items, but ETS's scoring machine had treated them as correct responses.) He also continued to point out security violations, receiving increasingly petulant responses from a variety of ETS personnel. In October 1982, he wrote to say that while waiting outside a TOEFL testing room he had looked in through the open door and noticed a number of violations, which he described. (That the door was open was itself a violation.) Eleanor V. Horne, ETS's "student concerns coordinator," wrote back not to thank him for the tip but to ask that he stay away from TOEFL test centers "because visits of unauthorized persons to test centers can be disruptive." Horne told Lowrance that the reason ETS had never investigated any of his charges was that he hadn't identified the test center in question. But Lowrance had done so several times, and the center's identity was obvious from the context of his correspondence. Horne assured Lowrance that "ETS devotes a considerable amount of time and attention to the training of test center supervisors." Lowrance wrote back to point out that *he* had never received any such training before being allowed to supervise ETS tests.

In 1983, after Lowrance had continued to press his objections, Robert H. Parker, director of test security, flew to North Carolina to talk to him personally. "What should have been a discussion," Lowrance wrote to me, "turned out to be a lecture by [Parker], who requested that I leave the 'institution' alone and let it identify and handle problems." Lowrance said later that Parker had been "very defensive" and that "every time I would bring up a point, Parker would just refute it and tell me, You don't know everything that's going on in the company; who are you to say that this is happening?" About two weeks later, Lowrance wrote to ETS again, pointing out another apparent violation of ETS's guidelines for administering TOEFL. Instead of answering this letter directly, ETS addressed its response to Sister Mary Boulus, the president of Sacred Heart College. Lowrance told me he thought ETS was trying to get him in trouble with his boss, not realizing that she supported him. Six weeks later ETS sent another letter to Sister Boulus, this time asserting that Lowrance himself had misadministered a test. This charge was quite extraordinary, because Lowrance had administered the test in accordance with written instructions he had requested and received from ETS. ETS now implied that those instructions had been incorrect. Lowrance wrote back to ask that ETS stop speaking to him through Sister Boulus and write to him directly. ETS did not respond.

Adam Robinson was waiting with a group of his students across the street from Julia Richman when I went to take the SAT again in May. He was plying them with orange juice and doughnuts and telling them not to be nervous. Most of the Princeton Review was taking the test at a better center across town, but there hadn't been room for everybody.

Finally it was time to go inside. Once again, no one checked my identification. My proctor this time was a young woman who was having a great deal of trouble reading her seating chart. She couldn't decide which end went where, and she couldn't figure out how the diagram related to the classroom. She turned it upside down, then right side up, then upside down. I simply found my name on the paper and took my seat. She didn't ask me who I was. I didn't even take my wallet out of my pocket.

The proctor was having so much trouble with the seating chart that the supervisor came in and told her just to seat us anywhere. A few students changed seats. The supervisor turned on the lights, which our proctor had forgotten to do, and left.

Then Anella Schmidt, the ETS observer, arrived. Schmidt was a solidly built woman with the stern look and patronizing demeanor of a minor government official on a tour of the provinces. Her gray hair was tied back in a bun. She wore a name tag identifying her as an emissary from "ETS, Princeton, NJ." Periodically she made portentous jottings in a green notebook. Her first act was to modify the supervisor's random-seating order. She explained that ETS needed to know where everyone was sitting so that it could later detect cheating. "Are any of these Perezes related to each other?" she asked, scowling at the seating chart. Then she went around the room noting where everyone was sitting.

Our proctor wasn't quite sure what to do. This was her first time giving the test. She apparently hadn't read her instruction manual, although she certainly had done something with it: it was torn, folded, and crumpled. Schmidt looked over her shoulder and told her what to do. "You've got to read all that," she said when the proctor skipped part of the instructions. By this time Schmidt had taken the seat next to mine. I may be paranoid, but I find it peculiar that, with several hundred students and more than a dozen classrooms to choose from, Schmidt decided to sit next to the person whose phone call had prompted her trip. If I were Schmidt, I'd have wanted to observe the proctor about whom ETS had received the complaint. I know she was there; I passed her in the hall.

It was hard to hear the instructions because the proctor had a quiet reading voice. She stumbled over some of the longer words. When she got to the part about using test books for scratch paper, she inserted the word *not* and made it sound as though we weren't supposed to. There was some confusion about this; eventually it was cleared up. Then a black girl in the back of the classroom asked if we were supposed to guess. The proctor deferred to Schmidt.

"I wouldn't guess unless you can eliminate two of the five," said ETS's official representative. "Guessing isn't going to help you."

As ETS knows, this is absolutely untrue. Several of Adam Robinson's students snickered. All the others, I presume, got the message that they weren't supposed to guess.

You can never really understand the difference $500 makes on the SAT until you see it in a test center. The Princeton Review students had brought candy and Cokes to keep their energy up. They had plenty of sharp pencils. They all had wristwatches. They knew almost everything there was to know about the test they were going to take. They had already memorized the instructions. And they knew that Anella Schmidt had not told them the truth about the SAT. The other kids, several of them black, were less fortunate. They had no wristwatches and their pencils were stubs. ETS had led them to believe that the SAT would put them on an equal footing with the kids from the private schools. But they might as well have been taking a different test.

Schmidt left when we began to work. Our proctor spent most of her time standing at the window with her back to us, watching some boys play basketball (noisily) on the playground below. It was a nice day and she didn't want to be doing what she was doing.

I found the experimental section easily and filled in that part of my answer sheet in a handsome zigzag pattern. I used the Force on a couple of questions and the corner of my answer sheet on a geometry problem. At break time students were excused, in groups of two or three, to go to the bathroom, which, as usual, was not proctored.

I talked to Katzman a couple of days after the test. He said that a bored proctor at one of the other test centers hadn't timed students on individual sections of the test but had merely told them that they had three hours to complete the whole thing. This meant that the students could work on any section they wanted to whenever they wanted to — an enormous advantage. Another proctor, for an Achievement Test, had fallen asleep at his desk. One hour went by. Then another. When he finally woke up, his students had been happily working on a one-hour exam for nearly three hours. The proctor asked the students not to say anything because he didn't want to get in trouble with ETS.

When I told ETS that I had been a firsthand witness to genuine, indisputable, unambiguous cheating on the SAT at Julia Richman High School — not to mention flagrant violations of the test administration rules — the company's only response was to send Anella Schmidt to show the Princeton flag at Julia Richman High. But ETS doesn't always show so little concern for test security. Periodically it cancels scores that it finds suspicious. Like income tax audits and public hangings, these measures are intended to serve partly as admonitory examples. Most such cases are routine; others are not. One of these occurred in 1982.[6]

Richard Becker, Lloyd Berkowitz, James Denburg, and Stephen Haskin signed up to take the SAT on May 1, 1982. All four were juniors at Millburn High School in Millburn, New Jersey. All four were members of the tennis team. At some point during the week before the exam, their coach, A. Edward Tirone, realized that the test would conflict with a tournament in which they were supposed to play. He informed the boys and said he would ask Louis Zuckerman, the school's ETS test center supervisor, whether some sort of special arrangement might be made. Zuckerman said that Tirone, an ETS proctor, could give the boys the test a few hours early, enabling them to get to the match on time.

The boys learned of this arrangement on Friday, the day before the test. It was late in the afternoon. They had just played a tennis match at another school. As they arrived back at Millburn High on the team bus, Tirone told them to meet him at six o'clock the next morning to take the SAT. Becker had been planning to spend the night at Haskin's house, which was close to the school. Since they all had to be up early, Haskin invited Berkowitz and Denburg to do the same. The coach went into his office, and the boys left.

When they arrived at Haskin's house, they talked briefly with his parents and then walked to a pizza parlor for dinner. When they returned, at eight or eight-thirty, they watched TV, listened to records, spent an hour or so — sometimes separately, sometimes together — looking at the *Barron's* SAT review book and some other coaching materials, talked with Mr. and Mrs. Haskin, and made periodic forays to the kitchen. Mrs. Haskin remembers hearing them turn in around eleven. They slept in separate rooms.

Early the next morning they walked to school and banged on the door until a janitor let them in. Tirone arrived a few minutes later. He arranged four desks so that the boys would be facing different walls with their backs to one another and to him. He did not leave the room during the test. Zuckerman looked in once or twice to see how they were doing and noticed nothing amiss. When the test was over, Tirone returned the test books and answer sheets to Zuckerman, and the four boys and their coach went off to play tennis.

ETS reported the results of the test in June. The boys' scores ranged from 490 to 630 on the verbal and from 660 to 730 on the math. Sometime either that month or the following September, one of their classmates, Paul Song, told another classmate, Jeffrey Leen, that he had heard a rumor that the four boys had stolen copies of the test on Friday, studied them that night, and returned them before taking the exam the next morning.

There was no evidence whatsoever that this had happened. Zuckerman had given Tirone the exam books on Friday, and Tirone had immediately locked them up. The four boys had spent that afternoon at the tennis match. After the bus had dropped them off in the evening, they had been away from the school until the following morning, when they arrived to take the test. Still, the rumor had a certain logic to it. The four boys were on the tennis team, they had taken the test at a special time, and their coach had been their proctor. The idea that they had stolen the SAT struck a raw nerve in Jeffrey Leen, and he became very upset.

"I couldn't believe it," he said later. "I thought it was unfair to the rest of the students. . . . It stands in their way of getting into the university that they might want to go to and I didn't think it was fair that some students should get away with beating the system at the expense of the other students."[7]

The university Leen wanted to go to was Brown. In the fall, he applied for early admission. Becker, whose father was a Brown alumnus, also applied for early admission. Becker and Leen had been close friends when they were younger, but in high school they had drifted apart. Becker was popular, outgoing, athletic. Leen was photography editor of the yearbook, but he spent most of his time on his schoolwork. He wanted very badly to go to Brown.

Brown mailed out its admissions decisions in the winter. Leen was rejected outright; Becker was deferred into the regular applicant pool (he was later rejected). A short while after the letters were sent, Louis Zuckerman stopped Leen in the hallway. Zuckerman was Leen's guidance counselor and a longtime friend of the family. He knew how much Leen had wanted to go to Brown and how disappointed he was to have been turned down.

"He said that he had been looking over the file of acceptances and rejections from early-action applicants," Leen said later, "and he could not believe that Richard Becker got deferred and I got rejected. So he simply called up Brown to have them give him some sort of explanation."[8]

Zuckerman told Leen that according to the admissions office, Becker had been deferred rather than rejected because his father was an alumnus. This explanation didn't fully satisfy either Zuckerman or Leen. "Mr. Zuckerman informed them that he would be watching closely, so to speak," Leen said, "because he was very annoyed with the fact that someone with lower credentials would be accepted over someone with higher credentials."[9] Zuckerman told Leen that his grades were better than Becker's but that their SAT scores were similar. This surprised Leen. "I didn't think he was capable of it," he said later.[10] He was annoyed to think that he and Becker had been considered on anything resembling an equal footing, and Zuckerman said that he was, too.[11]

Leen began to think more and more about the May SAT and about what Paul Song had told him about stolen exam books. The more he thought about it, the angrier he became. That night he went home and told his mother that the only reason Richard Becker had been deferred at Brown was that he had stolen the SAT. His mother was shocked. She didn't think that sort of thing should be allowed to happen. The next day she called Louis Zuckerman and asked if it was possible for students to steal copies of the test. Zuckerman said that it was not.

Zuckerman had done as much as anyone to arouse Leen's suspicions. Now that the boy's mother was involved, Zuckerman decided to talk to Tirone. He called Tirone into his office, and, in the presence of another counselor, grilled him about his conduct of the test. Tirone said that everything had gone well and that he had carefully locked up the exam books as soon as Zuckerman had given them to him. Six or seven months had passed since the test, and he couldn't remember whether he had locked them in his file cabinet or in his closet, but he remembered locking them up and then locking the door to his office. The door had still been locked the next morning. Getting to the tests would have required stealing two keys.

Still, under Zuckerman's intense questioning, Tirone had to admit that it would not have been absolutely impossible for someone to have stolen, and then replaced, the exams. Zuckerman called back Mrs. Leen and told her that he had been wrong and that it was indeed possible for someone to have taken the test books. Indeed, he now thought that it was likely. He had heard that another student in the school had told his guidance counselor that he had seen the four boys studying a stolen copy of the exam on the night before the test. He told Mrs. Leen this as well.

On January 7, 1983, Louis Zuckerman called ETS test security specialist Joan Honig and told her that he was "all but positive" that "a cheating incident" had taken place and that he and Tirone and others at the school were very upset. Honig said she would look into the matter. She told Zuckerman to call back in four or five weeks. In her record of the conversation, she wrote, "It is hoped that we may be able to develop something on Pre-Knowledge."[12]

Sometime later, Leen asked Zuckerman if he had done anything about "the possibility of the exams being stolen."[13] Zuckerman had discussed the case fully with Leen, giving him information about the four boys' SAT scores and telling him that it might have been possible for them to break into Tirone's office. Zuckerman now assured Leen that he had made a report to ETS and that he would check up on it soon. Leen's parents also asked him what he had done. When a month had passed, he called ETS again and was told that nothing had happened. He relayed this information to the Leens and said that trying to get information out of ETS was very frustrating.

Mr. Leen was upset. He decided to call Joan Honig himself. Using the pseudonym Philip Jones (but leaving his real telephone number), he asked what was being done about what he called the problem at Millburn High School. Nothing had been done yet, he was told. Zuckerman made more phone calls. Then Mr. Leen called again, using the same pseudonym. This time he got a response. On the day of the second call, the ETS Test Security Office put together a report on the Millburn case and passed it on for submission the next day to the Board of Review, the ETS committee that makes final judgments in cases of suspected cheating.

The more Jeffrey Leen thought about it, the more sense it made. In the yearbook adviser's office one day he found a binder full of quips and sayings that the seniors had provided to run beneath their photographs. There were nicknames, favorite quotations, inside jokes, and cryptic references. On James Denburg's form — among phrases like "beach bum whirlpool" and "the grunter toga" — Leen found the words "we stole it." He became furious. He told his mother that evening that he couldn't believe anyone would just come right out and boast in the yearbook that he had stolen the SAT. It was so brazen. It was almost like a taunt.

As it happened, the quotation had nothing to do with the SAT. It referred to an evening when Denburg and a friend named Chris Murray had found a moped in a driveway and taken it for a thirty-minute joy ride. But Leen didn't know that. All he could think of was his rejection at Brown and the incredible arrogance of the boys on the tennis team.

Around the time that Zuckerman had started calling Joan Honig at ETS, the four boys began to think that some of their teachers were treating them differently. One teacher interrupted class to give a lecture on cheating. Stephen Haskin noticed that two friends of his on the faculty had stopped coming to watch his tennis matches. Coach Tirone was different, too. "All of a sudden," Haskin said later, "he never had any time for me. I didn't understand it. I talked about it with my parents, and they said maybe he's having trouble at home or whatever."[14]

Later, after rumors had begun to circulate at school that the four boys were in some sort of trouble over their SATs, Tirone asked Jeffrey Leen if the boys or anyone else had been hassling him about it.

"At the time I was extremely baffled," Leen said later, "because I didn't know why they would assume that I had anything to do with trying to implicate them in the theft of the exams."[15]

"I remember being on the first committee on security," Martin Katz, an ETS research scientist, testified during a closed company hearing in 1982. "In those days Captain [Paul] Williams was in charge of security and his idea, I was horrified to find out, was to wring confessions from suspects, because it was only if he got a confession that you could be sure that someone had cheated. And he would call these people on the phone and try to get a confession over the phone or even arrange to interview them and put them through some sort of a third degree."[16]

ETS eventually abandoned Williams's strong-arm tactics, but procedures for detecting cheating remained crude. Even as late as 1980, in all testing programs except the SAT, the company was using a method that an ETS researcher had described in a 1978 internal report as being "extremely inadequate, almost primitive."[17] This procedure consisted of calculating the percentage of items on which two students had chosen the same wrong answer. The assumption was that when one student copied answers from another, he would copy incorrect answers along with correct ones. If the percentage of agreement between incorrects seemed high enough, ETS believed, then cheating had probably taken place. ETS had done no research on this procedure. The results were unreliable and highly ambiguous, and the employees charged with interpreting them were generally unaware of their limitations.

The procedure used in the SAT program wasn't much more sophisticated. On cases of suspected copying, ETS used Angoff's

Indices, two statistical formulas developed by researcher William Angoff. Like the procedure used in other programs, Angoff's Indices involved a statistical comparison of incorrect responses. They were used until early 1981, although their reliability was highly questionable. For one thing, they were based on a version of the SAT that was no longer in use.

In the 1970s, Angoff's Indices began to cause trouble for ETS. "The major problem that we were experiencing as an office was dissatisfied candidates because of the basis on which we were recommending score cancellations or retesting," said Robert H. Parker in 1982. ". . . Now, you got to realize, at this time, was the beginning, as I look back now, of the era throughout the nation in general against testing and specifically it seemed to be just everybody's against ETS too, at the time. And we found more and more client concerns with lawyers at the time."[18]

Fears about lawsuits, and ETS's familiar anxiety about the national mood, prompted a powerful interest in developing an inexpensive method of detecting copying that test-takers and their lawyers would find more persuasive. Frederick Kling, an ETS researcher and a member of the Board of Review, began to think he might be able to develop such a method. Kling had come to ETS after abandoning his intended career as a minister. He had done some graduate work in psychology and statistics, but he was not a scientist. His research output at ETS was small. On two occasions in his twenty-six years with the company he was nearly fired. Still, he began to work on the cheating problem in his spare time. In 1978, he made a proposal to the Board of Review, seeking money to finance validation research on the method he was developing. The Board rejected his proposal.

Kling's original idea was to modify Angoff's Indices in order to account for the fact that some wrong answers on tests are more attractive than others. "Our current practice," he wrote in a memorandum dated October 1, 1976, "is to treat all items equally and all distractors as if they had the same probability of being selected." But this, he said, was clearly unwarranted. "The simple fact is that not all items are equally likely to be answered incorrectly, or omitted, and that distractors can vary greatly in their attractiveness."[19] By looking at the statistical item analysis for a given test, Kling reasoned, it would be possible to determine the rough probability of a student's selecting any particular incorrect answer that had also been selected by another student. This would eliminate one of the major flaws in Angoff's Indices. If the new method were adopted, Kling believed, ETS would be able to support accusations of cheating with far greater confidence.

As Kling originally conceived it, the new copying-detection method would require two separate probability charts and several lengthy mathematical calculations. But the Board of Review felt that in this form the Kling method would be too cumbersome and too expensive to be of practical use. Angoff's Indices might be flawed, but they were quick and easy. Still, as time went by, in cases of suspected cheating where, in the words of Robert Parker, "there was a high likelihood of serious lawsuits or poor PR kind of feedback,"[20] the Board of Review would sometimes turn to Kling.

Eventually, in hopes of making it more palatable to the Board, Kling simplified his method. He abandoned the idea of individual probabilities — which he had first conceived as his method's distinguishing feature — and calculated average probabilities based on five old forms of the SAT, more or less as Angoff had. He also pared down his formula so it could be programmed into a Texas Instruments TI-59 calculator and used by untrained personnel. Running the routine took only a few seconds. All an operator had to do was punch half a dozen numbers — the number of items on the test, the number of incorrect answers shared by the presumed source and the presumed subject, the subject's estimated probability of selecting wrong answers, and two or three others — and then read a number from a paper tape. If the number was, say, .000001, that meant — according to Kling — that there was only one chance in a million that the wrong-answer agreement between the two test papers had occurred by chance. The new method came to be known as the Kling Index, or Index K.

ETS found that students, parents, and even lawyers tended to be very impressed by Index K. The stroke of genius in Kling's method was not the procedure but the product; there was something about those zeroes that stopped people in their tracks. "I find it's so much easier to address the question of copying, with the result of that statistic in front of you," said Shirley Kane-Orr, a senior test security specialist, in 1982. "When you have a series of eight zeroes, for instance, you would [say], '[one would expect to] observe this degree of comparison less than one time in one hundred million comparisons.' It's truly off-the-wall and it's off-the-wall to say, and the candidate knows that you have the statistic and they are very impressed with it. It usually ends discussions."[21] When ETS wheeled out Index K, lawsuits disappeared.

One of the best things about Index K was its simplicity. Despite their daunting titles, the members of ETS's Test Security Office are clerical personnel. Senior test security specialist Kane-Orr's academic background consists of an associate's degree in secretarial science and one year of art education. Before going to ETS as a temporary secretary in 1969, she had been a secretary at Bethlehem Steel for four years and an assistant manager in a small fabric store. But using Index K didn't require a background in statistics or in anything else. All that the company's five test security specialists had to do was punch numbers into a calculator.

On March 15, 1983, Kane-Orr performed some preliminary Index K calculations on the May 1982 SATs taken by Richard Becker, Lloyd Berkowitz, James Denburg, and Stephen Haskin. She passed this information along to a secretary, test security specialist Antonia Rosenbaum, who did more calculations and prepared an Investigative Summary. Index K can be used only for a pair of students, a source and a subject. There is considerable likelihood of error in the procedure, so ETS's general policy is to investigate suspected copying cases only when the Index suggests that there is less than one chance in ten thousand that the correspondence between wrong answers happened by accident. On the verbal exam, Rosenbaum found that of the six possible pairings between the boys, two — Becker/Denburg and Denburg/Haskin — had K values that, according to this arbitrary criterion, indicated that copying had taken place. Three of the other K values came fairly close to the criterion, although they didn't actually reach it. She found no worrisome K values for the math SAT. She did, however, find substantial agreement between *correct* answers on the math (although ETS has never considered agreement between correct answers to be evidence of cheating). On the basis of her study, she concluded that Berkowitz, Denburg, and Haskin had copied answers from Becker. Her report was submitted to the Board of Review, which was scheduled to meet the following afternoon.

Three members of the Board considered the case, devoting above five minutes to it. They looked at the numbers Rosenbaum had produced. They also read Joan Honig's original note mentioning a rumor at the school. They decided unanimously to inform the boys that their scores would be canceled unless they could provide information proving they had not cheated. One member, Thelma Spencer, decided that Becker must also have been cheating, since the four boys had taken the test together. She added Becker to the group.

The following day, four letters were mailed over Antonia Rosenbaum's signature. "I am writing to you because the ETS Board of Review believes there is reason to question your May 1982 Scholastic Aptitude Test scores," the letter began. ". . . The Board of Review is made up of experienced staff members responsible for determining the validity of scores that are questioned. In reviewing your scores, they found close agreement of your answers with those on another sheet from the same test center. Such agreement is unusual and suggests that copying occurred." The boys were given until April 1 to respond.

Nearly all of the two thousand students who receive such letters from ETS every year either do nothing, causing their scores to be canceled, or agree to take a retest, which ETS offers at no charge. The four boys, however, insisted to their parents that they had not been cheating. "You have to have faith in your child," Phyllis Denburg said later. "When your son looks at you and says, 'Ma, I didn't do anything wrong,' you believe him."[22] Richard W. Haskin spent a long evening questioning his son and concluded that he was telling the truth. "I am satisfied that he neither had access to the test before it was given," he wrote in a letter to ETS, "nor did any irregularities occur during the taking of this test. Since the test was given nearly 10 months ago, it does not seem fair or appropriate for Stephen to be required to take it again." He asked ETS for a written assurance that it would not cancel his son's scores and said that he had retained an attorney.[23]

A few days later, Harris B. Siegel, principal of Millburn High

School, also wrote a letter. He informed ETS that the test books had been secure before the test. He also said that copying answers during it would have required "a herculean effort" because of the way the boys' desks had been arranged. "I fully recognize that your analysis may have led to high correlations of incorrect responses and such," he wrote, "yet given the circumstances I find that this may indeed [be] that rare case in which statistics do not prove valid. . . . My investigation leads to the belief that the source of the rumor (who has subsequently recanted the charge) lies in one student who was disgruntled at one of the students involved."[24]

The next day, Nancy T. Siegel, a Millburn guidance counselor, wrote a letter to ETS on behalf of James Denburg. "It appears that the scores are being questioned as a result of a call placed by the [Millburn High School] test administrator based on remarks made to a counselor by a student in January of 1983 suggesting that some type of irregularity took place in the testing in May of 1982," she wrote. "It is most important to note that that same student now states he knows nothing of any irregularity and that his earlier conversation with the counselor was without basis in fact."[25]

A number of other letters were written as well. They pointed out that the four boys' SAT scores had not been unexpectedly high, that their characters and academic records were good, that they had had no reason to cheat on the test, and that the test had been administered under secure conditions. Louis Zuckerman, the test supervisor who had made the original complaint, submitted a statement saying that he had granted Tirone's request to give the exam at a special time, that "such a request is not unusual," that he trusted Tirone, and that on the day of the test he had visited the test room "on one or two occasions to make sure that everything was all right, and I stuck my head in the door of his room for this purpose. I didn't see anything irregular taking place."[26]

The Board of Review considered this new information on March 30 and April 6 but found it unpersuasive. On April 7, the boys went to meet with ETS. They learned that the charge against them was not copying, as Antonia Rosenbaum's letter had stated, but pre-access. They also learned that ETS was now challenging

Denburg's verbal score on an SAT taken in March 1982, two months before the May exam, because an Index K analysis suggested strongly that Denburg had copied his answers from Becker on part of that test. Furthermore, the Board had decided to challenge Becker's and Denburg's scores on a math Achievement exam taken in December 1982. The K values for that test did not meet ETS's general criterion for copying, and the two boys had taken the test in different rooms. But the Board found strong similarities between their answers. It also found similarities between their answers and those of another student, Ross Sullivan, who had been sitting near Becker. Index K actually seemed to suggest that Sullivan had been copying from Becker rather than the other way around, but Sullivan's score was not challenged. (It was later suggested privately that ETS didn't really think the boys had been cheating on these tests, and that the charges would have been dropped if the boys had abandoned their protest.)

On April 5 and 6, all four boys had taken and passed lie detector tests, backing up their claims of innocence. At their meeting with ETS on April 7, the boys' attorney asked ETS if it would consider the results of those tests before proceeding with its case. ETS said that it would not.

The boys filed suit on April 21.

ETS doesn't take kindly to lawsuits. It fights them with all of its considerable power, and it almost always overwhelms its opponents. In 1975, the American Student List Co. of Great Neck, New York, filed an antitrust suit against ETS and the College Board. ASL is a small company that sells colleges the names of graduating high school students. The suit contended that ETS and the Board, through their testing programs and the associated Student Search Service (SSS; see Chapter 1), enjoyed what amounted to a monopoly on the student list business. Marty Lerner, the president of ASL, felt that ETS and the College Board had an unfair advantage in the marketplace, partly as a result of their nonprofit status. "If they're doing exactly what I am," he said, "why shouldn't they have to pay taxes?"[27]

Lerner hired a local attorney. ETS brought in a team of lawyers from Wilmer, Cutler, & Pickering, its high-priced Washington law firm. The College Board hired Sullivan & Cromwell, an equally high-priced law firm from New York.

"My lawyer was scared of them, you know?" Lerner told me. "We're a small company. We have a couple of small offices. But because of their power they were able to obtain an order from the court giving them access to all our records. They used to have the right to come up here whenever they wanted and go through my files and my books. They were like a Gestapo group. I'd get a call from the attorneys and they'd say they were coming up the next week with Xerox equipment. And they'd arrive, three or four of them. They just harassed the hell out of me, hanging around, going through my files. We tried to get the same right to go through their records, but the judge denied it. I couldn't get to first base."

ETS and the College Board won a broad protective order keeping the court proceedings and virtually all information about SSS a secret. ETS refused to reveal even the number of names in its files. Lerner was prohibited from seeing most of what little information ETS did give up about SSS on the grounds that the information was proprietary and that Lerner would be able to make use of it in his business. "My attorney was prohibited from discussing the case with me," Lerner told me. "So he said to the court that he was having a hard time preparing for the trial because he couldn't talk to me. The judge said, That's too bad." The National Education Association filed a brief with the court requesting that the protective order be lifted, but the judge upheld it.

The case never got to trial. Lerner spent more than seven years and a quarter of a million dollars on it before giving up. How much did ETS and the College Board spend? They're not saying. "They're more powerful than the government," Lerner says.

Even when the stakes are small, ETS fights tooth and nail. In 1981, Christopher Laucks sued ETS for $38 in small-claims court in Trenton, New Jersey. Laucks had taken the Law School Admission Test (LSAT) that year and successfully challenged ETS on its scoring of one of the questions, a geometry problem. ETS had eliminated the item and rescored the test.

But Laucks didn't want the item eliminated. He wanted credit for the answer he had picked, which ETS had acknowledged to be the only correct one. When ETS refused, Laucks sought the help of

Jay Richard Rosner, a young lawyer who had recently been involved in another lawsuit against ETS. That suit (filed by Benjamin Walters, a black student who felt his SAT scores had suffered because he had believed ETS's claims that coaching didn't work) had nearly driven Rosner into debt. In defending itself, ETS had supplemented its regular corporate counsel both with outside lawyers from a local firm and with a pair of attorneys brought in from Wilmer, Cutler in Washington. During pretrial discovery — the period in which attorneys on both sides of a dispute exchange exhibits and take statements from witnesses — they had buried Rosner in paperwork and requests for information. The case dragged on for nearly two years. Neither Walters nor Rosner had much money. In the end, the court granted a motion by ETS for a summary judgment against Walters.

Rosner told Laucks he would help him with his case, but only if Laucks agreed to file it in small-claims court. There, Rosner said, the matter could be settled quickly and with a minimum of courtroom grandstanding by ETS, because there would be no discovery. Laucks agreed and Rosner filed the suit, arguing that ETS, by failing to give Laucks the score he had earned, had breached an implicit contract. The suit asked for a refund of Laucks's test fee.

Lawyers are a rarity in small-claims court. ETS sent two, William J. Brennan III (son of the United States Supreme Court Justice) and Alexander P. Waugh, Jr., both from the Princeton law firm of Smith, Stratton, Wise, Heher & Brennan. One of their first moves was to request that the trial be moved into the regular court so that they could have discovery. The judge, Coleman T. Brennan (no relation to the Supreme Court Justice), refused to move the case but said he would allow discovery. ETS then dragged out the proceedings for a year. Finally, ETS asked the court for a summary judgment against Laucks. Judge Brennan, in a fifty-eight-page opinion that took an hour and a half to deliver from the bench, agreed. After more than a year and thousands of dollars in legal fees, ETS had beaten a $38 lawsuit.

"I get the impression from judges that they view ruling against ETS as dealing a mortal blow to the status quo," Rosner told me. "Here you had ETS, one of the area's biggest employers, and they were represented by the son of New Jersey's pride. There's no

discovery in small-claims court, but the judge granted them discovery. You're supposed to be able to get a jury trial in New Jersey
small-claims court, but the judge granted their motion for summary judgment. There is no rule specifically on this point, but I
called court administrators in half a dozen counties and they all
said they'd never heard of a summary judgment in small-claims
before. But we didn't have the money to appeal the judge's ruling.
Finally, the judge delivered what must be the longest decision in
the history of small-claims court. He apparently felt he would have
had to shoot down the entire law school admissions process to rule
in our favor. The judges are so tied to the way things work that
they view ruling against ETS as a threat to life as we know it. I
guess you have to approach it with a sense of humor. It's theater of
the absurd."

In the Millburn High School case, ETS perceived a greater than
usual threat to life as we know it. All told, the company had a
dozen different lawyers working on its defense, including ETS
general counsel Stanford H. von Mayrhauser, associate general
counsel Russell W. Martin, Jr., and assistant general counsel Patricia E. Taylor; William J. Brennan III and Alexander P. Waugh,
Jr., from Smith, Stratton, Wise, Heher & Brennan; Howard Willens, John Rounsaville, Christopher Lipsett, and Jana Singer (not
to mention two paralegals) from Wilmer, Cutler & Pickering in
Washington, D.C.

When the Millburn case was being considered by the Board of
Review, ETS didn't send anyone to the high school to observe the
conditions under which the test had been taken or to talk to the
people who knew the boys or were familiar with the rumors that
had prompted the investigation. ETS's security guidelines provide
for such visits, but they are seldom made because of the cost
involved.

Now that a lawsuit had been filed, however, ETS spared no
expense in tracking down information that it believed would be
damaging to the students' case. After ETS's lawyers had learned
about James Denburg's yearbook quotation, John Rounsaville of
the Washington firm was dispatched to New Jersey to obtain a
copy. Rounsaville didn't seek permission from Denburg or his
attorney. He merely set up a meeting with Neal Vasarkovy, the

Millburn yearbook adviser, in the office of Dr. Paul W. Rossey, the superintendent of schools. Rounsaville asked Vasarkovy for the card on which Denburg had written out his yearbook quotation. "I looked at Dr. Rossey," Vasarkovy said later. "Dr. Rossey said, 'Give it to him.' We hiked on over to my office and I gave it to him." Rounsaville also asked Vasarkovy where the yearbook was being printed; Vasarkovy gave him the name of a company in Pennsylvania. ETS immediately sent lawyers to Pennsylvania, where — once again without permission, even from Vasarkovy — they requested and received a proof of the page on which Denburg's quotation would appear.[28]

ETS eventually realized that the quotation had nothing to do with the SAT. It was never mentioned in the trial. But ETS was tireless in its pursuit of unflattering information, even when there was no apparent connection to the case. Early in his deposition of Stephen Haskin, attorney Howard Willens made a lengthy effort to determine whether Haskin and his friends were drunks:

Willens: Have you had parties at your house at which liquor has been served for you and your friends?
Haskin: Yes.
Willens: And have you gone to parties at your friends' house where liquor has been served?
Haskin: Yes.
Willens: And on some of those occasions have one of or more of your friends gotten slightly inebriated?
Haskin: Yes.
Willens: Have you ever seen Lloyd Berkowitz get inebriated on alcohol?
Haskin: Yes.
Willens: More than once?
Haskin: Yeah. He is my best friend, I'm with him a lot.
Willens: And he does drink a lot?
Haskin: Well, the times that he does, he is with me. We're all together. It is not every weekend or anything.
Willens: How about Richard Becker, have you ever seen Richard overindulge in alcohol and become inebriated?
Haskin: Less frequently than Lloyd.
Willens: But you have seen him on more than one occasion over-indulge?

Haskin: I wouldn't necessarily call it over indulging.
Willens: Did he become inebriated or drunk or not?
Haskin: Well, he had a few drinks. It depends on what you call drunk, I guess.
Willens: Well, has he ever drunk so much that you didn't want to be in an automobile that he was driving?
Haskin: No.[29]

Willens can be an intimidating interrogator. His gaze is piercing, and there's an edge of contempt in his voice. My *Harper's* article was published around the time the four boys filed their suit, and their attorney, George B. Gelman of Rosen, Gelman & Weiss in Newark, asked me if I would look at certain questions from the test they had taken and analyze them the way I had analyzed similar questions in my article. I said I would. (One of them, involving the "intensity and vitality" of culture, is discussed in Chapter Five.) I wasn't paid, and I didn't testify at the trial, but I was deposed by Willens. "Is there any reason," he asked me at one point, "why ETS should look into your [SAT] scores?" I said there wasn't.[30]

The boys' two lawyers — Gelman and a young associate in his firm, Jill Haley — spent a great deal of time both before and during the trial trying to determine precisely what the evidence against their clients was. After all, no one had seen them cheat. No test books had been reported missing. The boys' SAT scores had not been suspiciously high. Neither the proctor nor the supervisor had noticed anything untoward at the time the test was administered. Cheating is rampant on the SAT, but these four boys, unlike most students, had taken the test under conditions in which copying from one another was impossible. ETS conceded both before and during the trial that the boys could not have copied; its only contention was that they had obtained prior access to the test. But ETS couldn't actually say how they had done this. It offered an occasional hypothesis, but these bordered on the absurd. Paul Holland, a member of the Board of Review, said in pretrial testimony that if the boys had not stolen the exams at the school, then "they might have gone out to Ewing Township and stolen books out of the warehouse."[31] None of the boys had a driver's license; perhaps one of their mothers had driven them to Ewing and waited in the car while they broke into the warehouse, sorted through boxes of exam books from ETS's several hundred testing programs, found the correct form of the SAT, and either memorized it or stole a copy without being detected. Confident that the boys had cheated, ETS found no scenario too fantastic.

The source of ETS's confidence was Index K.* It was the numbers, test security specialists and members of the Board of Review said repeatedly, that had convinced them the boys had been cheating. And ETS found the numbers extremely convincing. Asked if there was any evidence the boys could have presented to change ETS's judgment in the case, Board of Review member Protase Woodford said yes, he could think of one thing: "Confession by three of the persons exculpating the fourth."[32]

Index K was designed to detect copying, not preknowledge. Preknowledge cases are extremely rare at ETS — Board of Review members said they could recall handling them before, but they couldn't remember when — and there is no formal procedure for dealing with them. "We don't have a wealth of experience in dealing with preknowledge," Shirley Kane-Orr admitted.[33] The Test Security Office used Index K because it was handy and quick. ETS had done no research to prove the efficacy of Index K in detecting preknowledge. Indeed, it had done no systematic research on Index K at all. Even in copying cases, the procedure's utility was hypothetical. One of the company's first moves when it began to fear the boys might file a lawsuit was to hire Frederick Kling, the man who had invented the index but who was no longer

---

*Other evidence evaporated. Antonia Rosenbaum's original Investigative Report said that on eight occasions during the test, Haskin had erased an answer and changed it to one that agreed with Denburg's. Several ETS officials said this "erasure pattern" had influenced their decisions in the case. But the pattern turned out to be a clerical error, one of many in the report: Rosenbaum had hit the wrong key on her typewriter. ETS later conceded that there was nothing unusual about the erasures on the tests. Incidentally, ETS has no empirical basis for believing that "erasure patterns" mean anything at all. After reading about Rosenbaum's analysis, I went back and looked at my own SAT answer sheets. On the test I took in May, I discovered eight erasures in section 5 alone; in each instance, I had erased an incorrect answer and replaced it with a correct one. Had I been cheating? Of course not. I had simply been correcting careless marks made in haste. Section 5 was the last section on the test (except for the experimental section, which I filled out at random) and I was getting tired.

employed by ETS (and who might have been a witness for the plaintiffs had ETS not put him back on the payroll), to prepare a description of his invention — how it worked, how it should be used — that would be comprehensible to an intelligent layman.

That ETS felt it still needed such a description — even though by that time it had been using Index K for more than two years — is quite remarkable. After all, members of both the Test Security Office and the Board of Review were, generally speaking, laymen. Most seemed confused about precisely how the index was to be applied. Thelma L. Spencer — a Board member who, before going to ETS, had been a social worker, a schoolteacher, and a deputy probation officer — said she thought there was nothing odd about using a copying index in a preknowledge case, because preknowledge might also involve copying (even though ETS conceded that the boys could not have copied). "If there's pre-access," she said, "then there could be one candidate who would be able to be the source and the others would just sit and wait for that candidate to mark the answer sheet."[34] On the other hand, Aileen Cramer — a test security specialist who, before going to ETS, had also been a schoolteacher and a probation officer — thought that identifying a source and subject didn't make sense. "The fact that this was a preknowledge case," she said, "would indicate to me that technically nobody should be identified as the source."[35] Even so, she saw nothing wrong with using Index K — which requires identification of a source and subject — on the Millburn case.

Lawrence E. Wightman, a member of the Board, thought the matter was straightforward. "If a group of test-takers has had access to, early access to a copy of the test," he said, "it's very unlikely that any of the group will know all the correct answers. Therefore, they will agree on wrong responses."[36] On the other hand, Cramer thought that agreement between *correct* responses would be more telling in a preknowledge case. For this reason, she didn't find it odd that the K values for the boys had not met ETS's criterion for cheating in four of the six possible pairings. If the boys had been *copying* from one another, she said, the agreement between wrong answers would have been higher; but this *wasn't* a copying case, so the agreement didn't have to be as high.[37] Lack of evidence for the first charge became the only evidence for the second charge. (We now have a corollary to the kettle defense: the kettle accusation.)

The only part of the SAT that yielded suspicious K values was the verbal. And yet the boys' verbal scores — 490, 510, 510, 630 — had not been terribly high, either in absolute terms or in comparison with their previous performance in school or on tests. The verbal SAT is primarily a vocabulary test. Didn't it seem odd that the boys' scores were not higher, considering that if they had really had a copy of the exam book the night before, they would have been able to look up all the words on it in a dictionary? "I don't know how much help that would be to them," said Aileen Cramer, who would sooner abandon her faith in dictionaries than her faith in Index K.[38] James Denburg had canceled his score (510) immediately after taking the test, something ETS allows students to do. Did it seem odd to Cramer that a student who had gone to the trouble of stealing an exam book would then take the test and cancel his score? "No."*[39]

Index K, the Test Security Office's article of faith, is based on a number of very questionable assumptions. One is that cheating is the only explanation for similar response patterns on tests. Although it says it has done no research on the matter, ETS maintains that students from similar backgrounds are no more likely to select similar answers than randomly selected students are. It saw no significance in the fact that the four boys were best friends, that they had grown up together, that they had taken many of the same classes, that they had been exposed to many of the same books and movies, that they spent much of their time after school together, or that three of them had been tutored for the SAT by the same person.

ETS may not think that similar students make similar mistakes, but John Katzman *knows* they do. Classes at the Princeton Review

---

*ETS's statements to students about score cancellations are deceptive. Canceled scores aren't actually *canceled;* they are merely not mentioned on score reports. ETS secretly maintains canceled scores in its files and, although students are not allowed to find out what they are, uses them as evidence in security proceedings. One reason the Board of Review found Denburg's *math* SAT score (730) suspicious was that he had taken the test two months earlier and scored only 360. But Denburg had canceled that score. He had become ill shortly after the test began and, with the test administrator's permission, had canceled his score and gone home after answering only the first few questions.

are arranged so that they contain students who not only score similarly but also tend to make the same errors. And they *do* make the same errors, again and again and again. ETS's untested assumption that mistakes on the SAT are independent of one another is simply wrong. (After all, ETS picks answers in predictable ways; why shouldn't Jimmy Denburg?)

ETS ought to know this. In one of its own publications — a 1961 biography of Carl Campbell Brigham, the man who created the SAT for the College Board — ETS notes that Brigham had done a study indicating that "the errors which students made on test items seemed to follow definite patterns — that is, a large number of students made identical mistakes. Apparently a common factor was involved. His analysis indicated that the cause of these mistakes frequently was an incompleteness of learning and confusion in thinking common to many people."[40] ETS also knows that "because of careful test construction, distractors may consistently appear to a misinformed student to be more plausible than the correct answer," as it noted in a 1971 technical report prepared for the College Board.[41] Even more recently, in an issue of *The College Board Review* published several months before the four Millburn boys took the SAT, ETS research scientist Thomas F. Donlon described a statistical technique called distractor analysis, which showed that groups "of different composition can be meaningfully contrasted with respect to their patterns of response to these various [incorrect answers]."[42] But ETS conveniently forgot all this at the trial.

Becker and Denburg had also made extremely similar responses on the March 1982 SAT. Rather than seeing this as evidence that the boys thought alike, ETS hypothesized that Denburg must have copied from Becker. The two boys had originally been given seats four rows apart, far enough to make copying very difficult, though perhaps not impossible. But the sun was shining directly in Becker's eyes, and before the exam began he was given permission to move to the far corner of the room, seven rows *farther* away from the student who supposedly copied his answers. Why would he have moved if he and Denburg had been planning to cheat? How could Denburg possibly have seen his answer sheet from that distance? ETS also said that Becker and Denburg had copied answers from Ross Sullivan during the December 1982 Math II Achievement Test. Becker and Sullivan, though seated near each other, took the test at different times. Denburg took it in a different room. How did ETS suppose that they had copied from one another? "Well," said Paul Holland, a member of the Board of Review, "I assume that there's always the possibility of some sort of radio communication, there's — must be numerous things in the age of technology."[43]

Another questionable assumption on which Index K depends is that every incorrect answer on an SAT is equally attractive to a student taking the test. In the original version of Index K, individual probabilities were calculated for every distractor. But this was too complicated for the Test Security Office's clerical staff. An "empirical compromise," in the words of Paul Holland, was reached.[44] The operational version of Index K uses a *single average probability* for the entire test. This probability is geared loosely to a student's scoring level, but it is based on a handful of test forms that are several years out of date. For the four Millburn boys, ETS selected probabilities that ranged from about one chance in six to about one chance in five. In other words, ETS assumed that every time one of the boys agreed with another on a wrong answer, he arrived at his answer by making a random or worse than random guess. But this is ridiculous. If, say, a student has eliminated three wrong answers on an item — as students at these scoring levels very often do — then he has one chance in two, not one in six, of selecting the remaining one.

In all, there were forty-two items (out of a total of eighty-five) that at least one of the boys answered incorrectly. On seventeen of these, at least three of the four boys had selected the same wrong answer. ETS found this very suspicious. But according to ETS's national sample for this test, twelve of these seventeen answers were either more popular than the correct answer or the most popular wrong answer for students in the boys' scoring range. (Of the other five answers, three were C. All four boys had been taught to stick with a single letter when guessing. Three of them had received this advice from an SAT tutor who had an unpronounceable Polish name and was known to his students simply as "Mr. C.") The answers the boys chose, in other words, were logical choices. They weren't random selections, as Index K assumes.

Aileen Cramer didn't find this noteworthy. "If they indeed had access to the examination and were picking the most logical distractor," she said, "that would not surprise me greatly because if you had the opportunity to examine the question and you did not know the correct answer or the keyed answer to the question, then it doesn't seem to me so unusual that they would have agreed, you know, as a group discussing it, that they would have agreed upon the next highest, you know, the next most popular distractor."[45] But if ETS didn't think it was odd for a group to arrive at a popular distractor, why did it think it was odd for individuals? An attractive answer is an attractive answer.

Most of the matching incorrect answers occurred on items that at least one of the boys answered correctly. If the four had all huddled the night before and agreed on "the next most popular distractor," how did any of them happen to pick the *correct* answer the following day? Or perhaps they had figured out the correct answer the night before, and then two or three of them had forgotten it. But if this is true, it means only that the boys ended up answering the questions the way they would have answered them if they had never seen a copy of the test. Their agreement, in other words — assuming Cramer's scenario is correct — could not be the result of their having known the questions beforehand. It could only be the result of their having forgotten what they had seen. Since such answers can't be distinguished from honest answers, how can ETS maintain that the boys must have stolen a copy of the test? How can *expected* answer selections be construed as evidence of cheating?

On August 3, 1983, after a three-week trial in the Superior Court of New Jersey, ETS's dozen lawyers polled one another on how they thought the judge would rule. Their verdict was unanimous: they all thought ETS would lose.

The following day, Judge Richard S. Cohen surprised everyone in the courtroom by ruling in favor of ETS. He had limited the trial to the question of whether ETS had been fair and reasonable in its decision to question the four boys' scores. He did not rule on whether the boys had been cheating, and he said that ETS had not, either: the company had merely said that it had reason to believe their scores were "invalid." Cohen acknowledged that ETS's test security procedures "were not well suited to an investigation and adjudication of the guilt or innocence of the plaintiffs of the suspected improprieties." But he said that ETS's important "role in the academic world" gave it a certain leeway.[46]

In general, Judge Cohen said, he trusted ETS. "Ultimately," he wrote, ". . . one has to evaluate the testimony of ETS people who have seen the K Index in actual use and who say that special item analyses done for particular cases have never shown the K Index underestimating the actual likelihood of agreement on the questions analysed. I am inclined to trust that testimony."[47] He also said he was sympathetic to the company's predicament: if colleges and universities lost faith in ETS's ability to police its tests, then they would also lose faith in SAT scores.[48]

"It is in the public interest to permit ETS to fulfill its varied responsibilities to a wide range of test-takers and score recipients," he wrote. "It is, therefore, necessary that ETS have the authority to withhold or withdraw sponsorship of the reliability of test scores that it has reason based on sufficient credible evidence to doubt. . . . It may be difficult for ETS to convince its various publics that it deals with score validation and not with judgments on candidates' behavior. But it will not be required by this court to abandon a proper and reasonable method of dealing with test security problems solely because of the danger, however real, that its role may be misunderstood."*[49]

But the judge got it wrong. It isn't test security that's sacred to ETS. It's ETS. When I gave the company genuine, firsthand proof that SAT scores for an entire testing room were invalid, it referred my letter to one of its public relations departments. But when four boys from Millburn High School challenged the infallibility of Index K, ETS hired lawyers from Washington to find out if they were drunks. ETS refused to tell me how much it had spent on its defense in the Millburn trial, but a lawyer familiar with the case estimated that the total bill — including computer time, consulting payments (Frederick Kling alone received at least $15,000), em-

---

*Judge Cohen's wording here is from a 1980 ETS document labeled "Briefing Paper to Stimulate Discussion of the Philosophy and Objectives of Test Security": "Along similar lines, can we convince our various publics that we are interested not in establishing the guilt or innocence of candidates, only of assuring the validity of scores?" Cohen's opinion frequently echoes ETS documents or testimony.

ployee salaries, and fees for its far-flung cohort of attorneys —
must have come to a million dollars.* That's five times ETS's
entire 1980 test security budget for the Admissions Testing Program (ATP), or about 78 cents from every student who took the
SAT in 1982. In 1980, after ATP security costs had risen from
$136,000 to $204,000 a year, ETS had considered "discontinuing
the test security function altogether."[51] But when its public image
was threatened, it pulled out all the stops.

James Denburg had applied for early admission to Carnegie-
Mellon University and been accepted. When Judge Cohen handed
down his decision in August 1983, the university informed Denburg that it would not permit him to enroll unless he took the
SAT again and confirmed his original score. ETS confirms the
scores of students who take a retest and score within 50 points of
their challenged score. This cushion is less generous than it may
seem. After all, ETS says that 60- and 70-point score differences
on the SAT are statistically meaningless (see Chapters 4 and 10). It
also says, in its computerized cheating-detection program, that
score differences of less than 250 points are not suspicious. This
means that while a score difference of 60 points would not be a
sufficient basis for *suspecting* that a student had cheated, it would
be a sufficient basis for *proving* that he had cheated.

It was the end of the summer. Denburg had been away from the
classroom for three months, and the last thing he wanted to do
was take a test. But if he wanted to go to Carnegie-Mellon, he had
to take an SAT.

ETS itself administered the new exam under special supervision.
Denburg scored 520 on the verbal and 680 on the math — respectively 10 points higher and 50 points lower than his scores on the
day he had supposedly been cheating. His scores were automati-

---

*The real figure may actually be much higher. In the fiscal year ended June 30, 1983 — i.e.,
about a month before Judge Cohen's decision — ETS paid Wilmer, Cutler & Pickering
$786,446 in legal fees. Its total legal bills for that year amounted to $1.5 million. The
figures are listed in ETS's 1982 tax return, which can be obtained from the Internal Revenue
Service. (ETS doesn't release copies to outsiders, at least not to me.)[50] ETS's return for fiscal
1983 was not filed until late 1984 and was not available when this book went to press. In a
letter dated May 13, 1984, I asked ETS how much it had paid Wilmer, Cutler during fiscal
1983 as well as what its total expenses for the trial had been, but ETS wouldn't tell me.

cally confirmed. The case didn't even go back to the Board of Review. Also confirmed was Denburg's score on the March SAT, on which ETS had accused him of copying from Becker.

Stephen Haskin had been admitted to the University of Richmond. The university said it would not permit him to enroll unless he took an admissions test and earned a score comparable to the one he had earned on the day he had supposedly been cheating. He agreed to take the ACT, the SAT's chief competitor, administered by the American College Testing Program. He took the test at the university on the first day of freshman orientation. It was scored immediately. He was admitted to the university by noon. Becker had been accepted at Emory and Berkowitz at the University of Colorado. Both were admitted without retests.

In the spring of 1984, the Appellate Division of the Superior Court of New Jersey upheld Judge Cohen's decision.

9

The Cult of Mental Measurement

WE MUST FACE A possibility of racial admixture here that is infinitely worse than that faced by any European country today," wrote Carl Campbell Brigham in *A Study of American Intelligence,* "for we are incorporating the negro into our racial stock, while all of Europe is comparatively free from this taint."[1]

Brigham was a young professor of psychology at Princeton. His book, published by the university's own press in 1923, was a painstaking analysis of the Army Mental Tests, which Brigham had helped administer to recruits at the time of America's entry into World War I. Brigham's work with soldiers had convinced him that Catholics, Greeks, Hungarians, Italians, Jews, Poles, Russians, Turks, and — especially — Negroes were innately less intelligent than people whose ancestors were born in countries that abounded in natural blonds. In his book he argued passionately for stricter immigration laws and, within America's borders, for an end to the "infiltration of white blood into the negro."[2]

"The really important steps are those looking toward the prevention of the continued propagation of defective strains in the present population," he concluded, noting an "alarming" increase in the number of mulattoes. "If all immigration were stopped now, the decline of American intelligence would still be inevitable. This is the problem which must be met, and our manner of meeting it will determine the future course of our national life."[3]

Congress passed a tough new immigration law in 1924, assuaging Brigham's fears about the external contamination of American intellect. But the problem of eliminating "defective strains in the present population" remained. One solution, Brigham believed, was intelligence testing. By carefully sampling the mental power of the nation's young people, it would be possible to identify and reward those citizens whose racial inheritance had granted them a superior intellectual endowment.

Brigham's book and his work at Princeton deeply impressed the College Board, which hired him in 1925 to develop an intelligence test for use in college admissions. The test he developed was the SAT. Today Brigham is little remembered except by historians of mental measurement and by users of the Carl Campbell Brigham Library, the principal repository of enlightenment and learning at ETS.

The methodological forefather of the modern cult of mental measurement was Alfred Binet, a French psychologist who, in the early 1900s, developed a procedure for estimating the general intelligence of children. Binet had been asked by his government to find a method for identifying students with learning disabilities that might be ameliorated through special education. He created a test in which children were asked to copy figures, give their names, count coins, and perform other tasks drawn, for the most part, from everyday life. To express the results of his tests, he created a numerical scale that represented a child's intelligence as the difference between his mental age (as indicated by the test) and his actual age in years. This was the earliest version of what would later be known as the Intelligence Quotient, or IQ.[4]

Binet was reluctant to extend his method beyond the narrow, diagnostic purpose for which it had been devised. He didn't think his scale was an appropriate measure for "normal" students, and he thought the potential for abuse was enormous.[5] Others, however, found his work highly suggestive. Henry Goddard, an American psychologist who ran a school for the "feeble-minded" in Vineland, New Jersey, translated Binet's study into English in 1910. Goddard, who coined the word *moron*, was a eugenicist. He viewed his school as a sort of reproductive prison, a compound where people with inferior genes could be prevented from contaminating prime American breeding stock.

"It is perfectly clear," he wrote in 1914, "that no feeble-minded person should ever be allowed to marry or to become a parent."[6]

Goddard advocated using intelligence tests to identify people unsuited for human propagation. He also saw the tests as a scientific method for allocating the fruits of society. Speaking to students at Princeton University in 1919, he said, "Now the fact is, that workman may have a 10 year intelligence while you have a 20. To demand for him such a home as you enjoy is as absurd as it would be to insist that every laborer should receive a graduate fellowship. How can there be such a thing as social equality with this wide range of mental capacity?"[7]

Binet's procedure was further revised and popularized by Lewis M. Terman, a professor of psychology at Stanford University. The Stanford-Binet Intelligence Scale, as it has been known ever since, remains a sturdy fixture on the American educational scene. Like Goddard, Terman saw IQ as a lever with which to move society. "It is safe to predict," he wrote in 1916, "that in the near future intelligence tests will bring tens of thousands of . . . high-grade defectives under the surveillance and protection of society. This will ultimately result in curtailing the reproduction of feeble-mindedness and in the elimination of an enormous amount of crime, pauperism, and industrial inefficiency."[8]

Terman's hopes for intelligence testing didn't end at prison walls and factory gates. He envisioned an entire society calibrated to the Stanford scale. "The time is probably not far distant," he wrote, "when intelligence tests will become a recognized and widely used instrument for determining vocational fitness. . . . When thousands of children who have been tested by the Binet scale have been followed out into the industrial world, and their success in various occupations noted, we shall know fairly definitely . . . the minimum 'intelligence quotient' necessary for success in each leading occupation."[9]

There was something peculiarly American about this passion for measuring brainpower. In a nation without dukes or princes, "native capacity" provided the basis for a sort of alternative aristocracy. Intelligence tests gave the nation's privileged a scientific-sounding justification for the advantages they enjoyed. The wealthy lived in nice houses because they were smart; the poor were hungry because they were stupid. American society was just after all.

Even so, the cult of mental measurement might not have taken hold so firmly in this country had it not been for World War I. Before 1917, research on intelligence testing was diffuse and incomplete. But when the United States declared war, Robert M. Yerkes, a professor of psychology at Harvard, realized that the mobilization would provide an incomparable opportunity to test the intelligence of a large body of people. He received permission from the government and then, with the help of Terman, Goddard, and others, created the Army Mental Tests: Alpha, a written examination, and Beta, a pictorial test for illiterates. Results of the tests were to be used in assigning recruits to jobs within the army.

In April 1917, Yerkes went to Canada to learn, as he later wrote, "what use our neighbors were making of psychological principles and methods in their military activities."[10] In Canada he encountered a young psychologist attached to the Military Hospitals Commission. His name was Carl Campbell Brigham. Yerkes liked him immediately and persuaded him to come to the United States to take part in his bold new experiment. Brigham, who had found the Canadian army too small for his ambition, quickly agreed. Arriving in the United States the following fall, he rapidly become one of Yerkes's most valuable assistants.

The Army Mental Tests were ludicrously flawed. Alpha Test 8, for example, contained the following multiple-choice questions:

---

2 Five hundred is played with   rackets pins cards dice

3 The Percheron is a kind of   goat horse cow sheep

7 Christie Mathewson is famous as a   writer artist baseball player comedian

10 "There's a reason" is an "ad" for a   drink revolver flour cleanser

19 Crisco is a   patent medicine disinfectant tooth-paste food product

29 The Brooklyn Nationals are called the   Giants Orioles Superbas Indians

32 The number of a Kaffir's legs is   two four six eight

35 The forward pass is used in   tennis hockey football golf

38 The Pierce Arrow car is made in   Buffalo Detroit Toledo Flint

---

The Beta Tests — for men who either couldn't read or couldn't speak English — were also absurd. In Beta Test 1, recruits were given two minutes to trace paths through five mazes. Instructions were given in pantomime by an "experimenter" with the aid of a "demonstrator." The experimenter stood beside a blackboard on a platform at the front of a noisy, crowded barracks. "The blackboard was turned so that two sample mazes . . . appeared," Brigham wrote.

> The experimenter traced through the first maze on the black-board, and then motioned the demonstrator to go ahead. The demonstrator traced through the maze with crayon very slowly. The experimenter then traced through the second maze and motioned the demonstrator to go ahead. The demonstrator in tracing this maze made a mistake by crossing the line at the end of a blind alley, was corrected by the experimenter with vigorous shakes of the head and "no-no," and made to re-trace his path back to where he could start right again. The demonstrator then traced through the rest of the maze with great semblance of haste, stopping momentarily at each ambiguous point only. The experimenter then motioned to the group to do the same thing on their examination blanks. The experimenter and the orderlies walked about the room, motioning to the men who were not working, and saying, "Do it, do it, hurry up, quick."[11]

Yerkes and Brigham rubbed their hands over the results of these tests and drew dark conclusions about the brainpower of recent American immigrants. With so much new scientific data at hand, old misconceptions could be swept aside. "Our figures," Brigham wrote, ". . . would rather tend to disprove the popular belief that the Jew is highly intelligent."[12] Measuring mental capacity was such an inebriating activity that some of Yerkes's researchers found it difficult to return to ordinary academic life when the war was over. "It's hard to come back to a milk diet," said Professor John J. Coss of Columbia, "after having lived on raw meat!"[13]

In analyzing the army data, Brigham — borrowing the classifications of Madison Grant, a eugenicist who had published a book called *The Passing of the Great Race** a few years before —

*New York: Scribner's, 1916.

detected four distinct racial strains in American society. At the pinnacle were the Nordics, the blond, blue-eyed original settlers and the group to which Brigham naturally assigned himself. At the other extreme was the American Negro. "Between the Nordic and the negro," Brigham wrote, "but closer to the negro than to the Nordic, we find the Alpine and Mediterranean types."[14] The Mediterraneans were particularly worrisome, Brigham said, because they had bred "conspicuously" with "the Amerind and the imported negro."[15]

Brigham reserved most of his considerable scorn for blacks, whose arrival in America he described as "the most sinister development in the history of this continent."[16] In charts and graphs and throughout his text, he repeatedly treated blacks (and Jews) as being distinct from "Americans." Indeed, he seems to have considered blacks to be members of a separate species, referring at one point to the "sub-species" of various races.[17] He quoted very approvingly a passage from a recent book by Edwin G. Conklin, a colleague at Princeton, in which Conklin advocated "geographical isolation of races" in order to "prevent their interbreeding" but despaired that it might be only temporarily possible "to maintain the purity of the white race."[18]

In America, Brigham believed, the dilution of the master race had been a direct consequence of the abolition of slavery. "If we examine the figures showing the proportion of mulattoes to a thousand blacks for each twenty year period from 1850 to 1910," he wrote, "we find that in 1850 there were 126 mulattoes to a thousand blacks, 136 in 1870, 179 in 1890 and 264 in 1910. This intermixture of white and negro has been a natural result of the emancipation of the negro and the breaking down of social barriers against him, mostly in the North and West."[19] Brigham did not advocate the reestablishment of human bondage. But he did believe that blacks should be barred from mixing freely in white society.

Carl Campbell Brigham was a prime New England specimen, a worthy inheritor of the Nordic intellectual legacy he sought to protect from genetic contamination. "On his mother's side," wrote his biographer, Matthew T. Downey, in a celebratory volume published by ETS in 1961, "he was a descendant of William Brewster, the fourth signer of the Mayflower Compact, and of John Goss, who came from England with Governor John Winthrop in 1630." His father's family were Boston Brighams. Young Carl was born into great prosperity. Although he "inherited little of the traditional Yankee reticence," according to Downey, "he did retain throughout his life the poise, bearing, and social graces derived from the environment of an old and esteemed New England family."[20]

Brigham followed his brother to Harvard in 1908 but found the place drab. Without telling his father, and almost before he had unpacked his trunk, he transferred to Princeton. Brigham was a "socially gifted young man" who "fitted well into Princeton of the old days," in the words of his biographer.[21] Princeton, to be blunt, was a country club. Brigham had little patience for schoolwork. He spent his first two years on campus pursuing the life of privileged leisure for which his alma mater was justly renowned.

But in his junior year he discovered psychology. The field of mental measurement was emerging from its infancy — Binet's work was just being translated into English — and Brigham found his calling. Both as an undergraduate and as a graduate student, he pursued a growing fascination with intelligence testing, impressing his professors with his diligence and imagination.

The war, and Robert Yerkes, launched Brigham's professional career. The army experiment also boosted the credibility of his chosen specialty. "Within two or three years after the war," wrote Downey, "intelligence testing had developed a new and wide popularity in secondary schools, colleges, and universities across the country."[22] Brigham returned to Princeton after the war and field-tested Army Alpha on undergraduates. Finding the test too easy for college students, he created a more challenging version.

"The tests have proved most useful in the office of the Supervisor of Freshmen," Brigham wrote in the *Princeton Alumni Weekly* in 1923. "For the first time we have been able to locate, with some certainty, the men of good intellectual ability, who are neglecting their studies and are not realizing their maximum capacities along academic lines. Many of these men, when shown that they had been getting low academic grades simply because they had neglected their work, and not because of stupidity, realized the fact and subsequently made a good record."[23] In 1925, Princeton made Brigham's test a requirement for admission.

Intelligence tests were clearly the wave of the future, and several colleges were working to develop their own. Fearing that a flurry of independent activity might put it out of business, the College Board in 1924 asked Brigham, Yerkes (by then at Yale), and a psychology professor at Dartmouth to advise how it might go about administering "psychological tests" of its own. Brigham quickly took command of the group. "With his intellectual stability and tremendous driving power," wrote the Board's official historian twenty-five years later, he "was by common consent made the spokesman of the Board whenever decisions had to be reached."[24] In 1925, Brigham was officially appointed to direct the preparation and scoring of an intelligence test to be used in college admissions. He was assisted by a committee of psychologists, but the SAT was his test. He adapted it directly from Army Alpha, incorporating what he had learned in his experiments with Princeton undergraduates.

There is an air of the antique about the exam's first edition, but veteran ETS-test-takers would feel at home with the format. There are antonyms, analogies, sentence completions, and even primitive reading comprehension passages. One or two sections seem a bit odd. Brigham retained the army testers' penchant for esoteric information, quizzing students on brand names (Bon Ton, Congoleum, Atwater-Kent), cuts of beef (round, rump, sirloin), and chicken breeds (Plymouth Rock, Leghorn, Wyandotte). He also included a peculiar section on artificial language, in which students were given made-up vocabulary words and grammatical rules and then asked to parse sentences like "Ol thanto oteb" and "Ol pue bomem." By and large, though, the first SAT bears a surprisingly strong family resemblance to its modern descendant.

The SAT very quickly became Brigham's consuming passion. "The committee continued to meet irregularly for a year or two," his biographer wrote, "but the future development of the test was entirely in Brigham's hands."[25] The College Board funded him liberally, enabling him to set up an office and laboratory at 20 Nassau Street in Princeton.

The arrangement was ideal for Brigham. It gave him the freedom he needed to cultivate his fertile imagination. An inveterate tinkerer, he mounted his file cabinet on little wheels and attached the whole thing to his foot with a rope. When he wanted a file, he jerked his foot and the cabinet came skidding across the floor. When he was finished, he kicked it back across the room.[26]

Brigham also hatched bold plans for the future of mental measurement. In his laboratory on Nassau Street, he invented "an automatic testing machine to add a new dimension to test data." This device, according to his ETS biographer, was

> a box-like affair with a projection screen and dials on the front, and a moving-picture camera, a film projector, and a pair of stop watches inside. At the flip of a switch the gears whirred, a test item flashed on the screen, and the first stop watch began. After the subject had dialed his answer, he flipped a second switch. The camera then recorded the time and the response on 35 mm film, and the second stop watch timed the rest period until the next question. . . . Pervading his laboratory was the warmth of Carl Brigham's personality. One might find him, with the inevitable cigarette in his hand, sitting beside a table studying a pile of little wooden blocks, the material for a new spatial relations test. Making a last careful addition to the pile, he would look up and exclaim: "Testing is a cockeyed business!"[27]

In recent years, the College Board and ETS have described Brigham's virulent racism as a sort of irrelevant eccentricity. Brigham was asked to create the SAT, they say, because he was a testing expert, not because he was a bigot. His views were unfortunate, to be sure, but, like William Shockley's, they must be considered in isolation from his work as a scientist.

But in the 1920s Brigham made no such distinction between his eugenicist views and his professional life. Indeed, he had built his academic reputation *as* a racist. *A Study of American Intelligence* was his only book. It was just a year old at the time he was appointed, and the Board had studied it carefully. Hatred and vilification drip from every section. The notion that the Board somehow missed this fact is simply not credible. In his preface, Robert Yerkes said flatly, "[Brigham] presents not theories or opinions but facts. It behooves us to consider their reliability and meaning, for no one of us as a citizen can afford to ignore the menace of race deterioration or the evident relations of immigration to national progress and welfare."[28] There is no reason whatsoever to believe that the Board disagreed with Yerkes, whom it had also asked for advice on intelligence tests.

ETS and the College Board also say, when asked now about Brigham, that he eventually recanted his views. This is only partly true. In 1930 — seven years after *A Study of American Intelligence,* four years after the first SAT — Brigham published an article in the *Psychological Review* called "Intelligence Tests of Immigrant Groups."[29] He sketched contemporary notions of the nature of intelligence and then described a study that had found flaws in the method the army researchers had used to compare and combine scores on Alpha, Beta, and individual Binet tests. "As this method was used by the writer in his earlier analysis of the army tests as applied to samples of foreign born in the draft," Brigham wrote, "that study with its entire hypothetical superstructure of racial differences collapses completely."[30] The article concludes: "This review has summarized some of the more recent findings which show that comparative studies of various national and racial groups may not be made with existing tests, and which show, in particular, that one of the most pretentious of these comparative racial studies — the writer's own — was without foundation."[31]

These are Brigham's only references to his study. His ETS biographer made a virtue of this terseness by saying that Brigham "disposed of his own book in a few quick sentences."[32] Two quick sentences, to be precise. It's impossible not to wonder how much he was really giving up. His "recantation" is a wholly passionless document. He mentions his book by name only in a footnote, and he doesn't mention it at all until the end of the article. Nor does he say anything about blacks. He mentions the "foreign born" and, in the next to last paragraph, the unfairness of testing people in languages they don't speak.[33] But he is silent on the matter of his book's most conspicuous prejudice. Nor does he dismiss the *idea* of racial and national differences in intelligence; his quarrel is only with "existing tests."*

---

*Just two years before, in 1928, Brigham had published an article on the Army Mental Tests in *Eugenical News,* a journal that in 1933 reprinted an item called "Text of the German Sterilization Statute," by Adolf Hitler.[34]

Brigham has been blamed — most notably by Leon J. Kamin and Stephen Jay Gould* — for playing an instrumental role in the passage of the heavily restrictive Immigration Act of 1924. Kamin and Gould even implicate Brigham in the deaths of European Jews during World War II: denied American visas in the 1930s as a result of Brigham's proselytizing, they suggest, would-be emigrants were left to perish in the Holocaust.[35] More recently, in an article in the *American Psychologist,* Mark Snyderman and R. J. Herrnstein of Harvard have argued that the architects of the Immigration Act knew next to nothing about Brigham's book and were guided by little more than their own unspeakable prejudices. After reviewing transcripts of debates and hearings, they concluded that the results of mental tests "were surely not crucial in the congressional deliberation, and, most likely, they were immaterial."[36]

Snyderman and Herrnstein seem persuasive on this point. I had echoed Kamin and Gould's view in my *Harper's* article, describing Brigham as a major force behind the law. I now think I was wrong. Brigham would certainly have supported any effort to keep Jews and southern Europeans out of the United States. But Congress in the 1920s didn't need pointy-headed psychologists to convince it that foreigners were muddying the American gene pool. In making this point, though, Snyderman and Herrnstein miss a larger one. Their intention is to brighten the tarnished image of the early testing movement, but their effect is quite different. What their article proves is not that the testers were blameless on the question of race but that the "science" created by Brigham and others was driven by the same crude bigotry that led Congress to pass the Immigration Act. Brigham may not have influenced the lawmakers, but his motivation was the same. Brigham's remarkable ability to overlook the flaws in his method — flaws that Snyderman and Herrnstein ably document — was the unconscious product of his reprehensible point of view.

Snyderman and Herrnstein also argue that Brigham was something of a lone wolf in his profession and that his views were not

---

* In, respectively, *The Science and Politics of I.Q.* (Potomac, Md.: Erlbaum, 1974), and *The Mismeasure of Man* (New York: Norton, 1981). Both books are well worth reading. Gould's, I think, is the best book ever written on the history of mental (mis)measurement.

widely shared by his fellow psychologists. *A Study of American Intelligence* had its supporters, they say, but it was also greeted by "a chorus of critics."[37] Once again, their intention is to distance "the intelligence testing community of the period"[38] from individual racists associated with it. But if they are right, Brigham's appointment by the College Board — which the Board felt no need to justify at the time — is impossible to defend.

Brigham gradually retreated from his original ideas about the nature and distribution of intelligence. But his most enduring contributions to testing were made before his "recantation." Brigham quite literally created the culture of standardized testing. He invented the 200–800 scale, the delta difficulty rating system, the practice of testing new questions by burying them in actual tests, the equating of tests from one year to another, and the internally justified item-analysis method still used by ETS. The theoretical foundations of the SAT — and of numerous other descendants of Army Alpha — were laid down by a man who had blinded himself to reality in order to prove what he wanted to believe. The circularity of ETS's statistical method (and, indeed, of much of modern psychometrics) has its roots in efforts by Brigham and others to demonstrate "scientifically" what science could not demonstrate.

To say that Brigham and the College Board created the SAT to keep blacks and recent immigrants out of college would be quite misleading, however. Simply put, Brigham and the Board did not think of either group (or of women) as a threat to the Ivy League. The point of the SAT was to extend the Alpha standard to what Brigham and the Board viewed as mainstream American culture. Brigham intended his test to establish a "scale of brightness" on which the "native capacity" of the nation's best and brightest young men could be measured and compared.[39] The SAT was to be the cornerstone of a new American social order — the aristocracy of aptitude, the meritocracy.

The College Board suffered along with the rest of the nation during the Great Depression. Between 1926 and 1935, test volume declined by 30 percent, from 22,089 to 15,394. As the economy grew worse, fewer and fewer families could afford the luxury of a college education. For a few bleak years, according to the Board's historian, "it looked to the pessimists as if the Board were heading towards catastrophe."[40] Aggravating the problem was a minor rebellion by a handful of colleges that had begun waiving admissions test requirements for students with good high school records. The Board found this development extremely ominous. "It should be unnecessary to argue," it argued in 1932,

> that educational institutions that admit large numbers of students on the basis of the Board's examinations should refrain from any action likely to make the Board less efficient or to injure its academic standards. If institutions which make use of the Board's examinations should excuse from the examinations the cream of the student body, the Board's Readers would see chiefly the examination papers of second-rate students and would gradually be led to believe that really good examinations are within the power of very few students. . . . Furthermore, to excuse from the Board's examinations a large number of candidates forming a homogeneous group would seriously hinder any statistical study of the results of the examinations.[41]

Having established itself thirty-two years earlier in hopes of simplifying the lives of admissions officers, the Board now chastised colleges for complicating the lives of its essay graders and statisticians. The Board's lease on life was still tenuous, but the organization had already come to see its continued existence as a social good apart from its actual usefulness to colleges.

Fortunately for the Board, World War II arrived in time not only to pull the nation out of the Depression but also to secure the future of standardized testing. In 1940, when American entry into the European war seemed inevitable, the Board enthusiastically volunteered its services to the federal government. Carl Brigham offered to turn over to the military all the test materials and experimental data he had developed in connection with *A Study of American Intelligence.** "Anything which is copyrighted in my name is yours, if you want it," he wrote in a letter to a Major Holdridge.[42] He was promptly appointed "expert consultant" to the War Department.[43]

---

*This was a full decade after his "recantation." Brigham apparently still felt warm enough about his "pretentious" data on comparative intelligence to think they might be useful to the military.

Rumors of war brought a new excitement to the College Board. The meetings of the period were "lively and thrilling," according to the Board's historian. "Imaginative minds had taken hold of its operations. At committee luncheons the research workers from the Princeton laboratories were using technical terms which mystified the laymen. Nobody was afraid of new ideas, and a tonic pioneer spirit pervaded the discussions."[44]

When the Japanese attacked Pearl Harbor, the Board flew into action. It abandoned its traditional essay examinations, never to take them up again, in favor of the shorter SAT and the concomitant Achievement Tests. It also threw its staff and resources behind the war effort. For the army and the navy, it developed the A-12 and V-12 officer qualifying tests, which were administered to 316,000 men in 1943 alone. "Under one single contract," the Board's historian wrote, "the Board handled for the Bureau of Naval Personnel approximately one hundred service jobs, including the printing or reprinting of 133 tests, answer sheets, and bulletins — a total of 36,000,000 pages of material."[45] The Board also developed a college admissions test for veterans, entrance exams for the United States Naval and Coast Guard academies, and scholarship tests for Westinghouse and Pepsi-Cola. As the Board realized with satisfaction at the time, most of these new programs could be carried over into peacetime, ensuring the Board's future for years to come. They also provided an immediate and much needed economic boost. Having run deficits a number of times over the years, the Board found itself in 1943 with a wholly unexpected fund surplus of $300,000.[46]

The Board got an even bigger boost when the war ended. Suddenly college campuses were flooded with returning soldiers. Demand for the SAT grew rapidly as admissions officers sought a fast, inexpensive method for sorting through mountains of applications. Soon the College Board had more testing business than it could handle. In 1947, it joined with the American Council on Education and the Carnegie Foundation for the Advancement of Teaching and created the nonprofit Educational Testing Service to take care of the new demand. The Board's historian called the establishment of ETS "a notable act of renunciation and self-decapitation."[47] Henceforth, all of the Board's operational functions would be handled by the new corporation.

Carl Campbell Brigham, "who had continued to toil unceasingly even when he knew that his doom was upon him," didn't live to see the organization he had done as much as anyone to create.[48] He had died four years before, at the age of fifty-two. "A sword of good steel," wrote ETS in 1961, "had worn out its scabbard."[49] But Brigham's spirit lived in ETS. Indeed, the testing company's first president was a man very much after Brigham's heart. His name was Henry Chauncey.

Henry Chauncey was born in Brooklyn, New York, in 1905, the son of the Reverend Egisto Fabbri Chauncey and the former Edith Lockwood Taft. He attended Groton and then entered Harvard, his father's alma mater, in 1924. He earned his degree in three years and starred on both the baseball and football teams, becoming a hero in 1925 when he kicked the field goal that gave Harvard a 3–0 victory over Brown. After graduation, he turned down two attempts by the Boston Braves to sign him as a catcher and spent two years as a teacher and coach at Penn Charter, a private school in Philadelphia. In 1929 he returned to Harvard as an assistant dean and coach of the freshman baseball team.

Chauncey was eventually put in charge of Harvard's scholarship program, which used tests to allocate awards. By the outbreak of World War II, he was devoting virtually all of his time to testing. He took a leave from Harvard in 1943 and spent fourteen months helping to administer the College Board's Army-Navy Qualifying Tests. In 1945, he was named director of the Board. Two years later, he became the first president of the Educational Testing Service.

Housed in Carl Brigham's old laboratory on Nassau Street, ETS expanded rapidly under Chauncey. A writer for *Collier's,* in an article called "They Know All the Answers," described the busy scene in 1951:

> The youthful air pervading ETS is especially noticeable in the dozen offices where the 25 item writers work from eight to five figuring out test questions, at desks piled high with textbooks, dictionaries and standard works in their particular field. Most of them are girls and most Phi Beta Kappas. . . . Here's petite Jean Franklin, sitting at her desk, legs crossed, hand on forehead, working away at one

section of the Medical College Admission Test. . . . Jean knows little about medicine. Scholastically, her strong point is history. . . . But our medical colleges want students who have not only an aptitude for biology and chemistry but also an understanding of what's been happening to American society. . . . One test of this understanding, Jean decided, would be a question about leisure time — for example: *Why have leisure-time activities become increasingly important?*[50]

Petite Jean may have known little about medicine, but she knew plenty about doctors.

Chauncey's cotillion of item writers faced numerous difficulties. "Devising the right setting for a question is often their biggest problem," observed *Collier's*. "A math question based on the number of pounds of flour required to make a certain number of cakes would be ruled out for prospective West Pointers. But it would be okay for a high-school group, because it would get the girls interested — and in math tests the girls have to be interested, because they always do worse than the boys anyway."[51]

ETS in those days shipped out copies of its 368 different exams (including not only SATs, LSATs, and MCATs, but also Foreign Service exams, ROTC scholarship tests, Coast Guard Academy entrance exams, and many, many others) accompanied by a consignment of what it referred to as "special electrographic pencils" — mechanical pencils equipped with No. 2 lead. The pencils made marks that could be read by the company's twenty automatic scoring machines, crude devices that contained hundreds of tiny, electrified, five-tined metal prongs, one for each square on an answer sheet. The young women on the staff graded test papers by feeding them into the machines one at a time and lowering the prongs to the surface of the paper. Every time one of the prongs touched a blackened square corresponding to a correct answer, the graphite on the paper completed an electrical circuit. The young women read the number of correct answers from a dial on the front of the machine and recorded it on the paper.[52]

Some students tried to improve their chances by marking more than one space on items they weren't sure of. ETS guarded against this by assigning a corps of sharp-eyed Phi Beta Kappas to scan each answer sheet visually and put cellophane tape over double responses. A University of Chicago student beat this system for a while by marking his second and third choices with tiny pencil dots that were invisible to Chauncey's girls but not to the grading machines. ETS noted with considerable satisfaction that this miscreant was later convicted of murder.[53]

ETS soon outgrew its tiny Princeton headquarters. By 1954, the company had become wealthy enough to move to bigger digs. The change of address was prompted by a Christmas gift to Chauncey from his second wife, Laurie. "The gift was a $1.25 knapsack to carry the lunch they often took with them on hikes," says an ETS brochure published in 1977. "The Chaunceys, who then lived on the other side of Stoney Brook, crossed the stream the following Sunday — 'a bleak, raw December day' — and coming through the woods, discovered the open farmland area where ETS buildings now stand."[54] Ah, Brigadoon. Chauncey persuaded ETS's trustees to buy the entire spread and to plant him and his family, free of charge, in the house that stood on it. Laurie Chauncey liked to refer to their home, which had once housed the Stoney Brook Hunt Club, as "company housing."[55]

Chauncey's vision of ETS's future was a good bit grander than the College Board's. He saw ETS not as a testing company but as a sort of university without students — his own university. ETS employees still refer to the company grounds as a "campus," and productive researchers are rewarded with "tenure." Chauncey looked out over four hundred acres of pastures and trees and dreamed of an entire university devoted to mental measurement.

Like Carl Brigham, Henry Chauncey was an ardent admirer of Army Alpha. "This test turned out to be a remarkably good instrument," he wrote in 1963, "for assigning recruits to jobs with different intellectual demands, for picking out promising officer candidates, and for rejecting those who lacked sufficient mental ability to complete military training successfully."[56] Chauncey was fascinated by the idea of assessing mental powers. In Army Alpha, in the Army-Navy Qualifying Tests of World War II, and in the early experiments of Alfred Binet, Chauncey whiffed the intoxicating spoor of *science*.

"[Binet's] method was truly scientific," he wrote, "and remarkably like the method used by physicists forty years later to detect and measure the forces released by the atom. The cloud chamber does not permit the physicist to see the atom or its electrically charged components, but it does reveal the tracks of ionizing particles and thus permits the scientist to deduce the nature of the atom from which the particles emanate."[57]

Intelligence, for Chauncey, was a hard, smooth nut, buried somewhere deep in the brain, that cast off particles of merit. One might never hope to squirrel out the thing itself, but if one were scientific enough, the nature of the nut might be deduced from its "emanations." Chauncey saw standardized tests as tools with which to remake society. Writing in ETS's *Annual Report* for 1949–50, he described "an urgent need for a national census of human abilities," which, he said, would be of "critical importance for the National Military Establishment" and would also provide information about "the ability difference between men and women, and the trends of employment as between the sexes. . . ."[58]

ETS's tests, furthermore, would serve society by dampening the unreasonable aspirations of the undeserving. "To many," Chauncey wrote, "the prospect of measuring in quantitative terms what have previously been considered intangible qualities is frightening, if not downright objectionable. Yet, I venture to predict that we will become accustomed to it and will find ourselves better off for it. . . . Life may have less mystery but it will also have less disillusionment and disappointment. Hope will not be a lost source of strength, but it will be kept within reasonable bounds."[59]

Henry Chauncey was more a visionary than a scientist. He wrote a few technical papers, but always with the assistance of researchers on his staff. He liked to hire people who struck him as having fertile imaginations, even if they lacked a background in psychometrics, and put them on the ETS payroll as his own special assistants. Once, an ETS researcher told me, Chauncey became enthralled by "two crazy old ladies in tennis sneakers." The women weren't actually hired, but ETS staff members, on Chauncey's instructions, spent more than a year working on a "personality inventory," based on Carl Jung's ideas about introversion and extroversion, that the women had developed.

"It was an asshole business," the researcher told me. "Psychologists at the time thought the whole thing was laughable. I mean, here at ETS we had the most top-flight psychometricians and statisticians in the country, and they were examining the entrails of a bird — all because these two little old ladies, who hadn't been to college, had charmed Chauncey. Chauncey knew more about measurement and psychology than the average layperson, but sometimes he went beyond what he knew. It was like 'a little learning is a dangerous thing.' He had this kind of need to find something, to make his mark."

Technology always held a strong appeal for Chauncey. In the early 1960s, captivated by the idea of teaching machines, he hired a researcher to develop an audiovisual device that could be used in teaching small children. Chauncey was very interested at the time in a spelling system that eliminated the idiosyncrasies of English orthography and spelled words the way they actually sounded, and this system was used on the machine. The device was assembled piecemeal from materials in ETS's laboratories: a slide projector, a tape recorder, buttons for making responses. The finished product was christened Sequential and Regimental Reading for Children (SEARCH).

SEARCH was expensive and cumbersome, and it was already obsolete by the time a prototype could be built. The computer age was just around the corner, and SEARCH was as old-fashioned as a vacuum tube. In a last-ditch effort to win grant money, ETS tried it out on retarded children. But no one was interested, and the machine was never produced. At a closed ETS meeting in 1982, executive Robert J. Solomon explained why: "After years of work that had proved fruitless . . . despite the fact that . . . ETS had obtained some patents for it . . . despite the millions of dollars, billions of dollars available in the so-called education industry in the 1960's, the materials that were developed were not marketable."[60] SEARCH went the way of the Jungian personality inventory.

Chauncey didn't lose his faith in technology, though. In the late 1960s he initiated a research and development program called Project Moonshot, which consisted of ten separate projects, each intended to tap the huge market for educational technology that

SEARCH had failed to penetrate. According to ETS scientist Samuel Messick, one of the projects was intended to "incorporate some of the ideas of artificial intelligence as it was conceptionalized using . . . some games, particularly Go, as a way of getting a complex human problem solved."[61] But Moonshot was a bust. The only one of the projects that ever came to anything was SIGI, the computerized guidance counselor that told both Gregory Anrig and me that we ought to be clergymen.

Even when the computer age was fully under way and after Henry Chauncey had retired, ETS remained unable to cash in on the technology boom. In late 1979 and early 1980, the company invested great hopes in something it called the hand-held testing device, a small microprocessor-driven machine intended for use in the classroom. An experimental prototype — made from a Texas Instruments programmable calculator with all but five of the buttons covered with tape — was field-tested at a nearby prep school in 1979. The results were mixed. The project was abandoned soon afterward, when ETS realized that a more sophisticated version of the same idea was already being marketed. This intimidating rival was Speak & Spell, the popular toy that enabled ET to phone home.

Henry Chauncey never found the big technological breakthrough he dreamed of, but he made his mark in other ways. By the time he retired, in 1970, his company's multiple-choice tests had become one of the givens of American life. In the course of a very few years, he had succeeded in transforming Carl Campbell Brigham's cramped little Princeton laboratory into one of the most powerful institutions in the United States.*

Chauncey was a firm believer in the meritocracy — a social hierarchy in which status and opportunity are determined by individual "worth" rather than by, say, family lineage. Chauncey saw ETS as the meritocracy's clearinghouse. The company's tests would regulate access to schools, professions, and jobs, ensuring that the deserving were allowed to advance and that the undeserving were held behind. Test scores would be the equivalent of money in a

---

*I keep referring to Chauncey in the past tense. But he's still very much alive, still residing in Princeton, New Jersey, and still visible at ETS on ceremonial occasions.

new marketplace of opportunity. Rinsed of the subjective bias inherent in human decision-making, this new "objective" system would make it possible for society to order itself rationally and efficiently. The science of mental measurement would eliminate caprice from the distribution of society's goods.

"We believe that justice should be done each individual according to his merit," Chauncey wrote in 1961.[62] The meritocratic ideal is so tightly entwined with the American ethos that many people, maybe even most people, feel the same way. But how should merit be defined? ETS would say that merit is "aptitude" and that it can be measured with standardized tests. To accept this notion is to believe that "aptitude" is or should be society's organizing principle, and that multiple-choice tests are the proper instruments for allocating society's rewards. It is also to believe that the responsibility for ordering society belongs on the shoulders of the test-makers. This is precisely the role that Chauncey foresaw for ETS.

"The administration at the end of the eighth or ninth grade of an extensive battery of aptitude tests would . . . identify the boys and girls of particular promise for professional and scientific studies," he wrote in his annual report to the ETS trustees in 1951. "Successive retesting every year or two after that . . . would help to define, with increasing precision, desirable vocational goals for students whose interests and abilities point toward termination of formal education upon completion of the secondary level. In the case of high-level talent, the successive retesting would also provide progressively more accurate identification, more directly focused on the nature of the work for which each individual was particularly suited."[63]

If one decides to structure society according to the results of a test, that test becomes the blueprint for society. But how should the blueprint be drawn? Do lawyers have more merit than farmers? Do corporate lawyers have more merit than public defenders? Do whites have more merit than blacks?

In American society, "merit" is usually little more than camouflage for class. Through a meritocratic sleight of hand, society's rewards become their own justification: if the meritocracy is supposed to reward the worthy by giving them high salaries, then people with high salaries must be worthy. The rich must be smart; how else did they get to be so rich? And the poor, of course, must be dumb.

"It is interesting to remember," wrote James Fallows in *The Atlantic* in 1980, "that when Michael Young, the British sociologist, invented the term 'meritocracy' twenty years ago, he did so with satirical intent. His point was that a system of rewards based on 'ability' and 'merit' would not necessarily be any fairer or more pleasant than other systems of stratification the world has known. It would, he said, be a dull and dangerous society, run by single-minded technicians. So deep has been the American hunger for a 'fair' system of classification, one based on ability rather than accident of birth, that Young's term has been appropriated without its irony."[64]

The meritocratic impulse can be quite unmeritocratic. Far from being egalitarian, the new "fair" system perpetuates old injustices by making them look like the neutral workings of the merit market. The testing industry is the mighty engine of the status quo. The meritocracy, as interpreted by ETS, is eugenics by other means.

10

Brains

HENRY CHAUNCEY THOUGHT OF the SAT as an IQ test. "Intelligence tests and scholastic aptitude tests," he wrote in 1963, "have the same purpose: to estimate the capacity of the student for school learning. . . . For all practical purposes, and in all of their school uses, they are the same kind of test."[1]

No one at ETS would publicly claim this today. Chauncey's confident declarations have become an embarrassment. Indeed, the company's recent history as a public institution has consisted almost entirely of an unruly retreat from prior enthusiasms. *Intelligence* is now a dirty word at ETS; *IQ* is an out and out obscenity. Both expressions hark back to the days (still with us in many quarters, however) when smug testers acted as though a person's "mental power" were steady and unchanging — and as easy to represent numerically as his age.

In recent years at ETS, *aptitude* has become almost as unmentionable as *IQ*. Until 1982, the principal part of the Graduate Record Examinations (GRE) was called the GRE Aptitude Test. Now it's called the GRE General Test. ETS doesn't even refer to the Scholastic Aptitude Test as an aptitude test anymore. You can read *Taking the SAT* from cover to cover and not find *aptitude* in it anywhere except in the name of the test the booklet purports to describe.

Will ETS rename the SAT as it did the GRE? Of course not. Dropping *aptitude* from the title of its best-selling product would be a marketing disaster. Instead, ETS pretends it isn't there. The word *aptitude,* like the name of God, is never uttered. The new euphemism is *developed ability* or, more grandly, *higher-order reasoning abilities.*

What were once called intelligence tests, and were then sometimes also called aptitude tests, are now usually referred to as ability tests.* What is ability? Is it different from intelligence or aptitude? There is much confusion on this point. In 1982, the National Research Council's Committee on Ability Testing (on which ETS was represented) published a two-volume report called *Ability Testing,* which said that ability tests include not only "tests of knowledge, reasoning, and special skills" but also ones that measure "vocational interest, attitude, personality, motivation, or physical activity" — in short, virtually all tests. The NRC said that aptitude tests and achievement tests are both ability tests, and that there is little difference between them because "ability is always a combination of aptitude and achievement."[3] Elsewhere, the NRC defined ability as "the upper limit of what a person can do now," but warned that it "should not be confused with 'potential' or 'capacity.' "[4]

Actually, my *Webster's Seventh New Collegiate Dictionary* confuses ability with both aptitude and capacity, and confuses capacity with ability and potential. ETS is also confused. In 1971 the company cited a 1951 study defining *aptitude* as "capacity or potentiality" while maintaining that the SAT was designed to measure "aspects of developed ability."[5] Testers have always been elusive in the naming of their tests, abandoning old terms as soon as they become pejorative and then adopting their synonyms. (What will the tests be called next? Only your thesaurus knows.) As Walt Haney, the former director of the National Consortium on Testing, pointed out in a review of the NRC study, the Committee on Ability Testing didn't seem to know exactly what it meant by ability testing. He also noted that, given this confusion, it was ironic that the committee had "decried as a 'fundamental

---

*On the other hand: although ETS says that its aptitude tests are really ability tests, and that neither ability nor aptitude is the same thing as intelligence, the ETS Test Collection — the company's 13,505-entry compilation of tests from all over the world — lists intelligence tests under the heading Aptitude and makes no mention of ability.[2] Go figure it.

shortcoming' the fact that 'inadequate explanation of abilities . . . informs testing.' "*[7]

The inadequate explanation of abilities is ETS's stock in trade. I once asked Arthur Kroll, vice president in charge of the Admissions Testing Program, to define *aptitude*, which he had just referred to as "developed ability." "The propensity to be able to do well in a particular area, whether it's mechanical aptitude, spatial aptitude, artistic or whatever," he said. "If one were to look at an analogy, you might talk about aptitude, intelligence, achievement being perhaps on a continuum, aptitude being somewhere on that continuum between intelligence, which might be seen on one end, and achievement on another end. And aptitude — as defined, anyway — is probably closer to the intelligence end than to the achievement end, but not synonymous with intelligence. I think intelligence is whatever one brings in the way of intellectual capacity that eventually turns into developed ability."

Kroll also told me that there was "probably very little" difference between developed ability and aptitude, but that ETS had started referring to the SAT as a test of the former rather than of the latter because "aptitude has never been terribly well understood in our society." Even so, he said, ETS had no plans to rename the SAT the Scholastic Developed Ability Test (and thus clear up society's misunderstanding) because the SAT "does test scholastic aptitude."

Kroll is an executive, not a psychologist, so his inability to define *ability* may be understandable. But the meaning of *aptitude* has also been puzzled over by ETS's professional research staff. Noting that there is "considerable confusion . . . between achieve-

---

*In a response to Haney's review, Alexandra Wigdor, co-editor of *Ability Testing*, wrote that Haney "faults the Committee for its failure to 'directly address the question of what ability is, and how well ability tests measure it.' The mind is still largely uncharted territory, and we social and biological scientists approach it like the six blind men approached the elephant. Ability testing has allowed us to get our hands on the animal, to get some sense empirically of its size, shape, and movement — even perhaps to make some guesses about its capacities and potential [the capacities and potential of *ability?*]. But we are a long way from a definitive formulation of the nature of ability and, therefore, from knowing how well tests measure it." As Haney pointed out in his response to this response, if what Wigdor said was true, "then it might have been better for the Committee to have either (1) disbanded after offering only these insights, or (2) changed both its name and much of the language in its report."[6]

ment tests and ability tests," ETS scientist Samuel Messick tried to set things straight in a 1982 Research Report:

> Since tasks within the same operation-content-product category are more similar in shared activities than those in different categories, a specific ability should eventually develop via transfer for every cell of the operation by content by product cross-classification.[8] . . . Overall, then, a person's developed ability structure is conceptualized here as a multidimensional organization of stable assemblies of information-processing components that are combined functionally in task performance, learning, problem solving, and creative production.[9] . . . Thus, developed abilities influence the structuring and restructuring of knowledge while developed knowledge structures influence the organization and application of abilities, leading to increasingly more complex structures of each.[10] . . . Furthermore, the distinction between developed abilities and developed knowledge structures cuts across this aptitude-achievement contrast, as does Anastasi's continuum of experiential specificity and Snow's pyramid of referent generality.[11]

This is the sort of ratiocination that raises hair on the palms. Despite its formidable jargon, Messick's disquisition on "knowledge structures" is entirely speculative. How much aptitude can dance on the head of a pin? When you finally pull back the curtain, ETS's attitude about aptitude seems to be: Hey, come on, everybody *knows* what these tests measure. From Kroll's continuum of intellectual capacity to Messick's multidimensional organization of stable assemblies to Snow's pyramid of referent generality — what ETS is really talking about is what children refer to, much more economically, as brains. Now, children don't have a very clear idea what they mean when they talk about brains. And neither does ETS.

ETS hasn't always been so evasive. In 1959 it published a booklet called *YOU: Today and Tomorrow,* designed to help *grade school* children plan the rest of their lives on the basis of their performance on ETS aptitude tests. "Your scholastic ability is like an engine," the booklet said. "It is the source of your power and speed in school. It tells you how fast and how far you *can* go." Everything was so simple in those days. "Can you measure scholastic ability?" the booklet asked, comparing aptitude to height.

"This is where you can use your 'magic mirror!' Take a good look at the facts about your scholastic ability *now*."[12]

ETS has said frequently that it abhors the "common misconception" that its aptitude tests measure something innate and unchanging. But if this is a misconception, no one has worked harder to make it a common one than ETS.

For all its huffing and puffing about pyramids and mental continua, ETS doesn't officially claim more for the SAT than that it is a somewhat less accurate predictor of freshman grades than an applicant's performance in high school is. "Your high school record," says the 1982 edition of *Taking the SAT*, "is probably the best evidence of your preparation for college."[13] Even this is reaching a little. Most people, reading this, assume that a student's "high school record" includes teachers' comments, advisers' recommendations, notes on difficulty of courses, and all the other information schools compile about their students over three or four years. But ETS here means only simple grade point average (GPA) or class rank, not adjusted for school quality or course difficulty or anything else. Many college admissions officers say they use SAT scores as a uniform standard against which to judge grades earned in high schools they know nothing about. But it would actually make more sense, given the relationship between scores and grades, to use high school GPAs as a standard for judging the meaning of SAT scores.

How well does the SAT actually predict freshman grades? George Hanford of the College Board was quoted in the *New York Times* in 1982 as saying, "Most studies show validities for the SAT and for the high school record of .52 (each, separately)."[14] This number is known as a correlation coefficient. *Validities* is a testing term that refers to the statistical relationship between a test and the purpose for which it is intended. Since the purpose of the SAT is to predict freshman grades, ETS judges the test to be "valid" if the correlation between scores and GPAs seems high enough. A perfect positive correlation — which would exist if you could line up all the students at a given college according to their SATs and the order turned out to be exactly the same as if you'd lined them up by grades — is 1.0. A perfect negative correlation — which would exist if the students with the highest scores got the *worst* grades, etc. — is − 1.0. All other correlations fall somewhere in between. A correlation coefficient, according to ETS, is "generally the most accepted" way "to describe how closely what the test giver wants to know corresponds to what is actually measured."[15]

I don't know where Hanford got the correlation coefficient cited by the *Times* unless he made it up or did a study of his own. In a booklet ETS published in 1980, the "characteristic" correlation between high school record and freshman grades was indeed given as .52, as Hanford said, but the correlation between SAT scores and freshman grades was given as only .37 for the verbal test, .32 for the math test, and .41 for the two tests combined.[16] Hanford, at the very least, was exaggerating.

ETS and the Board have both been known to take liberties with correlation coefficients in defending the SAT. Warner V. Slack and Douglas Porter, in their 1980 *Harvard Educational Review* article (discussed in Chapter 6), showed that a 1977 research study by the two organizations misstated validity calculations in an apparent effort to make the SAT look better, and the high school record look worse, at predicting freshman grades. In a 1977 College Board study prepared by ETS, researchers S. F. Ford and S. Campos had concluded that "SAT validities for recent years for the combined [sex] samples average about .40 for SAT-V, .35 for SAT-M, .50 for HSR [high school record]. . . ." But Slack and Porter redid the arithmetic and found that the actual values (derived from Ford and Campos's own tables) were, respectively, .37, .32, and .52.[17] The errors were quite systematic, and always in favor of the SAT.

Leonard Ramist, the director of ETS's College Board programs, told me in 1983 that the average correlation for the math test had risen to about .37, lifting the combined figure to .43. ETS was quite enthusiastic about this "improvement." But what it means, if anything, is hard to say. ETS arrives at its overall correlation figures by performing validity studies, free of charge, for colleges that want them. The schools give the College Board a list of grades; then ETS runs the numbers through a computer and tells the schools how the SAT is working for them. Every other year,

ETS averages all the individual correlations it has calculated for the previous five years. Much of the information in new averages is thus simply taken from old averages. This smooths out trends from one year to the next and helps disguise the fact that ETS's calculations are based on a very small and unscientifically selected sample (only about 200 schools volunteer each year).

Even though ETS says correlation coefficients are the "most accepted" way of talking about what tests measure, most people don't know quite what to make of them, however they're derived. Many people, including some admissions officers and an occasional ETS or College Board spokesperson, think of them as percentages. They are not. Exactly what they are is harder to say, largely because the meaning of the numbers depends entirely on their context. Correlations that seem significant in one situation can be meaningless in another. As Stephen Jay Gould points out, the correlation "between my age and the price of gasoline during the past ten years . . . is nearly perfect, but no one would suggest any assignment of cause. . . . The invalid assumption that correlation implies cause is probably among the two or three most serious and common errors of human reasoning."[18]

Because context is so important, the beauty of statistical correlations is very much in the eye of the beholder. In 1980, in response to accusations by Allan Nairn[19] and others that performance on the SAT was closely related to socioeconomic status (see table), ETS calculated that the correlation between ETS scores and family income was "about .30."[20] ETS did not find this relationship disturbing, even though .30 is higher than the SAT-GPA correlation for many colleges and also higher than, for instance, the average

Family Income	Average SAT Scores	
	Math	Verbal
Under $6,000	353	418
$ 6,000 to $11,999	381	443
$12,000 to $17,999	408	469
$18,000 to $23,999	418	482
$24,000 to $29,999	429	498
$30,000 to $39,999	438	509
$40,000 to $49,999	447	521
$50,000 or Over	464	534[22]

overall correlation between scores on ETS's Graduate Management Admission Test (GMAT) and grades in business school.[21] At the same time, Nairn — who found the SAT-income correlation resounding — dismissed the SAT-GPA correlation as meaningless. As statisticians have long known, correlations can be used to "prove" almost anything.

One way to get an inkling of what correlations mean is to look at some simple examples. The correlation between SAT scores and college grades, for instance, is lower than the correlation between weight and height; in other words, you would have a better chance of predicting a person's height by looking only at his weight than you would of predicting his freshman grades by looking only at his SAT scores.[23] Another way to think about correlations is to look at some actual numbers. In the following table, the order of the numbers in each of the three columns on the right (B, C, and D) bears a correlation of .43 — just like the SAT-GPA — to the true order of the same numbers, which is given in the column on the left (A).

A	B	C	D
1	6	7	2
2	1	3	6
3	7	2	8
4	3	6	7
5	8	8	1
6	5	1	3
7	2	4	4
8	4	5	5
9	9	9	9
10	10	10	10

This is quite a crude and probably misleading little table. But for anyone who thinks a correlation of .43 is the last word in "validity," it's worth bearing in mind.

ETS, the College Board, and others have argued that the predictive validity of the SAT may actually be greater than the correlation coefficients imply (whatever it is they *do* imply). According to Fred Hargadon, dean of admissions at Stanford and former chairman of the College Board, "The true validity of the SAT in predicting academic performance is, at least in some instances, attenuated, first, by student self-selection, and then by college admissions decisions, resulting in clusters of very high scoring students at some institutions and very low scoring at others, institutions of both types distributing the same grades in roughly the same manner and each graduating classes with a top ten percent and a bottom ninety percent."[24]

This is true. To give an extreme example, if a college admitted only students whose combined SAT score was exactly, say, 1,000, the SAT would have no predictive validity whatsoever for that college: the correlation between scores (all identical) and grades (all different) would be zero. But the predictive validity of high school record is *also* attenuated, for the very same reason, although Hargadon does not say so. In fact, the predictive validity of high school record is even more attenuated than that of SAT scores. As Hargadon says, "Nothing even comes close to being as influential in determining college admissions as applicants' high school transcripts and grades."[25] But the more influential high school grades are, the lower their predictive validity appears, for the reasons Hargadon describes above. A school may admit only students with A averages, but each class will earn grades across the entire scoring range. The more a predictor is used, the more attenuated its validity. If grades, as Hargadon says, are used more than SAT scores, then their validity is more seriously underestimated by ETS than is the validity of the SAT.

Admissions officers would be wise to keep in mind what ETS told law school admissions officers twenty years ago (but has not often, if ever, repeated since). In the *LSAT Handbook* for 1964, ETS pointed out that correlations between LSAT scores and law school grades ranged from about .30 to about .50 — about the same as those for the SAT and college grades. "Whether or not correlations of this magnitude are thought to be high or low depends on one's point of view," ETS wrote. "Many statisticians would be wholly unimpressed. . . . Judged against a standard of perfect prediction, the correlation for Law School Admission Test scores is very low, and anyone using the scores for prediction should be prepared for many disappointments."[26]

Most college admissions officers don't know any more about correlation coefficients than George Hanford and I do. In general, they trust ETS when it says that the SAT's validity has been proven. As an admissions officer at Middlebury College told me, "Basically, I have a sense of the SAT measuring exactly what ETS tells us it measures. I take it pretty much at face value."

But what *is* the face value of the SAT? ETS sends out very conflicting signals on this point. On the one hand, it reminds students that the SAT is only one measure among many and that it is not even the best one available for doing what it is supposed to do.[27] On the other hand, in the 1983–84 *ATP Guide for High Schools and Colleges,* it says that users of SAT and Achievement Test scores "learn to understand and appreciate the meaning of a score of 430 in the same way that they have learned to understand and appreciate the meaning of 14 inches."[28] This is utterly irresponsible. Not even the most wild-eyed vice president at ETS thinks the SAT scoring scale is remotely comparable to a ruler. Statements like this are a direct throwback to the days of Carl Brigham. They suggest a precision for the SAT that ETS knows to be absurd, and they encourage exactly the sort of test misuse that ETS claims to abhor.

Elsewhere in the *ATP Guide,* ETS engages in some psychometric name-dropping, mentioning "Kuder-Richardson reliability estimates," "true scores," "the Dressel adaptation for formula-scored tests," and a number of others. The terms aren't defined in enough detail to make them comprehensible to the vast majority of admissions officers and guidance counselors, for whom the booklet is intended. ETS is just flexing its muscles, assuring readers that experts are in control.

ETS is often vague or misleading about information that would actually be quite useful to admissions officers. The booklet says that the standard error of measurement (SEM) for the SAT is "approximately 30 points on the 200 to 800 scale."[29] This is correct for the verbal SAT. But according to the three examples ETS gives in a chart, the SEM for the math SAT would appear to be approximately 35 points, not 30. This is consistent with every other statistical analysis I've seen of the SAT. ETS employs the only statisticians I know who round off 33, 34, and 35 to 30 instead of to 35 (or to 40, for that matter; see below).

ETS says further that SEMs can "vary at different places on the same scale. Some SEMs can be slightly greater for some scores than for others."[30] But it doesn't elaborate. For which scores is the figure in the booklet misleading? I called ETS to find out. The person I was referred to referred me to someone else, who said she would have to refer me to another person, who would call me back the next day. The next day passed. Four more days passed. I called back again and was told that ETS was still trying to find someone who knew about the standard error of measurement of the SAT. A few more days passed. My first child was born. When she was ten days old, I called ETS again. I was passed around on the telephone for about ten minutes. The person at ETS who understands standard error of measurement was ill, I was told. My call was finally transferred to a woman whose response to my predicament was to demand why I was bothering her. "Where are you calling from?" she asked in a hostile tone. "Are you an admissions officer?" I told her I was a customer. She was confused. "I take your tests," I said. She told me she wouldn't be able to help me unless I could tell her the name of the person I had talked to during my two previous phone calls. I said I hadn't bothered to note the person's name, since the person had taken my phone number and promised to call me back immediately. We had a very heated exchange on this point. Finally, when I persisted in wanting to know what I had now spent three weeks trying to find out, my interrogator said she would get an answer for me and call me back within an hour. I never heard from her again.

Two days later, I received a letter from ETS (although I had given no one my address) saying, "To our knowledge there is no publicly available discussion of the variability of standard errors except in a very technical form in chapter 4 of Fred Lord's *Applications of Item Response Theory to Practical Testing Problems* (Erlbaum 1980). We hope this information is helpful."[31] That was all. Since Fred Lord is an ETS employee, presumably he could have been asked to explain this variability, to which it seems he alone holds the key, in a comprehensible manner. He must have explained it in this way at some point to the author of the *ATP Guide*. Furthermore, the substance of the letter is simply not true. Two independent measurement experts I spoke with told me that information about the variability of SEMs is not as scarce as ETS implies and that, generally speaking, test scores near the extremes of the scale tend to have larger than average errors of measurement. The scores of high-scoring students and low-scoring students, therefore, would appear to be less reliable than is suggested by the average SEM, which is all ETS provides. Isn't this something that admissions officers ought to be told — or at least be allowed to find out?

ETS is every bit as unhelpful when it tries to define what standard error of measurement *is*. Although, in the *ATP Guide*, it says in one paragraph that "SEMs do not take into account day-to-day variations in individual examinees or differences in environment from one administration to the next," it says in another paragraph that taking account of SEMs is "the most realistic way to account for the effects of normal variations in the physical and emotional conditions of the individual, the test setting, or the test content." The first statement is correct; the second is not. ETS also says that the standard error of measurement is affected by "differences in student performance due to the sample questions on the test."[32] What ETS really means here is the sample *of* questions: every student's score is affected by which particular questions (out of all possible ones) ETS happens to ask. *Sample questions,* which of course are not scored, have nothing to do with SEMs. This sloppiness is typical of the entire guide.

ETS uses SEMs to calculate a figure called the standard error of the difference. "Score differences of less than 1.5 times the standard error of the difference have little significance," ETS explains in the *ATP Guide.* "For example, the standard error of the difference for SAT-verbal scores is about 43. Only when scores differ by more than 64 points (43 × 1.5) can there be reasonable certainty that there is a genuine difference in the abilities being measured."[33] As explained in Chapter 4, the only way for scores to differ by more than 64 points on the SAT is for them to differ by 70 points. Why doesn't ETS simply tell admissions officers that score differences of less than 70 points on the verbal SAT are not significant?

And why, furthermore, does ETS not mention that this rather large margin of error is even *larger* for the math SAT? For the three examples ETS gives, the standard errors of the difference are 47, 48, and 49. This works out to margins of 71 points, 72 points, and 74 points. Admissions officers should thus ignore score differences of less than 80 points on the math SAT. But the only way they can learn this is by doing the arithmetic themselves.

All these figures are derived from ETS's calculation of the *average* standard error of measurement. For higher-scoring students, therefore, the margin of error is larger still.

On another page, ETS defines *true score* as "the score a student would earn if the test could measure ability with perfect reliability."[34] This definition depends on the (unproven) assumption that what the SAT measures is (undefined) ability. Even ignoring this, the definition is incorrect. True score is a fairly simple statistical idea that is consistently misrepresented by ETS and almost invariably misunderstood by admissions officers. A student's true score is the score he would be expected to receive on a particular test at a particular time if the effects of the test's "random error" (as estimated by the standard error of measurement) could be eliminated. It is a hypothetical, formula-derived estimate of what his average score would be if he were somehow able to take that same test under the same "physical and emotional conditions" an infinite number of times without remembering the questions from one administration to the next.

True score is not a number etched on the inside of a student's skull. It implies nothing about what a test measures. It includes no information not included in the standard error of measurement. If a student's obtained score rises as a result of coaching, or of "anxiety reduction," or of learning in school, or of reading *Taking the SAT,* or of getting better at erasing stray marks from his answer sheet, or of breaking up with his girlfriend, or of discovering oil in Oklahoma — then his true score, as estimated by the formula ETS uses, rises as well. True score does not, as its misleading name implies, remain unchanged from test to test or week to week or year to year. A better name for it would be *expected score.*

Like many testing terms (*validity* and *reliability* are two others), *true score* is highly ambiguous. It has a precise technical meaning that is distorted by everything we subjectively associate with the word *true.* Now, because ETS maintains (subjectively) that what the SAT measures is "ability" or "aptitude" (whatever they are) and nothing else, it thinks of a student's true score as his exact amount of ability or aptitude, and it says that a student's obtained score usually comes within 30 or 35 points of this exact amount. But ETS's claims about what the test measures are purely speculative and entirely unrelated to the estimation of true score. When ETS talks about true score, what it really means is "true ability." True score can be calculated with a formula; true ability cannot. If it turned out tomorrow that what the SAT measures is not ability but hair color, the meaning of a student's true score on the SAT would change but the number itself would not. True score implies nothing about the SAT's ability to measure ability; it simply provides a sort of statistical metaphor for representing the likelihood that a given form of the test will produce the same result for the same person two times in a row.

In the face of so many conflicting signals, inconsistencies, and (in my opinion) deceptions, admissions officers are left to draw their own conclusions about the SAT. Many of these conclusions are idiosyncratic and unscientific. Despite all the talk about correlation coefficients and standard errors of measurement, the SAT wouldn't enjoy the stature it does today if college admissions officers didn't at some level think of it as an absolute measure of intellectual worth. The director of admissions at Columbia defined aptitude for me as "innate ability." Students who do well in high school but poorly on the SAT are referred to as "overachievers," not as "undertesters." The term implies a moral judgment: these are people who earn better grades than they "deserve." ETS both discourages and encourages this view. Even as it urges admissions officers to be cautious in their use of the SAT, it also winks at them and nudges them under the table. The SAT is the aptitude test that doesn't test aptitude — or is it the test of aptitude that isn't an aptitude test? All the halfhearted denials, qualifications, and elaborations serve only to increase the mystique surrounding the scores.

This mystique is the true secret of the SAT's popularity. It can lead admissions officers to wild exaggerations about the importance of the scores. On a radio show in 1984, Harold R. Doughty, director of admissions at New York University, was asked whether he thought NYU would be able to get by without SATs.

"Well, yes," Doughty said, "I think I could do without them —
as long as you would permit me to add a zero to the height of every
student and thereby begin to create some numerical measures, so
that a person who is seven foot tall then would have an 800, or
whatever number we use," and so on and so on.[35] Doughty went
on as though the SAT were all that stood between NYU and
feudalism. George Hanford of the College Board, a panelist on the
same show, looked on approvingly.

ETS and the College Board encourage this sort of nonsense by
exaggerating the usefulness of the SAT and hinting darkly that
society would crumble if the test were ever abandoned. But both
organizations, aware that critics say the SAT is overemphasized,
also maintain the opposite position. In 1983 Hanford bizarrely
asserted that "there are very few institutions today which absolutely require the SAT or achievement tests, the ATP elements, for
admission."[36] This is untrue, and Hanford must know it. The
College Board itself says that admissions test scores are "required
of all candidates" at 48 percent of all colleges (including two-year
institutions) and at more than 60 percent of four-year institutions.
Furthermore, 70 percent of all colleges require admissions test
scores of at least some of their applicants.[37]

The principal justification for using the SAT is the notion that it
provides an *objective* standard in an otherwise *subjective* process.
"Humans are just terrible at making decisions about other humans," a senior ETS researcher told me. "Most psychologists who
are interested in measurement feel the same way. The general rule
of thumb is that whenever you can find some other procedure to
use instead of a human, you should. Humans have their uses, but
insofar as you can find a substitute, you're better off."

People who feel this way deceive themselves if they think requiring SAT scores reduces the well-known problems associated with
human judgments. After all, test scores have to be interpreted (and
tests have to be written) by humans. You just can't get around the
fact (assuming you want to get around it) that humans are going to
be involved. Admissions officers are every bit as quirky in their
interpretation of test scores as they are in their interpretation of,
say, messy handwriting. You don't make an admissions officer
more "objective" by giving him a bunch of numbers he doesn't

understand, especially if you haven't been straightforward about how the numbers should be interpreted.

When I told Ernest Kimmel, the director of test development for ETS's College Board programs, that I thought ETS hadn't done a very good job of informing admissions officers about the meaning of SAT scores, he agreed. "Sometimes I think we've been more successful at educating the kids than at educating the professionals," he said. "Your real problems are those admissions officers in most schools. If you visit the admissions offices, you know that there are one or two senior people, and then they've hired a bunch of recent graduates and they're paying them about nine thousand dollars a year, with no preparation in any of the disciplines that are really relevant to the jobs they're doing."

With all due respect to Kimmel, I'm not at all sure that "the kids" are better at making sense of their SAT scores than college admissions officers are. Classmates who do poorly on the test are "morons" or "retards"; high scorers are "geniuses." ETS and the College Board didn't even let students *see* their scores until 1958. "There was great fear that students would have their values warped by learning their own scores," explained Board president Frank Bowles two years later, "but I have learned from hearing my own children that SAT scores have now become one of the peer group measuring devices. One unfortunate may be dismissed with the phrase, 'That jerk — he only made 420!' "[38]

Many defenders of the SAT, including ETS, hold that one of the most important uses of the test is as an aid in "self-selection." But given the level of sophistication at which students interpret their scores, it's hard to find this very encouraging. Most students who "self-select" do so by sitting down with a directory of colleges and eliminating schools whose average SAT score differs from their own. Furthermore, most such self-selection is done on the basis of PSAT, not SAT, scores. Since the PSAT represents a student's first encounter with SAT-type questions, these scores are especially misleading. "Self-selection" doesn't strike me as much of an improvement over misinformed admissions officers.

Jerks and geniuses aside, many people would say, the correct function of the SAT is to enable colleges to find promising students

who might otherwise be lost in the shuffle. The SAT, this argument goes, puts all students on an equal footing, giving them a
uniform, color-blind test on which to demonstrate their ability.
"Unlike the personal interview, the classroom test, or the teacher's
subjective evaluation," wrote Henry Chauncey in 1961, "the objective test is a common touchstone. It gives all students who take
it the same chance, asks them to run the same race — even though
they have had different economic backgrounds, different educational, cultural, and social opportunities."[39]

This is a cheerful thought, but it has no basis in reality. As ETS
and the College Board finally acknowledged with published statistics in 1982, there is a considerable gap between the average SAT
performance of whites and that of blacks, Mexican-Americans,
and Puerto Ricans, and between people whose families have a lot
of money and people whose families don't.[40] In 1983, 7,263
whites scored above 700 on the verbal SAT; so did 66 blacks. In
the same year, 54,277 whites scored 600 or above; so did 939
blacks. (The test population included 685,219 whites and 71,490
blacks.) The mean score for whites on the verbal SAT was 443;
the mean for blacks was 339.*[41]

If colleges actually used the SAT as a "color-blind" indicator of
academic ability, you wouldn't find many minority students enrolled in selective schools. Most minority applicants who are admitted to selective colleges are admitted *in spite of* their SAT
scores, not because of them. Admission to college in these circumstances carries with it a built-in slap in the face: you can come to
our school, but you're not really entitled.

Whether the SAT is culturally biased against minorities is another hardy perennial controversy in which ETS takes the kettle
position: the tests were never biased; they've now been fixed; but
the changes have had no effect. ETS naturally says that it has
proved statistically that its tests aren't biased. Just to make sure,
for the last few years it has used "an actual member of a minority"
(as one ETS employee told me) to read every test before it's published. According to an ETS flier, "Each test is reviewed to ensure

---

*ETS wouldn't send me the publication in which these 1983 statistics appear. It also turned
down my request for the comparable publication from 1982. I ended up getting copies from
the College Board.

that the questions reflect the multicultural nature of our society and that appropriate, positive references are made to minorities and women. Each test item is reviewed to ensure that any word, phrase, or description that may be regarded as biased, sexist, or racist is removed."[42]

But the actual "sensitivity review" process is much more cursory and superficial than this description implies. The minority reviewer simply counts the number of items that refer to each of five "population subgroups" and enters these numbers on a Test Sensitivity Review Report Form. On the verbal SAT administered in May 1982, actual minority member Beverly Whittington found seven items that mentioned women, one that mentioned black Americans, two that mentioned Hispanic Americans, none that mentioned native Americans, and four that mentioned Asian Americans (actually, she was stretching here; these particular Asian Americans were Shang Dynasty Chinese, 1766–1122 B.C.). Two items overlapped, so Whittington put a "12" in the box for Total Representational Items. She also commented "OK" on the exam's test specifications, "OK" on the subgroup reference items, and "OK" on item review. She made no other remarks. If she had discovered the word *nigger* in one of the questions, presumably she would have scratched it out. ETS made Whittington take a three-day training program in "test sensitivity" before permitting her to do all of this. When her report was finished, it was stamped E.T.S. CONFIDENTIAL and SECURE. Then it was filed and forgotten.[43]

SAT items don't have to be very representational in order to be counted as Representational. The pronoun *she* is enough to make an item "woman-oriented." The SAT I took in December 1983 contained a black-oriented analogy:

---

18. DASHIKI:GARMENT:: (A) spoon:utensil   (B) hat:coat
    (C) podium:conductor   (D) foot:shoe   (E) plate:table

Dashiki is a Yoruban word for a loose-fitting tunic worn in certain parts of Africa; it enjoyed a vogue among politically aware black American males during the late sixties and early seventies. ETS put this item on the SAT to symbolize the company's profound new regard for the black experience. But are black seventeen-year-olds any more likely than white seventeen-year-olds to know what dashikis are? Would ETS ever have asked a white-oriented SAT question about Nehru jackets? Does familiarity with either garment have anything whatsoever to do with scholastic aptitude?

Fifteen years ago, ETS Test Sensitivity Reviewers, had they existed, would have found few dashikis to count in the SAT. But in 1970 the company began adding one or two "minority-oriented" reading passages to each edition. Now, because of the way the SAT is equated, ETS could only add minority-oriented reading passages that performed exactly like non-minority-oriented reading passages, since non-minority-oriented reading passages were what the SAT had always had *before*. In the same sense, it couldn't snip the word *nigger* out of one item unless it could find some way to sneak it into another. But the company had been accused of being biased against minorities and, although it denied the accusations, it decided it ought to make a public gesture.

In 1974, Steven Brill, writing for *New York* magazine, asked ETS executive Marion Epstein about these new reading passages.

> *Q. If the tests weren't culturally biased in the first place, why did you make the change?*
> *A. Because minorities feel at ease reading this kind of passage.*
> *Q. If they feel at ease reading this one, does that mean they* don't *feel at ease reading the six or seven others in the text?*
> *A. No. It just means they feel more comfortable with this one.*
> *Q. Well, if they feel more comfortable, does that mean their scores will be higher?*
> *A. No, I don't think there will be any difference in "scores."*
> *Q. Well, if there won't be any difference in scores, why would you make the change? Was it just so you could look like you were doing something?*
> *A. No, it's because when people are more comfortable, they'll do better on the test. They feel less threatened.*[44]

Is the SAT biased against blacks? A senior research scientist at ETS, who asked not to be identified, told me that black students tend to do better in college than their SAT scores predict they will.

If you have a black student and a white student with identical scores, he said, you can expect the black student to earn a higher grade point average than the white student. No doubt the motive for this assertion is high-minded: to rebut accusations that unqualified blacks are being admitted to selective schools because of favored treatment. But if the assertion is true, the SAT is literally racist: it systematically gives blacks lower SAT scores than they deserve in terms of the sole criterion by which the test's validity is judged.

But maybe the research scientist was wrong.* When I asked Arthur Kroll if the SAT penalized blacks, he said, "If you mean, Does the SAT predict as well how minority students are going to do in college as majority students, then the SAT has done as effective a job for blacks as for whites." If I understand Kroll correctly (why do so many people at ETS have so much trouble with syntax?), this means that the SAT is not biased either for or against blacks. A different story. So I asked Ernest Kimmel. "I guess I'll disagree slightly with my boss," he said. "The scores do not work exactly the same with whites and blacks. If an admissions officer uses a single admissions equation based on a mix of white and black students with the same scores and the same high school rank, he's going to predict the same grade averages. But in actuality the black students in about 80 percent of the studies seem to do a bit worse." In other words, blacks get worse grades than their SATs would predict; the test is biased against whites.

I now had three apparently contradictory explanations. I took them to Richard Noeth, the ETS official who had told me (in Chapter 2) that essay exams are different from multiple-choice exams but are neither better nor worse.

"The thing is," Noeth said, "to my knowledge, there's support-

---

*Sometime after my *Harper's* article was published, the research scientist called me to say I had been wrong and that "blacks tend to do *worse* in college than their SAT scores predict they will." I checked my tape of our conversation and have no doubt that I had accurately reported what he told me. Perhaps he changed his mind. Whether he did or not, many admissions officers would say he was right the first time. James McMenamin of Columbia told me that "educationally disadvantaged" students (meaning, for the most part, blacks) generally did better at Columbia than their SAT scores had predicted. Admissions officers at several other schools told me the same thing and said they often adjusted such students' SAT scores upward to correct for the disparity.

ing evidence for each of the three positions that you mentioned. I tend to — I believe them all. I'm sure they're all true."

Well, we've certainly cleared up this bias business. But we're left with the disparity in scores. Several hypotheses have been offered to explain this:

1. *Whites are simply more intelligent than blacks; the rich are more intelligent than the poor.*

This explanation is favored not only by dyed-in-the-wool racists but also by meritocratic purists. Daniel Seligman, associate managing editor of *Fortune,* put it this way in his publication's May 5, 1980, issue: "E.T.S. tests persist in showing some people to be smarter than others. And if some people *are* smarter than others, there might actually be some justification for an economic system in which some people have more money and authority than others. . . . The really interesting question is not whether rich people are smarter, but why they are. Is it because of their superior environments or their superior genes? The answer — also attested to in endless studies — is 'both, obviously.' " Seligman's article is entitled "The Rich Are Different." It is illustrated with a drawing of a Rolls-Royce whose license plate reads "IQ 200."[45]

This is pure, unreconstructed Carl Campbell Brigham and the product of an almost unbelievable naiveté about American society. Once, on a reporting assignment, I sat in a bar at an exclusive country club and listened to a silver-haired millionaire tell me that the reason there are so few black professional golfers is that blacks aren't smart enough to grasp the intricacies of the game. The backdrop for our conversation was a golf course where blacks were not allowed to set foot even as guests. The idea that there might be a connection between all such prohibitions and the dearth of black golf pros had never occurred to this man.

To recast Daniel Seligman's argument: If the Professional Golfers Association persists in showing some people to be smarter than others, might there not be some justification for a society in which some people are allowed to join country clubs and others are not?

Racial prejudice is so pervasive and insidious that it can contaminate even the most "scientific" experiments. The history of psychometrics has been, in many ways, the history of self-deception. Terman, Goddard, Yerkes, Brigham — their private hatreds largely determined their findings. The fact that "endless studies" of comparative intelligence — from Army Alpha to Arthur Jensen's experiments with reaction time[46] — have shown similar results doesn't strengthen the case: If new findings correlate highly with discredited old findings, shouldn't that cast doubt on the quality of the new findings? Since no one knows what "intelligence" is (a high score on a multiple-choice test? a low score on a golf course?) or how to measure it directly, intelligence testing is extremely susceptible to the conscious and unconscious predispositions of the testers. Measures that seem to confirm these biases are held to be measures of intelligence; measures that don't confirm them are presumed to be measures of something else. When studies show that the wealthy in America generally score higher on aptitude tests than the poor, people begin to talk about genetically determined differences in "mental capacity"; when studies show that Japanese and Taiwanese first-graders score higher on aptitude tests than their American counterparts, people talk about "low teacher salaries and curriculum content."[47]

2. *The test is not a fair measure for blacks and members of various other disadvantaged social groups.*

This argument holds that questions on the SAT systematically penalize students from outside the American economic elite. The poor tend to do worse than the wealthy on the SAT, this argument states, because the questions on the test reflect only a white upper-middle-class point of view; if the questions were written differently, racial and economic differences would disappear.

ETS and the College Board are very sensitive about this issue, as their adoption of "minority-oriented" reading passages proves. But both ETS and the Board believe firmly that this was a solution without a problem; the passages were added to improve public relations, not to correct an injustice. ETS says that wealthy whites don't have an undeserved advantage on the SAT, and it says it has proven this statistically.

Thomas F. Donlon, an ETS research scientist, addressed this issue several years ago in the *College Board Review,* a quarterly magazine for Board members and others. "The SAT," he wrote, "by virtue of the breadth of its coverage, and the careful editing of its content, is a balanced instrument with relevance for a variety of candidates. Although it is now only two hours long, it covers a range of topics and tasks that tends not to favor any one sub-group."[48] To prove his point, Donlon analyzed an SAT item of the sort that critics often point to when they claim that wealthy whites have an unfair advantage on the test. The item was an analogy from a verbal SAT:

RUNNER : MARATHON : :

(A) envoy : embassy
(B) martyr : massacre
(C) referee : tournament
(D) oarsman : regatta
(E) horse : stable

Regattas, Donlon conceded, "are less frequently associated with the minority experience." But he said that most white people prob-ably don't know much about them either. And although he ac-knowledged that only 22 percent of black students — compared with 53 percent of whites — had selected the correct answer, he said that this did not make the question unfair. To prove it, he compared the performance of blacks with the performance of whites of "matched ability" (as determined by SAT scores). Looked at this way, the results were closer. Only 26 percent of the "matched" whites selected the right answer, compared with 22 percent of the blacks.[49]

"It is clear," Donlon concluded, "that these matched whites perform very similarly to blacks. The clear implication of this is that it is not a black subculture which influences these patterns (for whites are not raised in that subculture), but some sort of general lack of knowledge or understanding of this item. . . . When the responses are examined in depth, the patterns of success and error for racially defined groups of comparable ability are not differ-ent."*[50]

---

*Actually, the way I figure it, 22 percent and 26 percent *are* different, as are the "patterns of error" Donlon gives for other responses. If these differences are meaningless, Donlon should explain why.

But all of this begs the real question: What exactly can ETS mean by "ability" if one of the differences between having it and not having it is the difference between knowing and not knowing about oarsmen and regattas (or about polo and mallets, or golf and clubs — as other SAT questions have asked)? Surely the fact that rowing, polo, and golf are sports of the wealthy accounts in some measure for the mysterious "general lack of knowledge" that Donlon detects among the huddled masses. Donlon's wholly circular statistical argument does not prove that the SAT "tends not to favor any one subgroup." Obviously the SAT favors at least *one* subgroup: the subgroup that does well on the SAT. And if this particular subgroup has certain consistent characteristics (familiarity with polo equipment, for example) that have little to do with "ability" but much to do with success on the test, then the SAT is unfair.*

I can think of many subgroups for whom the SAT is unfair: the subgroup that believes coaching doesn't work; the subgroup that thinks guessing is wrong; the subgroup that takes the test under the supervision of incompetent proctors; the subgroup that takes the test under the supervision of incompetent observers from "Princeton"; the subgroup that doesn't cheat; the subgroup that believes the SAT measures what the College Board once called "the future worth of candidates";[51] the subgroup that attends schools where ETS tests are not a way of life; the subgroup that doesn't understand the way the test is constructed; the subgroup that uses the Arco strategy for answering analogy items; the subgroup that applies to colleges with uninformed admissions officers.

---

*In the mid-1970s, the Golden Rule Insurance Company of Lawrenceville, Illinois, sued ETS on behalf of five blacks who had failed an ETS exam used by the state to license insurance agents. Golden Rule argued that the test was biased against blacks, since white candidates as a group earned substantially higher scores on it. ETS fought the suit for years, dragging it through various courts in Illinois. Finally, in November 1984, when it seemed clear that the case would actually go to trial, ETS settled with Golden Rule. The testing company agreed to pretest questions for the Illinois exam (something it had never done before) and to eliminate those items on which there is a marked disparity between performance by whites and performance by members of minorities. The settlement applies only to the Illinois insurance exam, but in time the principle will undoubtedly be applied to other standardized tests, including the SAT.

Another fairness issue, and one that ETS has never addressed, is the fairness of the criterion against which the test's "validity" is measured. Even if ETS could somehow prove that the test itself gives no one an unfair advantage, could it also prove that freshman grades are as fair a criterion for, say, blacks as they are for whites? Did the 14 black freshmen at Middlebury College this year have the same academic experience as the 442 white ones? Did their isolation affect their grades? Can the SAT really be a "uniform" measure if the standard against which its results are judged is not itself uniform?

3. *The test doesn't actually penalize anyone, although it does prove that the educational opportunities available to blacks are worse than those available to whites.*

This is sometimes known as the thermometer hypothesis. It says that the SAT holds no more responsibility for the deprivations of the underprivileged than a thermometer does for a fever. Test scores, this argument holds, serve to remind us of how much remains to be done in correcting social injustices and improving the quality of certain schools. The SAT is only a messenger; it is not to be blamed for its message.

As is true on a great many issues, ETS and the College Board maintain virtually every conceivable position on this point. Many of these positions are contradictory. ETS tends to shift among them depending on which argument it thinks a critic is trying to make.

When I interviewed Gregory Anrig in 1983 and told him I thought the SAT had harmed blacks, he said, "All a test does is reflect what's happened to someone. Is there equal education in the United States? No. Nowhere near it. Does economic status affect the kind of education you have access to? Absolutely. Do tests reflect that? Yes. The test doesn't cause that. It's simply reporting."

This is the thermometer hypothesis in action: the SAT serves society by recording the educational "temperature" of the schools. "Don't throw out the thermometer because it reports a fever," Anrig declared at an educational conference in Washington in 1983. "If we blame it on the test, we throw away the best indicator that keeps the issue most in front of the public."[52] But ETS also holds the opposite opinion — that the SAT is *not* a valid educational thermometer. When the national SAT average is released every year, ETS reminds editorial writers that the SAT — as an "aptitude" test not based on any school curriculum — is not a suitable measure of the general quality of education. "I think the SAT is totally inappropriate," Arthur Kroll told me, "as a measure of both longitudinal trends and the quality of education in American schools." But if the SAT is an inappropriate measure of the quality of education, how can it possibly be an appropriate measure of the quality of *black* education, particularly when only a small and highly unrepresentative sample of blacks take the test in the first place? The picture the SAT gives of black schooling must thus be terribly distorted. What good is a thermometer that doesn't give accurate readings?

While it claims that the SAT only "reports" on educational opportunity, ETS also claims that the test *improves* educational opportunity. During the past twenty years or so, ETS has frequently asserted that the SAT has transformed American society by changing the rules that determine who gets ahead. The thermometer doesn't just measure the fever, this argument goes; it also cures it. Before the SAT, ETS said in 1980, "selective admissions to higher education was far more a matter of class and economic status"; introduction of the SAT "resulted in a substantial increase in opportunities for educational advancement of low-income students."[53] ETS and the College Board both become quite moist-eyed when they take up this theme. They very nearly claim credit for the civil rights movement, saying that the improving status of blacks in this country has paralleled the rise of the SAT. Former College Board chairman Fred Hargadon has even claimed that criticism of the SAT comes from society's privileged, people who " 'made it' on merit" but now want to "change the ground rules" because they fear that multiple-choice tests will "show their offspring to have less talent and less potential than the offspring of minority or low income families."[54]

All of this is fantasy. SAT scores have never been a threat to the social hegemony of the white upper middle class; indeed, they have reinforced it. Low-income and minority students, as a group, simply do not do as well on the SAT as wealthy white students.

ETS tries to have it both ways on this issue. In the same publication in which it claimed the SAT had brought about "a substantial
increase in opportunities . . . of low-income students," ETS also
said that "there is no evidence that use of test scores *per se* has a
dramatic impact on opportunities for low-income students."[55]
This second statement is meant to assuage the fears of those who
think that the underprivileged, because they score lower, are
penalized by the SAT. But it is a flat contradiction of the simul-
taneous claim that the SAT is a social equalizer.

Also in the same publication, ETS acknowledged that when
selective colleges admit certain students, they do so not only because the schools "place importance . . . on achievement, accomplishment, demonstrated ability, and special talents," but also because they "seek to redress effects of past inequality and to admit
groups of students that are diverse in terms of geography, family
economic background, race, and other characteristics."[56] This,
too, directly rebuts the absurd notion that the SAT is responsible
for the easing of social strictures against blacks and others in the
last quarter-century; if admissions officers have to overlook SAT
scores and other indicators of "demonstrated ability" in order to
admit blacks, how can blacks be said to have gained *as a result* of
their SAT scores?

If ETS insists on taking credit for the social progress of
minorities, must it not also take the blame for trends in the opposite direction? The number of blacks awarded bachelor's degrees
fell 1.6 percent between 1976 and 1981; the number awarded
master's degrees fell 16 percent in the same period. "There is a lot
of evidence that we are losing ground," said Samuel L. Meyers,
president of the National Association for Equal Opportunity in
Higher Education in 1984.[57] Is the SAT to blame?

ETS's notion that colleges adopted standardized admissions
tests in order to diversify their student bodies is strictly mythological. College Board candidate volume remained quite low for the
organization's first forty-five years. Only 11,470 took College
Board tests in 1930; 9,083 took them in 1935; 17,377 took them
in 1940. The vast majority of these students (73.1 percent in 1930,
78.5 percent in 1935, 77.0 percent in 1940) were from eastern
states. Virtually all of them were applying to eastern schools.[58]

The Board's candidate volume grew considerably in the late 1940s, but this was only because returning soldiers were swelling the nation's applicant pool to an unprecedented size. It was the GI Bill, not the SAT, that diversified higher education. The SAT merely provided an inexpensive and apparently "uniform" method for quickly sorting through thousands of applications. It did not create (and was not intended to create) diversity *within* institutions. As Michael S. Schudson wrote in the *Harvard Educational Review* in 1972, "More young people attend institutions of higher education now than ever before . . . and this fact has been used to argue that a young person's class origin is less important in determining his access to higher education than it once was. This may be true but is certainly misleading if it is meant to suggest a growing equalization of opportunity in American society. . . . As soon as higher education came to serve a large or mass public, it grew more stratified within itself."[59] One of the instruments used to create and maintain this stratification was the SAT.

If SAT scores reflect the fundamental inequality of American society (as Gregory Anrig said), then admissions decisions based on them do, too. The SAT is much more than a thermometer if it serves to maintain the unfairness it allegedly exposes. And it is much less than a social equalizer if it functions to reproduce the status quo.

The crime of the SAT is not that it conveys an unwelcome "message" about the level of education American society provides for the underprivileged; the crime of the SAT is that it disguises this inequality as a morally neutral difference in "aptitude." Wealthy whites don't see SAT results as proof that the poor are mistreated. Like the *Fortune* editor quoted earlier, they see them as proof that mistreatment of the poor is fair.

"Black children are educationally retarded because the public schools they are required to attend are polluted by racism," wrote Kenneth B. Clark in 1982. "Their low scores reflect the racial segregation and inferiority of these schools. These children are perceived and treated as if they were uneducable. From the earliest grades, they are programmed for failure. Throughout their lives, they are classic examples of the validity of the concept of victimization by self-fulfilling prophecy."[60]

Earning a high score on an ETS test can give a great boost to a student's self-confidence, altering his expectations. But, of course, earning a low score has the opposite effect. Researchers from the University of Virginia and Carnegie-Mellon University discovered in 1982 that they could improve the college grades of struggling freshmen simply by telling them that their sophomore grades would probably be better. This good news also produced an immediate improvement in the students' scores on a reading comprehension test. According to an account of the experiment in *Psychology Today,* "The idea of telling worried students that their academic problems would be temporary came from studies in 'attribution therapy' that suggest that people have a better chance of solving a problem if they think their difficulty comes from a tough situation rather than from their character."[61] We'll never know how strong this effect is with ETS tests, because ETS, like a bad doctor, buries its mistakes.

When directories rate colleges as "highly selective" or "competitive," they do so largely on the basis of SAT scores. A demotion in status can have a big impact on a school's attractiveness both to candidates and to potential donors. This puts pressure on admissions officers to keep their SAT averages high. The director of admissions at a selective liberal arts college told me that he had been sent a memo by an administrative higher-up asking, "What would it take to increase our SAT average by 100 points?" The president of the college, the admissions director told me, had "lost a grant, because our SAT average wasn't what this donor wanted." The president also thought it would be easier for the school to market itself to students if the SAT average were higher.

"I wouldn't do it," the admissions director told me, "but I'm tempted to do what some other schools are doing, which is to remove minority students and other subgroups from score calculations, to get the average up." A simpler solution, of course, would be to admit fewer minority students and take fewer chances on students with good grades but low scores. Black enrollment at many selective colleges has declined in recent years. Is the SAT the reason?

For all its public piety on the subject of equal opportunity, ETS has demonstrated remarkably little enlightenment in its own practices.

The company didn't hire its first non-white executive until 1970. Before 1982, when it made broad readjustments in its pay scales in response to protests and petitions from black employees, it paid white employees higher salaries than black employees in identical jobs. In 1979, black employees sent a memo to top management, pointing out that "there has never been a Black staff member elevated to the position of officer at ETS, there is a paucity of Black representation at the levels of administrative directors, area directors, division directors, program directors, and managers of operating departments. It is still possible to walk through areas at ETS and see only one or no Black members of the clerical staffs. . . . Why is it that when one sees Black people working at the Henry Chauncey Conference Center, one sees them working as waitresses and maids?"[62] Even by 1983, only 7.3 percent of ETS's officials, managers, and professionals were black (as opposed to 40 percent of its service workers and 42 percent of the people depicted in photographs in its 1983 annual report).[63]

An ETS research scientist told me in 1983 there was only one black psychologist in the research department. I asked him why there weren't more. "Well," he said, "what you have to realize is that all of these things have to do with how many are available. I'm talking about psychologists, people with Ph.D.'s. So a prior question is, why are there so few black Ph.D.'s? If there are a lot of black Ph.D.'s, then there are more people who could potentially be working at ETS. If there are none, or very few, then obviously there are very few. I think it reflects the fact that there are very few black Ph.D.'s in psychology."

This is every company's explanation for the absence of blacks on its payroll: we'd hire more of them, but we can't seem to find any. But of all the employers in the country, ETS has the least right to say this. If the SAT has been opening up educational opportunities for blacks for nearly half a century, why can't ETS round up a respectable number of black Ph.D.'s?

11

Mythology

IN MARCH 1980, the *Bulletin of the American Association for Higher Learning* published a paper that, in cautious academic prose, threatens the very existence of the Educational Testing Service. The paper, written by Rodney T. Hartnett and Robert A. Feldmesser, two senior research scientists at ETS, was called "College Admissions Testing and the Myth of Selectivity." It pointed out the curious fact that although virtually all American colleges require their applicants to take a standardized admissions test, hardly any actually use the scores in making admissions decisions.[1]

"Many of the institutions that accept large proportions of their applicants nevertheless require the applicants to submit an admissions-test score," the paper said. "Ninety-two percent of all institutions in the random sample from the [College Board's] *College Handbook* had such a requirement; even among those accepting at least 90 percent of their applicants, 88 percent had such a requirement. . . . These figures put admissions tests in a new light and raise interesting questions about the role they are playing in the admissions policies and practices of particular colleges and universities, and in higher education generally."[2]

The overwhelming majority of colleges and universities in this country require standardized admissions tests but aren't using the results. "There's no way they could be," Hartnett told me. "If you look at the distribution of American institutions of higher education with regard to selectivity, you'd probably be amazed to learn how many of them are either open-door institutions or accept virtually everybody who applies. They may turn away kids who have some record of drug use or something."

ETS essentially confirms Hartnett and Feldmesser's thesis. Ernest Kimmell of ETS told me that there are only "fifty or sixty colleges and universities" that are still selective. The month before Hartnett and Feldmesser's study was published, ETS issued a pamphlet, *Test Scores and Family Income,* in which it said, "Many colleges are not selective and admit nearly all applicants."[3] But ETS did not point out that most of these colleges require admissions test scores anyway.*

"At a large number of institutions," Hartnett told me, "requiring SAT scores for admissions doesn't make any sense at all. It's crazy. But they do, most of them. Some institutions will say, Well, we use the scores for non-admissions purposes; we use them for guidance, or for placement. Now, the SAT wasn't designed for guidance or placement. Other measures would be more appropriate for those purposes. But they don't do it anyway. Even when they say they do, they don't use the scores for guidance and placement."

ETS might argue that some colleges that admit virtually all of their applicants and thus appear not to be selective may nonetheless benefit from the SAT if their applicants tend to select themselves on the basis of their SAT scores. This idea has a certain plausibility. But ETS has never formally studied self-selection and is in no position to speculate about the thought processes of college candidates. ETS does not know how students select themselves, or whether they make good decisions when they do, or how

---

*Hartnett and Feldmesser's study is sometimes quoted as a sort of left-handed vindication for ETS. Robert L. Linn, a professor of psychology at the University of Illinois at Urbana-Champaign and former director of developmental research at ETS, wrote in the *American Psychologist* in 1982 that a "fact that is apparently too subtle to deal with, or that perhaps is ignored because it weakens the critics' argument, is that most colleges are not very selective. . . . Hartnett and Feldmesser have noted that 'for the great majority of the one and a half million students who currently apply to undergraduate colleges each year, test scores have virtually no effect in determining whether they will attend college,' yet ETS is painted as the keeper of a very narrow gate."[4] Linn means in part to justify continued use of the SAT: If most colleges don't use the SAT scores they require, how can ETS be viewed as a powerful, evil institution? But his argument really makes a very different point: If most colleges don't use the scores, why don't they stop requiring them?

all of this affects college admissions. Nor has ETS published explanatory materials that would enable students, parents, and guidance counselors to make intelligent interpretations of SAT scores. The *ATP Guide,* discussed in the previous chapter, probably does more harm than good.

Why would colleges require SAT scores they had no intention of using?

"We came to the suspicion," Hartnett said, "that most institutions that are nonselective but nonetheless require the test scores do so to maintain this aura of selectivity. They're imitating the truly selective institutions, and they think it's in their best interest to do that. One other reason they do it is that it doesn't cost them anything. It costs the kids. If, in fact, the institutions had to pay, you'd better believe they'd stop in a hurry."

Contrary to what most people believe, it doesn't cost a college anything to require and receive SAT scores, or Achievement Test scores, or any other ETS test scores. The entire cost is borne by the students. In New York State in 1983–84, ETS and the College Board charged $11.50 for every SAT and $18 for up to three Achievements taken on a single day. There is a slew of extra charges for things like late registration ($10), test center change ($10), standby fee ($22), score verification ($5.50), a copy of test questions and answers ($7), and extra score reports (three reports are free; any more cost $4 each). Advanced Placement tests cost $46 each. And so on.

That's what students paid. What did they pay for? They paid for things like the subsidized lunches in the ETS cafeteria, for mowing the grass on the baseball diamond, and for tidying up the little island in the middle of the goose pond. They also paid for dozens of ancillary studies and services that ETS provides to high schools and colleges — the real "customers" — free of charge, along with test scores. If fifty students in a high school took the SAT, they paid ETS to send their principal a free analysis of how they performed on the test. If 100 people in the world asked ETS to send their scores to a particular college, that college received a free summary of information all about them.

"We also allow the colleges to tell us which students followed through and applied," ETS's Leonard Ramist told me, "and which ones were accepted, which enrolled, and even which persisted after the freshman year, and then we give them other summaries that give them much more detail about the entering class as it progresses from initial scoring through enrolling to persistence. And there are many other services that go along with that: tapes for colleges, group reports for groups of colleges, lots of others. Colleges can also get up to four subgroups of students, enabling them to look at in-state students, or engineering students, or minority students, or whatever."

All of this information is less useful to the colleges than it is to ETS. ETS floods institutions with statistics to make itself seem indispensable and to uphold the "scientific" façade it has erected around its tests. If the colleges had to pay, few of them would bother.

One ETS employee I spoke to disagreed. "The colleges would just pay for it," he said, "and then pass the cost along to the students. It's no big deal. It's like: General Motors has to have airbags? Sure. So we'll add $300 to the cost of the car."

If memory serves, there are no airbags in General Motors cars. GM didn't think it could pass the cost along to consumers, so it resisted regulations requiring passive restraints in cars. The ETS employee's analogy does not best express the relationship between standardized tests and airbags.

When I told Gregory Anrig that I thought colleges ought to have to pay for the tests they required — and that students who apply to nonselective colleges shouldn't be forced to subsidize the cost of testing students who do — he just laughed. "The SAT is a *very small cost*," he said. "What's this year's fee — $11.25, or something like that? What else can you do in society for that price? You can go to a movie, but that's about it." Anrig also told me that ETS had nothing to do with setting the price of the SAT. "The fees are totally a decision of the College Board," he said. But this is not correct. In its contract with ETS, the Board agrees not to change test fees "without prior advice to and consultation with ETS."[5] In fact, ETS essentially determines the fee for the SAT.

ETS's principal product is paid for by people who have no choice but to buy it, and their purchase is required by people who pay nothing for that privilege. If the SAT were required by only those few colleges that actually use the scores, the cost would be prohibitive and the SAT — the cornerstone of the cult of mental measurement and of ETS's financial statement — would go bust. As Hartnett and Feldmesser began to discuss their research about test use, ETS put pressure on them to alter their findings.

"Over a period of time," Hartnett said, "at a series of meetings, people would try to get us to change our minds, and we became rather obstinate. And over a period of time our thinking about that, which was obviously so deviant from the corporate interests, was one that led them eventually to regard us as people you couldn't count on. Increasingly, they wanted their research staff to be 'team players,' and that phrase was used time and again. I perceived a definite change at ETS in that regard over the course of my fifteen-year stay there. When I went to ETS in 1966, ETS was a very confident organization. The attitude then would have been: If Hartnett wants to say something that smacks of anti-SAT-ism, let him say it; we're strong, we're healthy. But as ETS became less confident, more insecure, all that changed."

When higher-ups at the College Board caught wind of what Hartnett and Feldmesser were saying about the SAT, they became enraged and tried to make ETS prevent them from conducting a symposium on test requirements at a national educational meeting in San Francisco. ETS didn't forbid the symposium outright, but it permitted only one of the two researchers to attend.

"Hartnett and Feldmesser made ETS and the College Board very nervous," an ETS researcher, who asked not to be identified, told me. "They showed that the SAT is not really serving any purpose for the great majority of the kids who take it, except for the ones who apply to Harvard, Yale, and Princeton. That finding caused some dismay."

Hartnett and Feldmesser's transgression was not forgotten by ETS. In 1982, both were given the choice of either leaving the company or accepting new jobs outside research. Hartnett quit; he's now on the faculty at Rutgers. Feldmesser decided to stay and was put to work writing test questions, something ETS also hires teenagers to do. ETS officially described both actions as "cost-cutting" moves necessitated by a projected $3 million cutback in federal funding for the company's research projects. But both men were tenured researchers. Hartnett had to be given an extremely generous severance bonus (according to ETS's federal tax return for 1982, he was paid $74,927 for his final thirty days as an ETS employee), and Feldmesser continued to be paid his old salary.[6]

If ETS's real motive was to cut expenses, why did it offer to keep both men at full pay? Joy McIntyre of the Information Division told me that the men were offered new jobs "in another division of ETS that was fully funded by client work."[7] All this means is that ETS was quietly passing the cost of their salaries along to test-takers, who would never know they were being overcharged for item writing. But if ETS was simply going to bill the clients, why didn't it put the men to work doing research in those testing programs instead of writing items, a job for which they were overpaid and undertrained? Clearly the company's intention was to force the two men out by offering them assignments that senior research scientists could be counted on to find humiliating. Shortly after he went to work writing test questions, Feldmesser also quit.

ETS has some peculiar ideas about scientific research. "Beginning in the late 1970s," Hartnett told me, "ETS started to put pressure — at first subtle, and then, recently, not at all subtle — pressure on researchers and even senior researchers to write proposals or take part in research activities that were, in my opinion, stupid, or crazy. The only conceivable reason for ETS to be hustling some of those research grants was because they knew there was money out there to pay for them." In a closed company hearing in 1982, Martin Katz, a senior researcher, said that in applying (successfully) for a grant from the W. K. Kellogg Foundation, ETS had made "horseback estimates" of its costs because "we knew what the traffic would bear."[8] Researchers are often assigned to projects not on the basis of their expertise but on the basis of their availability or their ability to attract funding.

On some research projects, ETS is more selective. "When it came time to marshal a group of people or identify an individual to do research or write a position paper on a topic central to ETS's defense to the public — on, say, the question of whether the SAT is valid for blacks — they would never consider going to people they know are not true-blue ETS-ers," Hartnett said. "The people who were put to work on those projects were people who stepped forward and were good soldiers."

Now that the mood at ETS has changed, more and more of the company's researchers are trying to act like good soldiers. "ETS has become a mean-spirited place in the last few years," one of the company's psychologists told me in 1983. "It used to be a place where there really was this academic freedom. But now ETS has become very paranoid. When we write memos for internal use about something, one of the vice presidents will go through it literally word by word and say, 'Well, shouldn't we say something else?' He's even advocated censoring research reports so they don't give ammunition to the critics. I mean, I would never fake anything about saying whatever I felt. But you don't want to say something that will get you in dutch with one of your superiors. There've been several cuts in the staff in research, and the threat is that if you're not cooperative, they'll remember you the next time they fire people."

Hartnett and Feldmesser demonstrated that SAT scores are used at only a few dozen selective colleges. But how genuinely *useful* are they even at these schools? New research by James Crouse of the University of Delaware indicates that they may not be useful at all.

Crouse has yet to publish his findings in final form, but he summarized them in an early draft circulated among colleagues in 1984. In general, he drew three conclusions:

> 1. The SAT contributes little or nothing to the ability of admissions officers at most colleges to make better admissions decisions from among their applicants. Most colleges could ignore their applicants' SAT scores without appreciably altering either the accuracy of their admissions decisions or the academic performance and graduation rates of those they admit.
> 2. SAT scores contribute little or nothing to the vast majority of students' decisions about whether a college is appropriate to their ability. . . .
> 3. The SAT does not reduce the number of qualified applicants who are rejected who are from low income and poorly educated families, and nonwhite backgrounds. . . .[9]

When colleges attempt to determine the usefulness of the SAT, they generally perform (or ask ETS to perform) a statistical analysis that estimates the success of SAT scores at predicting freshman grades. They also compare this "predictive validity" with that of high school record* alone and with that of high school record and SAT scores combined. Whatever meaning one ascribes to the correlations thus derived (see the previous chapter), these studies have invariably shown that record and scores combined are better at predicting freshman grades than either factor on its own. It is this increase in predictive power that is said to justify use of the SAT.

As Crouse points out, however, such analyses can be extremely misleading. The goal of admissions is not the prediction of freshman grades per se but, rather, the selection of a freshman class. A student's SAT scores can be said to provide important information only when they differ so markedly from his high school record that they lead admissions officers to make decisions they would not otherwise have made. According to Crouse, this doesn't happen very often. A better way of thinking about the SAT, he says, is to examine the extent to which using SAT scores enables admissions officers to admit students they mistakenly would have rejected or to reject students they mistakenly would have admitted. His conclusion is not a happy one for ETS. "The SAT does increase the validity coefficient," he says, "but when this increment is translated into the percentage of correct admissions decisions, the SAT now appears to add virtually no additional information beyond the high school record."

The SAT in this view is something like a tachometer in a car with an automatic transmission: it provides information that has essentially no practical value.

"I think ETS can make a very strong case," Crouse told me, "that the SAT makes a big contribution to forecasting effectiveness and efficiency, in the sense that if you have a candidate with low grades but high SAT scores, or vice versa, the scores and grades really do forecast different college outcomes. The problem is that there aren't very many of those people. The SAT isn't telling you anything very interesting. It's a little like saying a person who goes to college for a thousand years will be rich. But no one goes to college for a thousand years. ETS is predicting for cases that don't exist in any great number."

---

*Remember that "high school record," in ETS's usage, means simply high school grade point average or class rank.

Crouse's first step was to compare the results of two admissions strategies — one using high school rank alone, the other using high school rank and SATs. The idea was to determine whether a strategy based on rank and scores combined would produce a significantly different freshman class from the one produced by rank alone. Using data from a national sample of 2,781 actual college applicants, Crouse found that the two strategies led to identical admissions decisions for 90.8 percent of the students. "Only 9.2 percent," he says, "would be accepted by one policy and not the other." Crouse also found that the results were essentially the same no matter where he set the cutoff for admission.[10] He confirmed his findings with data from another national sample, with summary data from ETS's own validity studies of 412 colleges, and with data from individual schools of differing selectivities. In each case, Crouse says, he found "strong support for the general conclusion that when admissions are based on predicted freshman grades, a policy based on high school rank and SAT scores will make admissions predictions that are very similar to ones based on high school rank alone."[11]

Crouse had thus determined that the addition of SAT scores to a simple admissions formula produced different admissions decisions in only a small percentage of cases. The next step was to determine whether using the SAT produced *better* decisions in the few cases where it made a difference.

At this stage in his research, Crouse examined the outcomes of actual admissions decisions. He followed the students in his data sample into college and analyzed their performance in relation to the two admissions strategies. The idea was to determine whether an admissions policy that incorporated SAT scores produced a better class than one that did not.

Using "successful freshman grade point average" as the criterion, Crouse found that adding SAT scores enabled admissions officers to make only 2.7 additional correct decisions in every 100 cases. (With a more stringent admissions standard, the improvement dropped to 2.2 students in 100.) Using "successful attainment of a Bachelor's degree" as the criterion, Crouse found that the SAT improved admissions decisions for only one student in a thousand. Using "mean freshman grade point average" as the criterion, Crouse found that addition of the SAT improved the freshman average by only 0.02 on a 4-point scale.[12]

Crouse found that in 1.3 cases out of 100, using both rank and SAT scores enabled colleges to admit an ultimately successful student (freshman grade point average above 2.5) who would have been rejected by a policy based on rank alone. But he also found that in 1.4 cases out of 100, using rank alone enabled colleges to accept a successful student who would have been rejected if his scores had also been considered. In other words, *not* using the SAT produced a very slight increase in successful admissions decisions.[13]

ETS might argue that SAT scores are nonetheless invaluable in those few admissions cases where class rank and SAT scores greatly contradict each other. But the actual admissions policies of colleges suggest that this is not the case. A number of admissions officers told me that the least attractive applicant they could think of was one with low high school grades but high SAT scores — someone ETS would call an underachiever. A former Harvard admissions officer told me that such a student was "the worst college candidate in the world — just not an attractive college student." At an ETS conference in 1983, Fred Hargadon, head of admissions at Stanford and former chairman of the College Board, said the same thing. He described as "unwise" admissions policies in which "a student with low GPA may offset that by having high test scores."

But the "unattractive" college student selected by the "unwise" admissions policy is precisely the one who benefits most from a selection strategy in which SAT scores are combined with class rank. In such a case, paying attention to SAT scores would lead admissions officers to make what many of them feel is a very bad decision.

What about students with good grades and low scores? Every admissions officer I've ever talked to has told me that no student with good grades was ever rejected solely because his test scores were low. Some excellent students simply don't do well on multiple-choice tests. In a case like this, admissions officers say they examine the rest of the applicant's file, assessing the quality of his high school and the difficulty of his courses, and look for clues in application essays and letters of recommendation. If the student earned his good grades in hard courses at a tough school, admissions officers say, his scores aren't held against him. But all this means is that a candidate like this is considered as though he had never taken the SAT.

What about schools that use SAT scores as an absolute cutoff for admissions? Some colleges and universities simply admit all students who score above a certain level and reject all those who score below. For these schools, the SAT provides an economical alternative to making individual admissions decisions. Certainly these schools would be at a disadvantage if they didn't have the SAT. But ETS and the College Board have consistently maintained that such practices constitute a misuse of the SAT. They tell admissions officers that the tests should not be used "as the sole basis for important decisions affecting the lives of individuals, when other information of equal or greater relevance and the resources for using such information are available."[14] ETS has also said, in publications for admissions officers, that it has always made a "specific advisement against the use of a cutoff score."[15] Surely ETS cannot now maintain that such *misuse* provides the ultimate justification for continued *use* of the SAT.

The use of absolute cutoffs also has a disproportionate impact on minorities. Since blacks as a group earn average scores approximately 100 points lower on each half of the test than those earned by whites, cutoffs necessarily exclude a higher percentage of them than of whites. In 1983, Massachusetts considered limiting admission to state colleges and universities to students with combined SAT scores of 800 and above. The proposal was rejected, but if this standard had been adopted nationwide, something like three-quarters of the blacks who took the SAT in 1983 would have been barred from public higher education.

"I believe," Crouse concludes, "that the widely given advice by the College Board and ETS to colleges on how they should use their applicants' score reports — to make better academic selection decisions from their applicant pools — is very difficult to defend. If there were no costs of using the SAT to anyone, then one might argue that a massive admissions testing program that harms no one, yet helps colleges better select from their applicant pools by even a tiny amount, is a good thing. But the SAT has substantial costs that would seem to far outweigh the tiny amount of help I find colleges can get from the SAT."

Bowdoin College, a top liberal arts school in Maine, stopped requiring SAT scores in 1970. The plan, devised by Richard Moll, then director of admissions, was adopted because Bowdoin's faculty "believed there was an unnecessary emphasis on scores for admission to the most selective colleges."[16] One reason Bowdoin made the SAT optional was that in the two years before the plan was adopted, only 31 percent of all Bowdoin's honors graduates had scored above the class average on both SATs, while 24 percent had scored below. The policy was also frankly intended to distinguish Bowdoin from other good small liberal arts colleges by giving it an image that would stick in the minds of potential applicants. An admissions officer at one of these colleges told me he thought the decision had been a "publicity stunt." Then he smiled, sighed, and said, "I wish I'd thought of it first."

ETS did not take kindly to the optional SAT policy. "Bowdoin can make whatever decisions it wants," Arthur Kroll told me somewhat snippily when I asked him in 1983 if he thought Bowdoin was irresponsible not to require the SAT. "I certainly wouldn't classify them as irresponsible."

Kroll went on to say that the SAT helped colleges weed out in advance students who probably wouldn't be able to hack it and that "there's not much benefit in admitting a lot of people who are going to end up flunking out." But if the SAT helps colleges do that, I said, isn't Bowdoin being just the teeniest bit irresponsible in not requiring it?

"It depends on what their goals are," he said. "They may not have a goal of maximizing every student's educational performance at Bowdoin. Bowdoin may care less as to whether all students in fact benefit from that experience. But if that were their goal, then I would say that they were being irresponsible."

There. I'm glad he got it off his chest. But it's been nearly fifteen years since the plan went into effect, and Bowdoin hasn't had to auction off its dormitories yet. Its academic reputation is still as high as it used to be. Last year the college evaluated the results of the optional SAT plan and decided to continue it. "We probably get a higher proportion of able students who have proven themselves to everyone but the College Board," said spokesman Richard Mersereau.[17]

If a college like Bowdoin can get by without requiring SATs, how many schools can convincingly argue that they can't? And if those schools really *do* believe they can't do without the tests, why shouldn't they have to pay for the luxury of requiring students to take them? Where is Milton Friedman when you need him?

12

Testing and Teachers

IN NOVEMBER 1983, the governor of Arkansas signed a bill requiring public school teachers to pass competency tests in order to keep their jobs. As you might expect, the new law was harshly criticized by teachers. As you might not expect, it was also criticized by ETS, which sells the examination Arkansas originally wanted its teachers to take.[1]

"It is morally and educationally wrong," said Gregory Anrig, "to tell someone who has been judged a satisfactory teacher for many years that passing a certain test on a certain day is necessary to keep his or her job." Anrig said his company would no longer sell its National Teacher Examinations (NTE) to states or school boards that use the tests to determine the futures of practicing teachers.[2]

"The current NTE tests were developed to provide information about a candidate's academic knowledge and skills, typically acquired through a teacher-training program," Anrig said, quoting from an ETS pamphlet, *Guidelines for Proper Use of NTE Tests.* "They do not provide a direct evaluation of teaching performance. For this reason, NTE tests should not be used by school districts (or state agencies), directly or indirectly, to determine the compensation, retention, termination, advancement, pay supplements, or change in provisional employment status of teachers once they are employed."[3]

Education writers generally applauded Anrig's announcement as an unexpected gesture from a company that has never been eager to acknowledge the limitations of its products. But the NTE controversy is more complicated than it may seem. The new ETS position arises more from self-interest than from concern about test use, and it raises hard questions about how standardized tests are used in our society. These are questions that ETS has consistently found it lucrative to ignore.

The decline of American schools has been a hot topic in recent years. Most people would probably agree with the National Commission on Excellence in Education, which determined in 1983 that deteriorating schools had produced "a rising tide of mediocrity that threatens our very future as a Nation and a people." Most would probably also agree with the commission's conclusion that American teachers are poorly trained, badly paid, and not very bright to begin with.[4] Indeed, most recent critiques of American education have held teachers largely responsible for the disappointing state of the schools. In *High School*, the Carnegie Foundation's study of secondary education, Ernest L. Boyer, a member of the ETS board of trustees since 1982, assembled a host of depressing statistics about teachers and then called for a "renewal" of the profession.[5]

State legislators have been quick to seize the teaching issue — perhaps partly to distract attention from their own complicity in the crisis. (After all, as Diane Ravitch pointed out, those same legislators have aggravated the problem for years by burdening schools with "new requirements for nonacademic courses [drug education, family life education, consumer education, etc.] while cutting the ground away from science, math, history, and foreign languages.")[6] One of the most popular legislative approaches has been to require that prospective teachers pass competency tests before receiving teaching certificates. At least sixteen states now require such tests. Most use the NTE. "You're eventually going to have to pass it," a spokesperson for the Louisiana Board of Education told me, "if you want to get a regular teacher certificate."

This, apparently, is a use of the NTE that ETS approves of. Indeed, the company's confidential "Corporate Plan" for fiscal 1984 called for the addition of "two new states as users of the NTE programs for certification." In addition, ETS has begun actively marketing a Pre-Professional Skills Test (PPST), a shortened knockoff of the NTE, as an "employment test."[7] The PPST, which was first administered in February 1983, is now required for teacher certification in Delaware.

But if using the NTE and its offspring to test *practicing* teachers is "morally and educationally wrong," as the president of ETS has asserted, why is it right to use the same tests to determine which *aspiring* teachers will be allowed to enter the profession? If the NTE doesn't test knowledge that teachers need, why should people have to pass it in order to earn teaching certificates? And if it tests knowledge that teachers do need, what's wrong with requiring teachers to take it?

The NTE is also used by a number of colleges and universities to determine eligibility for teacher education programs. But the same questions arise. If it is immoral, as Anrig says, to use the NTE to measure the competence of practicing teachers, why should schools of education be allowed to use it in making admissions decisions? A test that is unfair for teachers must also be unfair for prospective teachers. Anrig told the *New York Times* in November 1983 that using the NTE "as a sole criterion for determining employment or pay scales violates all kinds of Federal laws about the relevance of tests to the workplace."[8] But if the NTE bears no relevance to the workplace — in this case, the classroom — then education students shouldn't have to take it either. (See Appendix B.)

Anrig and others at ETS defend the use of the NTE in teacher certification as long as "multiple criteria" are employed.[9] In other words, according to ETS, using the test to certify teachers is all right if passing it isn't the only requirement. But for anyone who fails to score above the cutoff point, the existence of *other* criteria is meaningless. The NTE is, in effect, the sole requirement for anyone who fails to achieve the necessary score. As they say in Louisiana, you can't get a certificate if you don't pass the test. The existence of "multiple criteria" may somewhat dilute the influence of the NTE in certification decisions, but it cannot make an irrelevant test relevant.

The true source of Anrig's concern about the NTE is surely not fairness but rather the flood of lawsuits that would inundate his company if veteran teachers began losing their jobs (or their raises or promotions) as a result of their performance on an ETS multiple-choice examination. Prior to his announcement, the Arkansas Education Association had said that it would go to court to challenge the state's new testing law.[10] ETS doesn't run into this problem with most of its other tests, because most other test-takers — unlike practicing teachers — aren't represented by powerful unions. Nor are most test-takers in a position to prove ETS wrong by demonstrating that they are actually capable of doing what ETS says they are not. A high school student who scores poorly on the SAT and as a result is rejected by the college of his choice could never prove in court that he had been treated unfairly.

Anrig is correct when he argues that teachers shouldn't have to pass tests that are irrelevant to their jobs. But he is not persuasive when he claims that those same tests can properly be used to judge people who have not yet been hired. If the National Teacher Examinations are not a fair measure of what it takes to be a teacher, they ought to be abolished, not confined to people who lack the means to defend themselves.

Gregory Anrig says the NTE is irrelevant to the classroom, but this is actually a point on which ETS has yet to make up its mind. In a booklet the company gives to people who register for the test "through Ticketron and Tele-Tron," the "Test of Professional Knowledge," a section of the NTE's Core Battery, is described as being "intended to assess examinees' achievement of that core of knowledge and those cognitive processes *that are of direct relevance to teaching.* The test reflects what appears to be a consensus among educators as to the knowledge important for a beginning teacher" (emphasis added).[11] Of course, the brochure is simply wrong. There is no "consensus among educators" about what teachers need to know, and ETS has no basis for claiming to have discovered one. Still, the booklet suggests that Anrig's professed reluctance to make unsupportable claims for the NTE does not yet have the full backing of his organization.

How relevant is the NTE? The only way to find out is to look at the test. Since ETS claims that educators appear to be unanimous in believing that the content of the exam, or at least of the "Test of

Professional Knowledge," is important for beginning teachers, settling the matter ought to be simple.

Here's a sample question, published in an ETS booklet, from the "Test of Professional Knowledge":[12]

Which of the following directions focuses on cognitive processing at the analysis level as it is defined in the *Taxonomy of Educational Objectives* by Bloom and others?

(A) Name three generals who fought on the side of the North during the United States Civil War.

(B) Identify the border states on a map of the United States.

(C) List in chronological order the Presidents of the United States who preceded Abraham Lincoln.

(D) Refer to the 1860 transportation map and contrast the transportation systems of the North and the South.

(E) Look at the 1860 political map and name the ten largest cities in the North.

Some would argue that American schools would improve overnight if aspiring history teachers stopped studying cognitive processing at the analysis level and started studying the Civil War. But no matter. If nothing else, we have discovered that educators who have delved to the Core of Knowledge agree that beginning teachers need to have read *The Taxonomy of Educational Objectives* by Bloom and others. If the book is required reading, though, perhaps ETS ought to say so somewhere in the information it distributes to test-takers. (There are a great many hidden requirements in the NTE. A question for English teachers requires test-takers to know that Toni Morrison's *Song of Solomon* is "a novel about familial bonds and conflicts in a wealthy Black family in the Midwest."[13] Morrison is a popular contemporary writer, but a passing knowledge of her works is hardly the sine qua non of good teaching.)* On the other hand, perhaps the object of the item is

---

* Obviously, this question is intended not to test teaching skills but to mollify blacks, who have complained (correctly) that the NTE excludes disproportionately more blacks than whites from teaching positions. ETS's inclusion of the Morrison item is a typically meaningless gesture of racial "sensitivity." If test-takers complain, as they should, that the item has no bearing on their ability to teach, ETS can throw up its hands and profess astonishment at the fickleness of its critics, who just the other day were complaining about racial bias.

nothing more than to determine whether test-takers can wade through the psychobabble in which the question is couched.

Lucid prose is not a virtue of the NTE. The test's authors disdain concrete examples and almost invariably prefer jargon to standard English, as in this item from "The Examination in Guidance Counselor":[14]

Since significant research findings indicate that counselor attempts to be "value neutral" are generally unsuccessful, what is the best method for counselors to use in countering the effects of conflicting counselor-client values?

(A) Taking a nondirective approach in the helping relationship
(B) Participating in value-clarification training workshops
(C) Exercising value restraint in the helping relationship
(D) Becoming consciously aware of their own values
(E) Diagnosing the client's value conflict

Many items are barely literate. Choosing the desired answer to a sample item from the test for kindergarten teachers requires test-takers to form this sentence: "The skill that is prerequisite to the successful completion of this experiment is the ability to be able to make accurate observations."[15] Other items are worded so that selecting a single answer is impossible:[16]

Of the following aids to the pronunciation of an unknown word, which would ordinarily be used by a reader after all others have failed?

(A) Configuration clues   (B) Context clues
(C) Phonic analysis   (D) The dictionary
(E) Structural analysis

Since this item requires the test-taker to assume, in evaluating each choice, that all other choices have been tried without success, any of the choices is correct. It doesn't matter which one you choose if the necessary assumption with each is that you have eliminated all the others.

Frequently the Core of Knowledge is simply wrong, as in this item from the test in "speech communication":[17]

Which of the following is the most effective way for a newspaper to protect itself against libel suits?

(A) Avoiding the use of the names of celebrities
(B) Giving the source of questionable information
(C) Avoiding ambiguous headlines
(D) Printing an immediate retraction if challenged
(E) Obtaining the consent of persons being quoted

I once worked as a researcher for a magazine that was sued for libel with great regularity. In no case that I can remember did "obtaining the consent of persons being quoted" — ETS's "correct" answer — provide any protection whatsoever, because people typically do not sue a publication over something that they themselves have said; they go to court over something the publication has said about *them*. Furthermore, if I made defamatory remarks about someone to a newspaper reporter, the newspaper couldn't protect itself against libel suits by getting *my* permission to repeat those remarks. I showed this question to Slade Metcalf, a partner in the New York law firm of Squadron, Ellenoff, Plesent, & Lehrer. Among other things, Metcalf defends Rupert Murdoch's publications against libel suits. He is a man, in other words, who knows something about libel suits. "This is an outrageous question," he said. "I just don't know the answer. None of the choices are any good."

It probably doesn't matter whether "speech communication" teachers know even the first thing about avoiding libel suits. But they shouldn't be denied jobs just because they know more than ETS.

The NTE examinations are written by ETS employees with the help of "professional educators from all sections of the country," according to the 1983–84 *Bulletin of Information* for NTE programs. In the case of the test for introductory reading teachers, ETS was assisted by an Advisory Panel consisting of two representatives from California State University, one from the University of Southern California, and one from the Pasadena (California) Unified School District. Most other tests have Committees of Examiners, whose members number as many as ten (General Knowledge) or as few as two (German).[18]

Tests created by committees have a tendency to resemble, well, tests created by committees, particularly in areas where the subject matter is less than well defined. In the following item from the examination in home economics education,[19] choosing the "correct" answer depends more than anything else on intuiting the thought processes of the Committee of Examiners:

Under which of the following conditions is work most likely to provide personal satisfaction as well as income?

(A) When one has perfected the necessary skills to perform the required tasks
(B) When the amount of money earned is equal to the efforts put forth in performing the task
(C) When the job is related to one's interests and the required tasks are done well
(D) When the performance of the job contributes to the productivity of society
(E) When the amount of income is sufficient to meet the cost of living and also cover the cost of recreation

---

The desired answer is C, which certainly seems to be a plausible choice. But the imprecise wording of the entire item leaves the thoughtful test-taker in a quandary. For example, C makes no mention whatsoever of income, which is one of the two conditions stated in the question. (Actually, the question doesn't make it clear whether "income" is *a lot* of income or simply any income at all.) Nor is there any necessary link between personal satisfaction and a job that is (merely) related to one's interests. Selling newspapers on a street corner would be a job related to my interests (journalism), but it would neither earn me much income nor give me any personal satisfaction. The only choice that mentions both income and satisfaction is E — if, that is, one assumes that satisfaction and "recreation" can be equated. The wording is so vague that any of the choices can be supported — or dismissed — for perfectly sound reasons.

Approaching this question in a truly objective or analytical frame of mind would make it impossible to answer. But of course the test-taker isn't really supposed to do that, even though ETS describes this as an "objective" examination. What the test-taker has to do instead is to identify the kinds of clichés, platitudes, and buzzwords that are likely to have been tossed around the conference table when ETS and the Committee of Examiners discussed the nature of human happiness. "Interests" and "done well" are the tipoffs — not because they refer back to the question (they do not), but because they are typical of precisely the sort of lazy thinking that leads to questions like this in the first place.

That this question was asked at all is a little odd. You might think that home economics teachers — who, if they pass the NTE, can expect to earn incomes — might be trusted to form their own ideas about personal satisfaction. What purpose is served by requiring them to divine the collective opinion of Mildred Barnes Griggs, Lilla C. Halchin, Dorothea M. Nixon, Maie Nygren, and Joyce Thompson — the philosophers of home economics to whom ETS gives credit for this exam?[20]

More interesting than how the tests are written, though, is how they are "validated." Validity, in testing, is a technical term that refers to the relationship between a test and the purpose to which it is put. ETS measures the validity of the Scholastic Aptitude Test, remember, by comparing students' scores with their first-year college grades, which are referred to as the "criterion." If the correlation between the scores and the criterion seems high enough, ETS judges the test to be valid for its intended use in choosing among college applicants. (Despite all the numbers and equations, of course, deciding whether any test is "valid" or not is still wholly subjective.)

Validating the NTE is much more difficult, because there is no criterion against which to measure test scores. Teachers don't receive grades the way college students do. No one knows how to measure good teaching. But the courts have consistently held that employment tests are illegal unless their validity for their intended use can be proven.[21] The NTE would be valid, ETS decided, if the material covered on the test bore a sufficient resemblance to the material taught in teacher education programs.

"The evidence for this validity exists in several different forms," according to the NTE *Bulletin*.

First, the test specifications or content outlines are developed by recognized authorities who are knowledgeable about current college curriculums in each field tested. Second, studies have been conducted by several states investigating the relationship between the NTE tests and the curriculums of colleges in those states. Third, studies have been conducted showing the relationship between the curriculums of particular colleges and the examinations.[22]

When I called ETS to ask for a copy of one of these validity studies, I was told that they all belonged to the states and that I would have to talk to them. So I called the State of Delaware, for which ETS had recently undertaken such a study, and asked for a copy. Ervin C. Marsh, supervisor of the Certification and Personnel Division in the Department of Public Instruction, told me he would look into the matter. He never called me back, so I called again to find out what had happened. He said the state's attorneys had advised against giving me a copy, but that he would check with them again and get back to me, which he never did. I eventually obtained a copy of the Delaware study, although not from the State of Delaware and not from ETS.

The NTE tests that Delaware uses are called the Pre-Professional Skills Tests (PPST), which ETS describes as "reliable measures of reading, writing, and mathematics that can be administered in a very short time frame."[23] The PPST is a new test; the questions in it — at least in the early editions — are drawn directly from the lengthier NTE Core Battery. (They are also similar, and in some cases identical, to items on the California Basic Educational Skills Test, CBEST, which is also published by ETS.) Edward Masonis, the ETS official in charge of the NTE Programs, admitted to me that "there's an overlap in the content" between the Core Battery and the PPST but claimed that "the questions are different." However, all of the sample questions in the *PPST 1983 Bulletin of Information* are drawn verbatim from corresponding Core Battery publications. The instructions are also very nearly identical. Core Battery: "Because writing is an important professional activity for every teacher, the Test of Communications Skills allots 30 minutes for examinees to write on an assigned topic."[24] PPST: "Because writing is an important professional activity, the Writing test allots 30 minutes for examinees to write on an assigned topic."[25] The cheapest way to market a new test is to take an old test and change its name.

To determine whether this versatile test was valid for certifying teachers in Delaware, ETS submitted a copy of the PPST to a professor from a teacher training school, a public school administrator, and twenty-two elementary, junior high, and high school teachers.* That ETS called on *practicing* teachers to pass judgment on the test's validity was, at the very least, paradoxical, since ETS simultaneously maintains that the test is unfair to precisely such teachers. How can a teacher for whom a test is unfair be asked to determine whether the same test is fair for someone else? But ETS saw nothing peculiar about the arrangement. It assembled its twenty-four experts one day in Dover and asked them to answer the following questions about the PPST: (1) "Will those who must pass the tests have had the opportunity to learn the basic skills tested?" (2) "Are the tests valid assessments of the basic skills needed to teach in Delaware?" (3) "What would the minimally qualified teacher candidate have to score to pass the test?"[27]

When ETS added up the results, it was mightily impressed. Although only one member of the panel actually worked in a teacher training program, "panel members overwhelmingly reported that candidates would have had the opportunity to learn the skills tested" in teacher training programs, according to the final report, which was written by ETS's Gary Echternacht. Furthermore, although "most panel members reported finding some questionable test items, most panel members believed that fewer than 13% . . . of the items on any one test were questionable. . . . These results strongly support the validity of the test." (They also strongly sup-

---

*According to ETS's report, "All school districts in Delaware were asked to nominate teachers to serve on the panel. Requests were mailed to district superintendents for nominations. We requested that two elementary school teachers, two middle school teachers, and two high school teachers be nominated. . . . Our only request was that the prospective panel member have demonstrated competence in teaching, and in the superintendent's judgment, know what basic skills are needed in teaching. We also asked for the nominees [sic] race, sex, and teaching areas." Final selections were made so that every school district in the state was represented; so that there were roughly equal numbers of elementary, junior high, and high school teachers; and so that junior high and high school teachers were "equally represented by quantitative (e.g., math and science), verbal (e.g., English, social studies), and vocational specialty areas."[26]

port the elimination of a number of test items, but this was not done; the test was later administered without alteration.) The only real sour notes, according to Echternacht, had come from a vocational education teacher who thought the test might be too difficult "because some voc-ed teaching certificates do not require college educations" and from a panel member who thought that spelling ought to be tested in the multiple-choice writing test.[28]

Setting the passing score was also easy. Panel members were instructed to arrange individual items from the test into "homogenous groups" and then estimate what percentage of the items in each group a "minimally qualified candidate" might be expected to answer correctly. These percentages were then multiplied by the number of questions in each group, and the resulting figures were added up to provide a minimum passing score for the test. Of course, panel members could have achieved the same result in less time by simply counting the number of items on the test that they felt were important. But ETS prides itself on its scientific approach to testing, and estimating percentages and performing multiplication seem vastly more sophisticated than merely adding up the number of relevant items. In his report, Echternacht refers to the percentage and multiplication procedure as "Ebel's method."*[29]

The estimates panel members arrived at through Ebel's method varied widely. On the forty-item math test, for example, the panel's suggested passing scores ranged from 15 to 38 — from a little more than a third to all but two of the questions. To arrive at a single score, ETS suggested averaging all the estimates and then adding a small cushion to allow for "measurement error."[30] This is what Delaware did.

Using an average as a cutting score is an interesting idea, since it means that one half of the expert panelists must believe that Delaware is now certifying unqualified teachers while the other half

---

*Named for its creator, Robert L. Ebel, a former ETS researcher. Incidentally, there is no provision in this method for eliminating the items that panel members find to be unimportant. A prospective teacher can win a certificate in Delaware without knowing everything the panel believes a "minimally qualified candidate" needs to know, so long as he knows enough of what he *doesn't* need to know.

must believe it is rejecting qualified ones. But a test without a passing score wouldn't be of much use.

Scores for each of the PPST's three sections (reading, writing, and mathematics) are reported on a scale that runs from 150 to 190. Of course, a 150–190 scale is no different from a 0–40 scale, which a layman might have been tempted to use instead. But ETS likes three-digit numbers, and it knows that a score of 178 seems more meaningful and scientific than a score of 28. Since there are forty questions in each of the reading and math sections of the PPST, every question is worth one point. (The writing section contains forty-five multiple-choice questions and one short essay; these are graded separately and then combined and converted to the 40-point scale.)* Every question answered incorrectly or left blank is worth none. Since there is no penalty for wrong answers (as there is on the SAT and most other ETS tests), test-takers will improve their scores, sometimes dramatically, by guessing wildly whenever they don't know an answer. The expert panel settled on a passing level of 175 for the reading section; guessing wildly would be expected to produce, on average, a score of 158. A test-taker who knows nothing at all thus knows roughly a third of what it takes to be a teacher in Delaware.[32]

Finding qualified teachers isn't the only, or even the most important, purpose of the PPST. ETS recommended to Delaware that it review its passing score every year "to take into account the supply and demand of teachers."[33] In other words, according to ETS, the test should be used not to identify a pool of qualified teachers but to control the competition for available jobs. If there aren't enough qualified teachers in Delaware next year, no problem; just lower the passing score on the test. Gregory Anrig told me in 1983 that ETS's methods for setting cutoff scores were very sophisticated and that "you can't have a cutoff score unless you prove in that state that that cutoff score, at that level, is related to the job performance that you want the person to have. In all frankness,

---

*The expert panel determined the passing score for the essay by reading several sample essays that had been "previously scored" by ETS and then deciding whether each was either good enough or not good enough for a teacher in Delaware. "The passing score is found," according to Echternacht's report, "by choosing the essay with the lowest score for which a majority of panel members passed."[31]

it's not like picking a number out and having no idea of its implications. You can't use our tests if you do that." Except in Delaware?

Frank B. Murray, dean of the University of Delaware's College
of Education, doesn't think ETS's methods are as sophisticated as
Gregory Anrig does. In a letter to William B. Keene, superintendent of the state Department of Public Instruction, Murray said, "I
am concerned that the procedure we are following to set a cut-off
score is not wise. Apart from the fact that the expert panel procedure (Ebel's method) is *only* recommended when you cannot get
data from a sample of test-takers, I am worried that the whole
point of the competency testing of teachers will be defeated because expert panels, where they have been used, have uniformly
set the score too high. To have to lower the cut-off score at some
later time would be a public relations disaster. (There are also real
questions about whether the panel even understood the Ebel procedure. . . .)"[34]

Despite the threat to its public relations, Delaware now uses the
PPST as a requirement for teacher certification, and ETS is working hard to ensure that other states will join it. ETS also hopes the
test will be adopted by employers, state agencies, and licensing
boards in many other fields, because, according to a promotional
flier, "professionals should be able to demonstrate competence in
communication and computation."*[36] (There are no plans, however, to make the PPST a requirement for employment at ETS.)

"As far as I know, there is no such thing as a test of teacher
aptitude or potential, and I know of no test, including the NTE,
that proports [sic] to measure teacher effectiveness. One problem
in judging is that there is no general agreement about what an
effective teacher is. The number of definitions is about equal to the
number of professional educators."[37]

These are not the words of an enemy of testing teachers. They
are the words of Edward Masonis, the administrator of ETS's

---

*The PPST was originally conceived as a test for teachers, but demand for it was less than
ETS had expected. At the time this book went to press, Delaware was still the only state
using the PPST for certification. The decision to promote and market the PPST as a universal "employment test" was made in fiscal 1983.[35]

NTE Programs, as quoted in an ETS publication called *FOCUS: Making the Public Schools Work*. If the NTE, despite what it purports to do, measures neither teacher potential nor teacher effectiveness, you might think that the wisest course would be to get rid of it, since these are the uses — however veiled they may occasionally be — to which the tests are put. But ETS's principal response to this problem has apparently been only to stop calling the tests National *Teacher* Examinations. The new official name — NTE Tests — doesn't mention teaching at all.[38]

Most people don't distinguish between the question "Should teachers be competent?" and the question "Should teachers be required to pass competency tests?" But the two are entirely different. No reasonable person would advocate the hiring of incompetent teachers. But a reasonable person might very well advocate the abolition of teacher competency tests or at least of the NTE. In fact, one could argue that using the NTE and tests like it actually works to *reduce* the quality of the nation's teachers. There are several reasons:

1. The NTE adds yet another layer to the educational bureaucracy that makes it difficult to reward good teachers and nearly impossible to remove bad ones. If you think it's hard to get rid of a bad teacher now, just try firing one whose "competence" has been certified by ETS. A passing score on an NTE test is a meaningless credential that does nothing but move teachers one step further from accountability.

2. Minimum competency tests have a way of becoming maximum competency tests. School districts that have imposed competency tests as requirements for high school graduation have often discovered that the tests tend to establish ceilings rather than floors for student achievement.

3. The emphasis on testing distracts attention from the real problems with our teachers and our schools. Walt Haney and George Madaus, writing about minimum competency tests in 1978, pointed out that the clamor for tests "is part of a much broader national reemphasis on improving educational achievement in basic skills" but wondered why the movement had "taken the form of calls for more testing, rather than for more schooling. In the 1950s, a similar concern over educational quality led, not to

minimum competency tests, but to more direct efforts to reform curricula."[39]

4. Far from facilitating such reform, the existence of an NTE requirement makes it nearly impossible to improve teacher education programs, which in turn makes it nearly impossible to change the NTE. Since ETS bases the content of the NTE on its understanding of what is taught in teachers colleges — and since teachers colleges not only admit students on the basis of NTE scores but also dedicate themselves to helping those same students prepare for NTE certifying tests — the tests and the school programs are mutually reinforcing. If the NTE asks questions about the taxonomy of educational objectives, then you can be certain that the taxonomy of educational objectives will be taught in teachers college. This is a disturbing phenomenon, particularly since there is now substantial agreement that one of the major causes of the current educational crisis is the dismal quality — and irrelevant curricula — of teacher training programs.

5. Tests like the NTE are often used less to screen potential teachers than to limit the size of the job market — hence ETS's recommendation that Delaware adjust its passing score annually to reflect supply and demand. Since minority candidates, as a group, tend to score lower on the NTE than white candidates, the effects are particularly unfortunate.

6. States afraid of Delaware-style "public relations disasters" set passing scores so low they might as well not set them at all.

Is there an alternative to the NTE? The question assumes that the tests now perform some necessary function. This is not the case. The easiest way to improve on the NTE would be to get rid of it. Beyond this, there is no easy answer. Using the NTE is a simple-minded response to a very complicated problem. State legislators find the tests irresistibly appealing because they already exist and because requiring them costs taxpayers little. The NTE enables all of us to believe we're taking concrete steps to improve our schools.

When I implied, in an article in *The New Republic* in 1984,[40] that the NTE Programs were profitable for ETS (as indeed I had believed them to be), I received a letter from Joy McIntyre of the

Information Division saying that "NTE operates at a *deficit* and has for five years. Because of its importance to states trying to maintain educational standards for teachers, however, ETS continues to support the program."[41]

This is disingenuous at best. If the NTE Programs really do operate at a deficit (the figures are not published anywhere, and ETS refused to let me see them, saying they were confidential), no one is more surprised than ETS. The company's $500,000 Booz, Allen management consulting study, completed in 1982, identified twelve "revenue growth areas" within ETS that had the greatest potential for producing increased short-term profits. One of them was the NTE.[42] In the company's confidential Corporate Plan for 1984, President Anrig, citing ETS's "need to increase revenues in the future," called for continued expansion of the NTE Programs.[43] If the NTE loses money, ETS views it as a loss leader and expects it to be profitable soon.

If the NTE *does* lose money, this can only mean that ETS believes current client states would be unwilling to pay the full cost and that ETS is subsidizing the program with income from profitable tests until enough new states can be solicited and signed up. (The Corporate Plan called for a minimum of two new states to be added in 1983 and at least two more in 1984.)[44] Is part of your $11 SAT fee being used to underwrite the cost of testing teachers in the dozen or so states that require NTE examinations? If this is true — as ETS admits — then students are being ripped off and teachers are being required to take a test that might not exist if the states that use it had to pay the true cost.

One of ETS's favorite fantasies is that it is "an independent third party of unquestioned objectivity"[45] that doesn't actually promote the use of tests but merely supplies them to businesses, government agencies, and others who express a need. Joy McIntyre suggests that ETS's support of the NTE is philanthropic. Richard Burns, the head of ETS's Center for Occupational and Professional Assessment (COPA), the division that sells tests for barbers, golf pros, and plumbers, told me that ETS never actually tries to "create demand" for its tests but merely "looks at areas where there is testing already going on but where it may not be adequate to the task." An Information Division employee told me that ETS has no sales force but merely waits for clients to come to it. But none of this is true. ETS actively promotes its tests, and, as with the PPST, it encourages the spread of testing into fields where it does not already exist. The company also very definitely has a sales force. In 1982, ETS hired the Consultative Resources Corporation to teach its sales personnel the "dynamics of a selling interaction," "the needs-driven selling sequence," and other "basic and consultative selling skills."[46] If ETS doesn't make money from the NTE, it's not because it doesn't try.

13

Testing and Society: What Can Be Done?

As the case of the NTE demonstrates, testing's effect on society extends far beyond the matter of who is admitted and who is rejected, of who is hired and who is not. Since what is tested directly influences what is taught, ETS's ubiquitous multiple-choice exams have an enormous impact on education, from kindergarten up through law school and beyond. And since what is taught influences how we live, the effect of the tests reverberates through society.

The power of tests to shape schools and lives is clearly evident in Japan. Admission to Japanese universities is based solely on entrance examination scores, and much of the nation's educational system is focused on enabling students to pass these exams. Because a college-educated Japanese person's opportunities in life are determined largely by the prestige of his alma mater, students are very serious about preparing for the tests. Between the first and twelfth grade, Japanese students spend the equivalent of four more years in class than American students do. Japanese high school students eat lunch at their desks, attend school until 12:30 on Saturdays, and do an average of thirteen hours of homework each week. Beginning early in elementary school, many students spend additional hours after school each day in private tutoring. Some especially diligent students do their homework at expensive desks with "built-in alarm clocks especially equipped with timers for speed tests, high and low intensity lights, swivel executive chairs, globes that light up, and in one case even a built-in calculator."[1]

Many Americans, viewing this single-minded dedication to schoolwork as the likely source of Japan's considerable economic success, advocate rebuilding American schools at least partly on the Japanese model. But educational reformers should take a closer look at the Japanese system before concluding that it offers a panacea for ailing American schools. Indeed, the real lesson of the Japanese experience has to do with the perils of ordering society on the basis of standardized tests.

College entrance examinations are the focal point of Japanese secondary education. Each university prepares its own test, but they are all very similar. Virtually all questions are multiple-choice or short-answer. Here are two brief but typical sections from the 1974 exam given by elite Kobe University.[2] Students were supposed to fill in the blanks:

The philosophy that arose in ancient Greece had an enormous influence on subsequent human thought. The earliest form, _____ philosophy, arose in the _____ century in the _____ region. Liberating itself from the mythological approach to natural phenomena, this philosophy aimed to explain the fundamentals of nature in a rational manner. _____, who explained the origin of things to be water, and _____, who treated the basis of matter mathematically, were representative scholars of the age. Following the war with _____, democratic government was implemented with Athens as its focal point, and a school of teachers, the _____, arose to give instructions to citizens in the arts of public debate. This development began the division of philosophy into component fields.

The Rhine turns north from Basel and the view suddenly opens up before it. This indicates that the Rhine has entered _____, a long and narrow plain 30 km. wide and 300 km. long bounded by _____ on the east and the Vosges mountain range on the west. The surrounding area consists of forests, swamps, and _____.

And on and on and on. Since the only function of academic secondary schools is to prepare students for these tests, high school curricula precisely mirror their superficiality. According to Thomas P. Rohlen,

> Greek thought . . . receives an average of ten pages out of 220 in the various texts for the year-long required course "Ethical Thought and Society." These pages read exactly like an encyclopedic entry on the subject. The authors skim from topic to topic at a rapid pace in order to introduce as much as possible in a limited number of pages. The result is a high density of items to memorize, from ten to twenty per page, but no textual material to chew on and no real basis for class discussion or individual speculation. Greek schools of thought, for example, are typically encapsulated in a single sentence.[3]

Teachers who stray from the textbooks except to provide additional facts are criticized by their students. If it isn't going to be on the test, Japanese students don't want to waste time learning it.

Because the tests are so important, revisions are not taken lightly. "Each announcement of an intention to change the exams significantly is met with near panic by parents, teachers, and students," Rohlen writes.[4] Universities have to announce changes up to ten years in advance. If scientists discovered tomorrow that the world is made up of only four elements, this new information couldn't be taught in Japan until teachers had been consulted, examination changes had been announced far in advance, and textbooks had first been revised and then introduced gradually into the schools, beginning in junior high. The old view of matter would have to be retained until all the students who had memorized the periodic table had taken their entrance exams.

Getting into college is so important in Japan that actually being there is an anticlimax. Most Japanese students don't do very much at the universities they have dedicated their lives to entering. "You sleep late, and you play a lot of mah-jongg," according to one.[5] Many students view their four years in college as a well-earned vacation — the first real vacation of their lives.

Japanese society is "meritocratic" to an extent that far surpasses even the most ambitious fantasies of ETS executives. A single score on an "objective" multiple-choice examination is translated directly into a universal currency of opportunity. The content of the exams is irrelevant except as it provides the symbolic ordeal that determines which students will advance and which will fall behind. Students prove themselves worthy of embarking on a wide variety of careers and opportunities solely on the basis of their ability to memorize and regurgitate a single vast collection of disconnected, trivial facts. This is the ultimate "aptitude" test: an examination whose only true subject matter is itself.

Japanese and American cultures are so different that attempting to see either through the lens of the other is almost invariably misleading. But the Japanese example demonstrates in an extreme form the impact of testing on schools and on society. Standardized tests send powerful signals throughout a culture, and their impact is directly proportional to their perceived importance. As their importance grows, tests begin to define the rewards and opportunities they were originally intended merely to allocate. Japan's college entrance examinations precisely determine not only the content of high school curricula but also the outline of Japanese society.

That standardized tests in America have had a similar (though clearly less sweeping) effect is not in doubt. When the College Board seventy years ago began its shift from the measurement of knowledge to the measurement of "aptitude," it did so in part because teachers had complained that its original examinations were having an adverse impact on schools. The Board's essay tests had left English teachers "shackled year after year to specified 'classics,' some of them repugnant to youthful minds," in the words of the Board's historian in 1950.[6] The new examinations, the Board believed, would free schools to devise their own curricula. Coaching would disappear as "curriculum-free" examinations made it irrelevant. Testing would become a neutral factor in education.

But clearly testing today is anything but. The SAT's impact on schools is every bit as large as that of the old College Boards. All the Board did by making its admission test "curriculum-free" was to put pressure on high schools, which had once been SAT-free, to adapt themselves to the test. The new tests have exacerbated the problems they were meant to solve. By helping to shift emphasis from learning to test scores, ETS has contributed greatly to the very decline in quality it elsewhere claims to have served the country by measuring.

In the winter of 1979, I spent a semester posing as a senior at a large public high school in Stratford, Connecticut.[7] In English class, we spent six weeks reading a fifty-five-page book and devoted most of the rest of our time to memorizing lists of vocabulary words and solving SAT-like multiple-choice word problems: antonyms, analogies, sentence completions. We almost never had to write anything and, aside from our weekly ten-page assignments, we didn't have to read. In large measure our time was spent doing multiple-choice busywork. One of the reasons for this, I think, is that over the years ETS has made busywork seem like real work. With its PSATs, SATs, GREs, GMATs, LSATs, and dozens of other tests, the company has given the multiple-choice question a credibility it does not deserve.

This is not to suggest that teachers would immediately start assigning papers again if ETS disappeared. But as school budgets have declined, ETS has given teachers an easy rationalization for abandoning time-consuming assignments. If multiple-choice tests are good enough for the experts down in "Princeton," they must be good enough for English 12. As long as the tests provide, or seem to provide, the standard by which society's rewards are allocated, schools will inevitably remake themselves in the image of the tests. When this transformation also lightens the loads of overworked teachers, it takes place all the more quickly.

SAT preparation courses have become standard fixtures in high school curricula. Hours that were once spent reading books and doing real schoolwork are now devoted to cramming vocabulary and learning how to pick through ETS analogies. More and more students are supplementing this coaching in school with expensive commercial SAT courses. Coaching schools are thriving even as public schools are struggling to survive. John Katzman pays his Princeton Review teachers between $20 and $30 an hour — up to five times what New York's public high school teachers receive. Parents who vote against increases in the school levy gladly pay private tutors as much as $50 an hour to improve their children's SAT scores.

The impact of the SAT is not felt equally by all our schools. Students still read books at Exeter and Andover, even if they also take coaching courses. But in schools where money is scarce and incentives are few, tests like the SAT provide a plausible excuse for cutting back. If the SAT can see through the differences in schools, as the official mythology states, does it matter if a city's poorest school district stops offering algebra, chemistry, and French? By emphasizing "ability" over content, the SAT sends a tragic signal to teachers and administrators.

In a broader social sense, ETS perpetuates the very inequalities it sometimes claims to eliminate and sometimes claims merely to measure. For all its sermonizing about equal opportunity, ETS is the powerful servant of the privileged. The company's executives wax lyrical about ghetto children rescued from poverty by their 600s. But the real beneficiaries of "aptitude" testing are the offspring of the advantaged, who ascend from privilege to privilege on the strength of their scores and come to view those numbers as a moral justification for the comforts that are the trappings of their class. Tests like the SAT convert the tainted advantages of birth and wealth into the neutral currency of merit, enabling the fortunate to believe they have earned what they have merely been given.

The same is true in Japan. Although described as "objective" and "impartial" measures that put all students, regardless of background, on an equal footing, Japan's entrance examinations function more as a private proving ground for the already privileged. Japanese society is vastly more egalitarian than American society, but social and economic differences exist and they translate into differences in opportunity. Only students from prosperous families can afford the marathon preparation that passing the tests requires. The exam-based system jumbles up the pieces of society, but it puts them back together largely as they were before, justifying each new version of the old order on the basis of merit.

As ETS extends its reach through American society, the impact of the meritocratic fallacy becomes more pervasive and more insidious. Do we really want to grant a company like ETS such a vast responsibility for ordering our lives?

Even in purely pragmatic terms, tests like the SAT represent an enormous squandering of common resources. High school students and their parents paid ETS and the College Board roughly $50 million last year just for the SAT and half a dozen other programs and services directly related to college admissions. They spent an additional $10 million or so on SAT coaching courses, tutors, and books (not to mention $200,000 on No. 2 pencils).[8] They wasted an uncountable number of hours memorizing words like *termagant* and *tergiversation* and studying strategies for taking multiple-choice tests. And all for what? To enable a small handful of elite colleges to make slightly less expensive admissions decisions about a small handful of their applicants on the basis of one small part of an unfair and badly written multiple-choice test?

The SAT isn't perfect, many people would concede; but what would you put in its place? This question is thought by the test's defenders to be unanswerable; critics of ETS, confronted by it, throw up their hands and vanish in puffs of gray smoke. But there are excellent alternatives to the SAT and other standardized tests. There are even some excellent alternatives to ETS.

Before looking at them, though, we need to look at the major justifications usually offered for testing. Supporters of the SAT consistently make certain arguments in the test's defense. The most compelling of these, along with responses, are:

1. *College admissions officers need the SAT because they can't get by without an objective, uniform measure that puts all applicants on an equal footing regardless of their educational or cultural background.*

College admissions officers get by without this now. The SAT isn't the same test for everyone who takes it. Well-coached students have an advantage over uncoached students. Suburban whites have an advantage over urban blacks. Students who cheat have an advantage over students who don't. Students who think like Pamela Cruise have an advantage over students who don't. One reason the debate about testing is so acrimonious is that most people don't distinguish between what the tests should be and what the tests are. The fact that it would be nice to have a test that would put everyone on an equal footing doesn't mean that the SAT is such a test.

2. *If the SAT didn't exist, college admissions officers would be forced to study individual high schools in order to learn how to compare grades and class ranks.*

Colleges do this anyway. I don't think I have ever met an admissions officer from a selective school who didn't at some point ask me where I was from and then reel off the names of half a dozen local high schools. Kansas City, eh? Shawnee Mission? Rockhurst? Southwest? Pem-Day? *Ah, Pem-Day.* The idea that selective admissions officers don't keep track of high schools is pure fantasy. So is the idea that these admissions officers routinely accept students with high SAT scores from schools they've never heard of. A former Harvard admissions officer told me that there are some high schools from which Harvard simply does not accept students, even if they do well on the SAT. These are schools whose students made an indelibly bad impression at some point in the past or whose guidance counselors don't cooperate with Harvard. I asked a former *director* of admissions at Harvard whether high SAT scores alone ever gave her confidence in the qualifications of an applicant from a school she knew nothing about. She said, "No. Harvard has this enormous network of alumni interviewers, so that you would always have had someone you knew interview the kid, even if he lived in the middle of nowhere."*

3. *The SAT may be unscientific and imprecise, but surely high school grades, interviews, letters of recommendation, and other subjective measures are every bit as likely to be misleading.*

Even considering that high school grades are *better* than the SAT at doing the only thing the SAT claims to do, this argument sounds convincing. Who would deny that grades, interviews, and letters of recommendation are subjective? It's easy to sympathize with Fred Hargadon, director of admissions at Stanford and former chairman of the College Board, who said in 1983 that "it never ceases to amaze me that grades and grading systems, as characterized as they are by incomparability from school to school, department to department, course to course, and teacher to teacher, generate so little heat and controversy when compared to that which surrounds the use of national standardized examinations."[9]

Actually, though, this isn't amazing at all. The reason grades don't generate the same sort of controversy is that everyone *knows*

---

*This is not meant to imply that Harvard thinks test scores are unimportant. Fred Jewett, the current director of admissions, told me flatly that he couldn't get by without "a factor that cuts across an educational system which is as idiosyncratic as ours is. If the SAT didn't exist, you'd have to invent it."

they're subjective. The trouble with the SAT is that most people — largely as a result of what ETS and the College Board have told them — think it's not. To be sure, getting rid of the SAT wouldn't make college admissions any more "scientific." But it wouldn't make admissions any *less* scientific, either. All it would do is make the process more honest by preventing colleges, high schools, and students from deceiving themselves about the meaning of numbers they don't understand.

4. *Without the SAT, minorities would disappear from college campuses.*

As I have tried to argue, minorities are generally admitted to selective colleges for reasons other than their SAT scores. If selective colleges wanted to *reduce* the number of blacks in their student bodies, they could do so simply by paying more attention to SATs. ETS is not and never has been an instrument of social progress. Quite the contrary.

For some unknowable reason, ETS executives talk about the SAT as though it were primarily a test for poor blacks. After New York's truth-in-testing law went into effect, ETS gleefully pointed out that virtually all of the people who requested copies of their questions and answers were wealthy, high-scoring whites.[10] This fact, ETS said, discredited the law's supporters by proving that the whole stink had been raised by a small group of rich, white grade-grubbers. But the simple fact is that, to the extent it is used at all, the SAT is used mostly to help determine which wealthy young whites will attend which wealthy white colleges.

Whatever its executives say in public, ETS exists to test rich, white grade-grubbers. Pretending this isn't true won't make it untrue. The only way to get minorities into colleges is to admit them. The SAT makes this less likely, not more.

5. *The SAT may be harmful for minorities and pointless for almost everybody else, but if it didn't exist, wouldn't admissions procedures at truly selective schools become prohibitively expensive?*

Admissions procedures at these schools are expensive now. It's just that the cost is spread across hundreds of thousands of SAT-takers who are forced to pay but don't stand to benefit. The admissions offices of the few schools that use the SAT are subsidized by students who apply to the many schools that require SAT scores but pay no attention to them. If Harvard, Yale, and Princeton really think they need the SAT, let them pay the true cost and devise some method for passing it on to their own applicants.

Some people will argue that the decision whether to use the SAT shouldn't be an economic one. But it's an economic one right now; colleges require the test because it's free.

6. *If colleges abandoned the SAT, the children of wealthy alumni would have an unfair advantage over applicants with superior intellects but inferior trust funds and family connections.*

Well, really. Go stand in the middle of the Princeton campus on a warm spring day and look around. The children of the wealthy and the children of alumni have always had an advantage in selective private college admissions, and they always will. Colleges that have to pay their own bills know that unhappy alumni don't respond eagerly to annual fund drives. You may think this is good or bad, but the SAT has nothing to do with it, and getting rid of the SAT won't change it.

Furthermore, if wealthy people tend to do better on the SAT than poor people (and they do), you can't *reduce* the advantage of wealth by making selections on the basis of SAT scores. To exaggerate considerably, you couldn't reduce the number of rich people at a college by admitting the applicants with the most money.

7. *The SAT is a check on grade inflation.*

Grade inflation is as rampant in college, where students don't have to take the SAT, as it is in high school, where they do. If there's any evidence that the existence of the SAT prevents teachers from giving too many A's, I haven't seen it. Some people worry that without the SAT, students would put pressure on their teachers to give them better grades than they deserved in order to increase their chances of getting into college. But you could argue as easily that *using* the SAT causes undeserving students to put pressure on their teachers to give them better grades to make up for their poor SAT scores.

You could even argue that the SAT *encourages* grade inflation. According to ETS, the predictive validity of the SAT has increased in recent years, a period in which collegiate grade inflation has worsened. In other words, the SAT would appear to be better at predicting inflated college grades than it was at predicting uninflated ones. Could it be that students who do well on the SAT are the sort of students who are unusually successful at talking their teachers into giving them better grades than they deserve?

8. *Without the SAT, we wouldn't know whether secondary schools were getting better or getting worse.*

Defenders of the SAT like to say that the test serves society by alerting educators to deficiencies in the schools. But because of the importance ascribed to the tests, educators too often respond to such deficiencies as though they were nothing more than deficiencies in SAT scores. Instead of asking how they can improve the schools, they ask how they can raise their scores.

Even more to the point, as ETS has said repeatedly, the SAT is a lousy measure of the quality of secondary schools. If you want to assess the schools, you want to know about more than opposites and fill-in-the-blanks. Even to the extent that it does reflect school quality, the SAT paints a very distorted picture, since the test is only taken by students planning to go to college. If the SAT distorts our knowledge of the quality of secondary schools, getting rid of it would improve our understanding of our schools.

9. *Even if you got rid of the SAT, colleges would still have to make admissions decisions. Some people would still be admitted, and some would be rejected.*

ETS talks about its critics as though they were wild-eyed communist agitators bent on destroying American society. But it's possible to want to get rid of the SAT without also wanting to make everyone wear gray tunics and drive the same kind of car. Obviously colleges would still have to make admissions decisions. But they would have to do so without hiding behind the pseudoscientific hocus-pocus of "aptitude." Virtually all colleges make virtually all of their admissions decisions without the help of the SAT right now. Why not make it unanimous and spend all that money on something else?

10. *Most high school students, including minorities, think the SAT is a good thing.*

ETS and the College Board frequently cite a public opinion poll, commissioned by the Board in 1978, which indicated that students like the SAT. "By a margin of 2 to 1," an ETS flier reports,

". . . students favored retaining the SAT in the admissions process because, they said, it is an impartial and objective measure of student ability." This statistic is illustrated with a silhouette in which two students have their hands raised while a gloomy nay-sayer — slump-shouldered and withdrawn — stands off to the side, one step behind. The flier further reveals that blacks like taking the test most and that girls like taking it least.[11]

But what is this supposed to prove? ETS wouldn't abandon the SAT if students suddenly decided they didn't like it. The fact that two-thirds of high school students generally believe what ETS and the College Board have told them for the last sixty years doesn't make the SAT a good test. And the fact that blacks enjoy taking it doesn't mean that the SAT is fair to blacks. ETS's electioneering is irrelevant to the real questions about the test.

11. *If the SAT were abolished, ETS would go out of business.* Hmmmm.

What would I put in place of the SAT? I don't think we *need* to put anything. If the SAT simply disappeared tomorrow, admissions officers would squawk for a year or so, the foundations of the Henry Chauncey Conference Center would tremble, and life would go on as before. The SAT plays virtually no useful role in college admissions right now. Getting rid of it would not, by itself, make admissions very different.

As long as we're being so radical as to chuck the SAT, though, we might as well take the opportunity to improve college admissions procedures in general. I think there are a number of fairly modest changes that would not only simplify the lives of many admissions officers but also raise the quality of our high schools and colleges. I don't see these proposals as *alternatives* to the SAT; I see them as improvements on an irrational system in which the SAT is, at best, superfluous.

If Japanese and American experiences with standardized tests can teach us anything, they can teach us that even an "impartial" method of selection has an effect on the people being selected and on the society in which they live. In thinking about how to choose people for admission to colleges (or to graduate schools or to jobs), we need to consider the nature of this effect. Might it not be possible to design a method of selection whose influence on individuals and on society would actually be beneficial?

The one inescapable fact about any method of selection is that people who want to be selected are going to try to improve their chances of being selected. If Columbia University suddenly decided to base admissions on the results of the New York State lottery, people who wanted to go to Columbia would buy more lottery tickets than people who didn't. If the SAT is believed to be important in determining who goes to which college, then students who want to go to college are quite understandably going to try to improve their SAT scores. They may not buy desks with built-in alarm clocks, but they may very well enroll in coaching schools. No amount of sermonizing (or outright lying) by ETS or the College Board is going to change that. As long as admissions officers continue to speak idolatrously about SAT scores, multiple-choice busywork and test-taking strategies are going to be facts of life in classrooms, and coaching schools are going to continue to make their owners rich.

Since students are going to expend all this effort anyway, why not adopt a selection method that would encourage them to expend it in some more obviously useful manner? ETS and the College Board pay lip service to this principle, since they maintain that one of the chief virtues of the SAT is that scores can't be improved except through genuine, high-quality education. But no one except them believes this.

Many educators — including, notably, Christopher Jencks and James Crouse — have argued that "achievement" tests should be favored over "aptitude" tests in college admissions, because doing so would send healthier signals to students and to secondary schools. "If selective colleges," Jencks and Crouse have written, "were to base admission on high school grades and tests that measure mastery of the secondary school curriculum (instead of basing it on grades and tests that measure vocabulary, reading comprehension, and basic mathematics), high school students who wish to attend selective colleges might take their academic work more seriously."[12]

This is probably true. As Jencks and Crouse also point out, "The name of a test has more influence on how both educators and students interpret the results than technical manuals and scholarly articles can ever have."[13] The word *aptitude* in connection with tests has seldom produced anything but misery and confusion (sometimes even for ETS). The word *achievement* would certainly remind students and teachers that there is something to be said for actually *doing* a few things rather than simply demonstrating an apparent potential for doing them.

The only trouble with "achievement" tests is that when most people talk about them, they usually mean Achievement Tests — that is, the fourteen Achievement Tests produced by ETS for the College Board. These tests have all the flaws of the SAT and a good many more besides. As John Katzman said (in Chapter Seven), ETS's Achievements are even easier to coach than the SAT — not because, as some have said, their subject matter is more finite but because the method by which they are put together is more transparent. Because the Achievement Test program has a vastly smaller candidate volume than the SAT program (just 270,000 spread over fourteen tests in thirteen subjects in 1983 as opposed to 1.2 million for the SAT), ETS cuts more corners in developing the exams. (Small candidate volume is also one of the reasons that the NTE is such a rotten test.)

ETS's Achievement Tests also vary extremely in difficulty. Because different Achievement Tests tend to attract different kinds of students and because all Achievement Tests are individually graded "on the curve," some tests are much easier than others. The physics test, for example, is vastly harder than the biology test because physics is usually an accelerated course in high school and biology is usually not. I fairly breezed through the biology Achievement one evening with no firmer background than several years' casual attention to the Science section of the *New York Times*. But I couldn't get to first base on the physics test.

In order to smooth out these differences, scoring formulas for the various tests differ widely. ETS reports Achievement Test scores on the same 200–800 scale it uses for the SAT, but the scores are not otherwise comparable. Simply leaving the physics test blank (or filling it out entirely at random) would have resulted in a score of 370 on a recent edition;[14] a comparable score on the SAT would have put a student at roughly the fiftieth percentile.

The same was true of the Latin test (on which, incidentally, a student could have marked an incorrect answer for *every single question* and still received a score of 270).[15] A student with SAT scores in the 300 range might slightly improve his chances with an unwary admissions officer by signing up for both the Latin and physics tests, marking them blindly, and presenting himself as a candidate whose far-reaching interests compensate for a modest level of accomplishment. On a recent Spanish test, on the other hand, a student who answered every one of the questions correctly would have received a score of just 780,[16] while on the European History and World Cultures Achievement Test, he could have left sixteen of the one hundred items blank (or answered thirteen items incorrectly) and still received a perfect score of 800. (To score a 200 on this test, he would have had to answer forty-eight items incorrectly and leave the other fifty-two blank.)[17]

Harvard is currently (though very tentatively) considering the possibility of one day offering its applicants the option of submitting five Achievement Test scores (two or three of them in specified subjects) instead of its current requirement of the SAT plus three Achievements. Critics of the SAT have hailed this vague proposal as a victory of some kind. But even if it were adopted nationwide, all it would do is make admissions officers treat the English Composition Test and the Mathematics Achievement Test like the verbal and math SATs. Students would have to take the same number of tests, but they'd pay more for the privilege, since Achievements are more expensive than the SAT. Harvard is lukewarm about the whole idea anyway. "Our assumption," says Fred Jewett, "would be that a relatively small number of people would use that option even if it were available."

The aptitude-achievement debate ignores a crucial question: Why is it necessary or desirable to base an admissions decision, even in part, on a student's score on *any* one-hour multiple-choice test? A few dozen simple-minded questions answered on a Saturday morning toward the end of eleventh grade — is this really the best way (or even a good way) to judge a student's readiness for higher education? The College Boards have been an American middle-class rite of passage for so long that we seldom stop to consider what a peculiar device they are.

*   *   *

One plausible alternative to this sort of testing would simply be an increased emphasis on academic requirements for admission, to *encourage* readiness rather than merely attempt to measure it indirectly. Colleges are in an excellent position to improve the quality of their own applicant pools by encouraging high schools to be better at preparing their students for higher education.

All selective colleges have at least some requirements. Students are supposed to take so many years of science, so many years of math, perhaps a year of a foreign language. But most colleges' requirements aren't much more detailed than that. What if colleges were very specific about what they expected their applicants to have accomplished in high school? What if a group of colleges announced tomorrow that they would no longer admit students who hadn't had four years of high school English (and that courses in film comedy don't count as English courses), that certain books have to be read, that a certain number of papers have to be written, and so on? One of the many crimes of the SAT is that it has led both colleges and high schools to behave as though differences in course content — Shakespeare versus Groucho — were less important than differences in, say, size of vocabulary. An emphasis on genuine accomplishment would be a useful corrective to the superficiality promoted by the SAT.

Most selective colleges strongly favor students who take uniformly solid courses rather than gimmicky electives. Some schools, like Stanford, even recalculate student grade point averages to reflect the presumed seriousness of courses taken. But few colleges, in the materials they send to potential applicants, are explicit about what sort of courses they like and what sort of courses they don't or about how they compare different transcripts. Frivolous high school courses would lose much of their appeal if students knew they were reducing their prospects for college by taking them. Nervous parents would stop demanding SAT preparation in the schools and start demanding term papers.

A few years ago, the College Board made what it believed was a step in this general direction when it published "a statement of what academic preparation for college in the 1980s ought to be." This statement was the work of the Board's so-called Educational EQuality Project, an unfortunately named enterprise that consumed ten years, "countless meetings," and untold thousands of dollars in the process of identifying "the Basic Academic Competencies." What are the basic academic competencies? "They are academic," announced the Board with the assurance of a decade's labor. "They are basic."[18]

The EQuality Project detected six essential skills (a better word than *competencies,* I would have thought): reading, writing, speaking and listening, mathematics, reasoning, and studying. "Without such competencies," the Board concluded, "the knowledge of literature, history, science, languages, mathematics, and all other disciplines is unattainable. . . . Teaching that is done in ignorance of, or in disregard for, such competencies and their interrelationships to each of the subject-matter areas is inadequate if not incompetent." (The Board, as usual, could use some competent instruction in writing competency.)[19]

Furthermore, the Board divided each competency into half a dozen subcompetencies, such as: "The ability to make estimates and approximations, and to judge the reasonableness of a result," "the ability to conceive ideas about a topic for the purpose of writing," "the ability to separate one's personal opinions and assumptions from a writer's," and so on. The College Board hands out little leaflets with these competencies listed on them. Teachers are supposed to read them and get with the program. If they do, their students will surely be rewarded when freshman grades are handed out. "The support of college people," proclaims the leaflet, "suggests these competencies have intrinsic validity for improving the chances for success in learning at the first-year level in college — possibly lowering the immense burden of remediation now done by many colleges."[20]

All of this is a huge waste of time and money. Partly as a result of the Board's long-standing commitment to simple-minded testing, students are already being pecked to death by "basic skills." Although it may be true that a student of literature requires "the ability to vary [his] reading speed and method (survey, skim, review, question, and master) according to the type of material and [his] purpose for reading," it does not follow that inculcation of this "competency" (subcompetency, rather) should be given first priority in the teaching of reading. It's easy to imagine high school teachers, armed with leaflets from the College Board, drilling their students on surveying, skimming, reviewing, questioning, and mastering instead of actually giving them good books to read. My personal experience has been that the acquisition of "basic competencies" follows rather than leads good instruction in "subject-matter areas." The Board and ETS are infatuated with basic competencies because basic competencies are all that can be measured with multiple-choice tests.[21]

A better model for reform is the Advanced Placement (AP) program (discussed in Chapter 2), in which participating high schools offer accelerated courses based on specifications promulgated by ETS and the College Board. The AP program as it is currently set up is a joke, but the form is appealing. The nice thing about the concept is that it emphasizes serious learning and promotes the notion that taking challenging courses is a good thing. Couldn't high schools and colleges come up with a similar program that would encourage real education and at the same time give admissions officers something resembling a common ground on which to judge candidates from different schools? An organization like the College Board could serve as a neutral forum at which high schools and colleges could meet to iron out what these courses ought to cover, how they might be taught, and what sort of materials they should use. The new program could simply be built on the bones of the old one. As with the AP, it would be possible to give teachers substantial leeway while at the same time making certain that general standards were upheld.

With colleges providing steady, systematic guidance to high schools, I don't think there would be any need for a national admissions testing program (indeed, I don't think there's a need for one even *without* such steady, systematic guidance). If colleges can't bear the thought of giving up test scores, however, then we need tests that are very different from the ones we have now. Once again, I think the AP program, for all its many faults, provides a general outline for what such testing might be.

Like AP tests, any new admissions tests should be directly tied to curriculum so that learning and "coaching" would be indistinguishable. But unlike AP tests, any new tests should not contain multiple-choice questions, and they should not be so trivial or transparent that they encourage short-cut preparation. They should be incorporated directly into the curricula they measure and be treated as a part of the educational process rather than as a "barometer" of the quality of schools. Like AP exams, they should be conducted by the schools and not by ETS or the College Board. At the very least, admissions testing, if it is done at all, should not take place in a single hour on a single Saturday morning.

Such testing would be enormously expensive (unless colleges were willing to dispense with centralized grading and let teachers mark the tests themselves and incorporate scores into class grades, perhaps in accordance with some common formula). But we shouldn't fool ourselves into thinking that a test like the SAT is good simply because it can be administered and scored with ease. The features of the SAT that make it quick and easy are the same ones that make its content so superficial and unfair and its effect on schools so pernicious.

An admissions system centered on explicit requirements and guidelines would not necessarily be any fairer to the under-privileged than a system based on SAT scores. As Leon Botstein, the president of Bard College, pointed out at the College Board's annual meeting in 1982, colleges can effectively exclude minorities simply by requiring their applicants to take courses that aren't taught (because they're too expensive or because qualified teachers can't be found) in inner-city schools. Given this fact, it seems to me that colleges have an additional responsibility to help less fortu-nate schools fulfill commonly accepted requirements for admis-sion. It is in the interest of colleges to make this possible. The only way to produce qualified minority students is to ensure that they have a chance to learn what they must know to succeed.

To meet this goal, colleges need literally to invest in disadvan-taged schools and school systems. Harvard recently spent five years raising a third of a billion dollars for its already oceanic endowment. A number of other prestigious colleges have raised similar sums, and still others are planning monumental fund drives of their own. Why not spend some of this money on helping high schools prepare qualified candidates (or on helping elementary schools prepare qualified high school students)? A useful role for an organization like the College Board would be as an intermediary between colleges and high schools, channeling expertise, subsidized teaching materials, and other aid to needy schools. The Board and ETS loudly extol the idea of equal opportunity, but they have never done anything to bring it about. The SAT, as I have argued, actually undermines such efforts by creating the illusion that differences in school quality don't matter. Since all colleges would be better off if high school students were better prepared, colleges could look at such contributions as expressions of pure self-interest. Many colleges now have expensive and time-consuming remedial programs. But colleges wouldn't have to offer high-school-level courses if high schools did.

Reforming schools and admissions systems along these or similar lines would not be terribly difficult, but it would require a conscientious effort by the colleges and high schools. Is such an effort likely to be made? I don't think so. The simple fact is that the selection of applicants at the vast majority of colleges isn't terribly important to the colleges: schools that have few applicants worry more about filling dormitories than about making fine distinctions between candidates; prestigious colleges with vast surpluses of qualified applicants (that are thus forced to turn away students who would succeed if admitted) know that the consequences of "incorrect" decisions are very slight. Colleges wouldn't hire undergraduates, scholarship athletes, and unemployed young alumni to read application folders if they were genuinely worried about making precisely "accurate" admissions decisions. This will be even more apparent in the near future, since the teenaged population is declining while applications to the most prestigious schools are increasing; the least selective colleges are becoming less selective while the most selective ones are becoming more so. Both trends make it very unlikely that colleges will devote more time, money, and energy to admissions (they also essentially eliminate the final justification for requiring the SAT).

In the old days, college admissions decisions were made by faculty members, not by nonacademic admissions staffs. Such a process is too expensive and time-consuming to be practical nowadays, and most professors would prefer not to be bothered anyway. But faculty members ought to take an active interest in how their institutions select freshman classes. If colleges put a little effort into helping high schools produce better candidates, the colleges would benefit too, and professors wouldn't complain so much about the shortcomings of the students they're forced to teach. Professors have tended to moan about inadequate high schools without realizing that they are in an excellent position to do something about improving them. After all, colleges created the multimillion-dollar coaching industry and transformed high school curricula simply by requiring their applicants to take the SAT; what would happen if they explicitly required their applicants to read books, write papers, and take challenging courses?

The first step in creating both a humane admissions system and healthy secondary schools is as simple as shifting emphasis from the rewarding of "aptitude" to the fostering of preparation. Before we can do this, we have to abandon the notion, cultivated by ETS, that each of us harbors a finite consignment of merit to be bartered for educational and economic opportunity. We will never eliminate inequalities and injustices from our schools or our society by maintaining an "objective" testing system that perpetuates both.

Since none of the foregoing is likely to come about, I will prudently suggest a few halfway measures that would offer varying degrees of transitory relief from the present tyranny of ETS and its multiple-choice mentality. Some of these suggestions are mutually exclusive or redundant. For example, if ETS were simply abolished (hear, hear), there would be no need to change the name of the SAT, since it would no longer exist. But I offer them all in the hope that nearly everyone will be able to find something to agree with. Hundreds of reforms are possible; I've boiled my list down to fifteen:

1. *Change the name of the SAT.*

There is wide agreement in measurement circles that test-makers should not make unsupportable claims for their tests. ETS calls the SAT an "aptitude" test but is unable to define *aptitude* or to prove that the SAT measures it. Anne Anastasi, a measurement expert recently honored with an award by ETS, has written: "To claim that a test measures anything over and above its criterion is pure speculation of the type that is not amenable to verification and hence falls outside the realm of experimental science."[22] The criterion of the SAT is freshman grade point average. Predicting this average is the only use for which the SAT is "valid." I propose, therefore, that the SAT be given an honest name: the College Freshman Grade Point Average Predictor Test (CFGPAT). Students could refer to the test colloquially as "the Grade Predictor." This simple change would go a long way toward demystifying the test and loosening its grip on both the anxieties of test-takers and the fantasies of ETS vice presidents.

2. *Give ETS an honest address.*

ETS is in Lawrence Township. It is not in Princeton and it has no connection with Princeton University. ETS's shameless exploitation of the Princeton name is deceptive and dishonest.

3. *Give ETS an honest name.*

Simply (and accurately) adding "Inc." to the company logo would be an improvement. Calling ETS something like Multicorp or Testco would be even better. Merely getting ETS executives to admit that their employer is a "company" and not an "institution" would be a start.

4. *Rescind ETS's nonprofit status.*

As long as ETS is going to act like a profit-hungry company, why not be honest about it? ETS hides behind its tax exemption and fools outsiders into believing it has no economic motive in promoting its tests. ETS claims to be concerned about public misconceptions about testing. One way to begin clearing up those misconceptions would be to make ETS present an honest picture of its role.

5. *Report SAT and other test scores on a 5-point scale.*

Since it is clear that the margin of error in SAT scores is vastly larger than ETS admits — and since even ETS concedes that many admissions officers and others read too much into small score differences — why not eliminate the problem by employing a scoring scale that more accurately represents the (modest) precision of the test?

6. *Make colleges pay for the scores they use.*

Obviously they'd just pass the cost along, but they'd have to do some soul-searching before they did. The SAT would seem much less necessary if the few colleges that actually use the scores had to hand over $150 or so every time they wanted to see one. If I ruled the world, students would pay nothing to take the SAT and the College Board would cover the cost of the program by assessing its members according to some prorated scale that reflected each institution's size or number of applicants. College Board members now pay annual dues of only $150, recently lowered from $200. Given the economic burden that students are forced to bear, this strikes me as obscene. The colleges should pay the full cost of programs they inflict on the rest of us and then make honest decisions about which ones they really need.

7. *Require ETS to state explicitly how test-takers' fees are spent.*

ETS uses income from its profitable tests, chiefly the SAT, to finance money losers in other fields, pointless research, inflated salaries, legal action against students, and wholesale deception on issues of direct concern to test-takers. Students ought to be told what proportion of their test fees is spent for such purposes.

8. *Disband the ETS research department.*

ETS has a large research department because Henry Chauncey yearned to run his own university. Much of this research is financed by unwitting test-takers who have no say in how their money will be spent. Most studies are intended to serve no loftier purpose than to provide scientific-sounding justifications for ETS's self-serving positions on such controversial topics as coaching, racial bias, and validity. When ETS cites "scientific studies" supporting its position on various issues, it is almost invariably citing studies performed by people in its employ. Obviously such research is biased and undependable — particularly when ETS executives put pressure on researchers to trim their findings to fit corporate objectives.

It would make much more sense for universities and other independent bodies to do the background research on ETS tests. Under such an arrangement, ETS would simply make testing data freely available to outside researchers. Naturally, ETS will never agree to this. But we should all ask ourselves why it makes sense to give ETS the primary responsibility for determining whether ETS is doing a good job. The fox has been minding the henhouse for nearly forty years now. It's time to change the guard.

9. *File a class action suit against the College Board on behalf of the students it has been overcharging for years.*

The suit should demand that the College Board put its testing contracts up for competitive bidding and that it pay back the exorbitant profits it has taken for itself and for ETS for years.

10. *Eliminate the Test of Standard Written English (TSWE).*

This is the mini Achievement Test ETS tacked onto the SAT in an effort to stabilize the SAT's market. The test is badly written, and it distracts students from the more important business of taking the SAT. Colleges are supposed to use the TSWE in making "placement" decisions, but they don't. Every admissions officer I've talked to has told me that he uses TSWE scores in making admissions decisions, a purpose for which the test is not designed and has not been validated. There has been some vague talk of a TSWE boycott among guidance counselors in New York City. The idea should be taken up nationwide.

11. *Prohibit ETS from spending test-takers' money to lobby against test-takers' interests.*

According to its original conception, ETS was supposed to be an impartial and disinterested supplier of examinations required by others. The company recently described itself as "an independent third party of unquestioned objectivity."[23] This is fantasy. ETS has become the single most active force behind the promotion of unnecessary testing in our society. In the past five years, the company has spent more than $1 million in test-takers' fees on direct efforts to dissuade legislators from voting for truth-in-testing laws. It has spent even more money indirectly.[24]

12. *Require ETS and the College Board to publish their first honest statement about coaching and the SAT.*

If no one at ETS or the Board wants to write it, I'd be happy to.

13. *Spin off the Center for Occupational and Professional Assessment as a separate, for-profit corporation.*

Much of the market for COPA tests wouldn't exist if this burgeoning ETS division couldn't hide behind the inflated reputation of its parent company. "As the nation's largest testing organization," boasts a current COPA brochure, "ETS is able to provide its clients with the same expertise, experience, and resources used to create such well-known programs as the Scholastic Aptitude Test (SAT), the Graduate Management Test (GMAT), and the Graduate Record Examinations (GRE.)"[25] This is grossly distorted. A member of the ETS research staff described COPA to me as "a shoddy operation" and said that the division cuts corners to fit the budgets of its customers. Most of COPA's tests serve not to "protect consumers," as ETS claims, but rather to restrain trade (by limiting access to jobs, as in the case of Delaware's PPST) or to stroke the egos of ordinary mortals by enabling them to embellish their business cards with grandiose professional titles (Certified Business Forms Consultant).

14. *Require ETS to make all its hiring, compensation, and promotion decisions for its executives and test development personnel on the basis of test scores. These scores should be published each year in the company's annual report.*

When I asked President Anrig why ETS doesn't make its own employees take the sort of tests it sells to others, Joy McIntyre interrupted triumphantly to point out that there are "417 different jobs at ETS." Testing so many different people, she implied, would be impossible. But there must be as many different college majors in the country; ETS sees nothing absurd about using a single test, the SAT, to cover all of them. Besides, ETS already publishes a test that it claims is "appropriate for a wide variety of potential users," including "educators, employers, and others."[26] This test is the Pre-Professional Skills Tests, the NTE test Delaware uses to certify teachers. (See Chapter 12.)

"Professionals should be able to demonstrate competence in communication and computation," says a PPST promotional brochure.[27] According to an ETS staff summary from 1982, the company employs 607 "professionals."[28] Since these are precisely the people ETS claims the PPST was designed for, wouldn't it make sense to require them to take it? Doing so wouldn't cost very much. As ETS says, the PPST is "inexpensive," and it can be "administered in a very short time frame."[29]

ETS undoubtedly believes that the PPST wouldn't tell it anything very important about its employees. It ought to bear this in mind when it presses the test on other employers. Making the test a company requirement would render this lesson impossible to forget.

15. *Abolish the Educational Testing Service.*

Appendix A

A Poisoned Question

AFTER MY EXPERIENCE with the four verbal questions discussed in Chapter 3, I more or less gave up on the idea of persuading ETS to concede that it had ever published even one ambiguous verbal item. Then, on the SAT I took at Julia Richman High School in May 1984, I found a question so flawed I didn't think ETS would be able to talk its way out of rescoring it. The question was based on a reading passage concerning the toxic effects of various "chemicals in our atmosphere." Following is the second paragraph of the passage and the question to which I object.[1]

Even before 650 B.C., lead ore was mined on a small scale in order to extract the silver from it. With the invention of coinage, the demand for silver led to an enormous increase in the amount of available lead ore. At the time of the Roman Empire, the wealthy used elegant metal containers for food and drink. Since acidic wine leached copper from bronze or copper vessels, producing obvious toxic effects, containers came to be lined with lead, which did not cause vomiting and actually tasted good. In fact, however, lead is more toxic than copper, and yet the members of the Roman aristocracy added lead to their diets in more than a dozen ways.

22. The passage suggests that by Roman times lead containers were widely used for which of the following reasons?

    I. Lead was in abundant supply.
   II. Lead imparted a pleasant taste to food and drink.
  III. Lead was considered an antidote to copper poisoning.

(A) I only
(B) II only
(C) I and II only
(D) II and III only
(E) I, II, and III

ETS's answer to this question is C. On June 18, 1984, I wrote to the company arguing that a better choice was E. "Your question writers," I said,

> hold that [the Romans did not consider lead an antidote to copper poisoning], presumably reasoning that a person suffering from copper poisoning could not cure himself by lining his wine goblets with lead. But my *Webster's Seventh New Collegiate Dictionary* gives the second meaning of antidote as "something that relieves, prevents, or counteracts." Since the lead lining prevented copper poisoning, and since the Romans knew this, ETS's answer on this item would seem to be incorrect.
>
> Even if you reject the dictionary definition, the question is still ambiguous. Copper poisoning was a societal as well as an individual problem for the Romans. Even if they didn't think lead cured individual cases of copper poisoning, they clearly thought of lead as a remedy for copper poisoning in general. In this sense [too] they clearly thought of lead as an "antidote to copper poisoning."[2]

How could ETS argue with both the dictionary and common sense? I mailed my letter and eagerly awaited a reply. Ten business days passed, then ten more. On July 16, I called ETS to find out why I hadn't received a response to my complaint. After being transferred from department to department, I was connected with a man who asked me for my name and date of birth, then put me on Hold for several minutes. "We'll have to refer you over to our test development office," he told me when he returned. "It's quite possible that they have received your letter and may be looking into it now." He said that he would send a note over to test development and that "you should be hearing from them within a couple of days." At 7:45 that night, he called me back to say that the people in test development had received my letter and that they were going to answer it, although he couldn't say when.

I finally heard from ETS a few days later. The letter — dated July 17, one day after my phone call, roughly twenty business days after my original complaint, in clear violation of ETS's vaunted "uniform complaint procedure" — read as follows:

Dear Mr. Owen:

We have received your inquiry about question 22 of the first section of the Scholastic Aptitude Test administered in May 1984.

Question 22 requires the candidate to decide whether the Romans considered lead, with which they lined their copper drinking vessels, to be an antidote to copper poisoning. As you know, Webster's defines 'antidote' as '1: a remedy to counteract the effects of poison   2: something that relieves, prevents, or counteracts.' The example given by Webster's New Collegiate Dictionary to illustrate the second meaning is 'an (antidote) to the mechanization of our society,' which suggests that, in its second sense, the word is used metaphorically. The meaning that seems relevant to the question is the first one, and one cannot infer from the passage that the Romans thought that they could counteract copper poisoning by ingesting lead. Yes, the Romans did think that lead prevented copper poisoning, but to say that lead is an antidote to copper poisoning is like saying that sun-screen lotion is an antidote to sunburn; a statement like that would sound unidiomatic, if not illogical, to most ears.

You also assert that, while the Romans may not have believed that lead cured individual cases of copper poisoning, they did consider lead to be a remedy for copper poisoning in general. It would seem that here you are applying the second, and metaphorical, meaning of 'antidote,' the sense evident in the statement 'Education is the antidote to the poison of superstition.' But the passage doesn't treat poisoning metaphysically [sic]; it describes, in a literal fashion, the effects of lead on the human body. Thus, it would be inappropriate to say that the Romans considered lead an antidote to copper poisoning.

Thank you for writing to us about this matter. We appreciate comments that may help us improve the accuracy of our tests.

Sincerely,
[signature]
Nontas Konstantakis
Assistant Examiner
College Board Test Development[3]

Well, ETS is certainly an antidote to boredom. If the company put as much effort into writing test questions as it puts into contriving after-the-fact excuses for them, the SAT would be a better test.

Konstantakis's assertion that Webster's "suggests" that the second definition of *antidote* is solely "metaphorical" is specious. Even so, his argument has no bearing on the matter at hand. There is nothing in the passage that precludes interpreting the word *antidote* in this "metaphorical" sense.

Konstantakis also says that this usage of the word *antidote,* though correct, is "inappropriate" because the passage deals only with the literal "effects of lead on the human body." If I understand him correctly, he is saying that the statement "Lead was considered an antidote to copper poisoning" is true ("metaphorically") but irrelevant to the theme of the passage and therefore incorrect as an answer. By this reasoning, though, ETS must also eliminate choices I and II, since neither the abundance nor the taste of lead is relevant to the specific purpose of the passage as Konstantakis describes it. Like choice III, both these statements are true; but by his reasoning, must they not also be considered "inappropriate"?

Even here, though, Konstantakis is wrong. The passage *does* discuss metal poisoning as a societal (and therefore "metaphorical") problem, and not just as an individual (and therefore "literal") one: the paragraph quoted above is not about the effect of metal poisoning on just any human body; it's about the effect of this poisoning on a particular social class, described as "the wealthy" and as "the Roman aristocracy." According to the passage, copper drinking vessels were poisoning these privileged people. Lining the "elegant" containers with lead was considered a remedy for this problem. Using the word *antidote* in this sense violates neither the context of the passage nor the dictionary definition of the word as Konstantakis interprets it. Indeed, according to the passage, the fact that lead provided a remedy to the aristocrats' copper poisoning problem was the *single most important reason* why lead containers were used by the Romans; this is *precisely* what the question asks.

I didn't have time to assemble a panel of "independent external subject matter experts" to review this item. If there are any such experts out there who would care to volunteer opinions, I will happily forward their remarks to ETS.

Appendix B

Illegal Test Use

PRESIDENT ANRIG'S CONCERN about the illegal use of ETS tests does not extend to other programs. A number of employers require college graduates to submit their SAT scores when they apply for jobs; many law firms make hiring decisions in part on the basis of LSAT scores. Both practices are presumably against the law for the reasons Anrig enumerated in connection with the NTE. ETS knows that such misuse is common, but both it and the College Board look the other way, perhaps because they earn $14 for every SAT score they supply.

In April 1984, I told Vernyce Danells of ETS that I knew of at least three companies — Morgan Stanley, Morgan Guaranty Trust, and Bain & Co. — that had programs with SAT requirements. I reminded her of Anrig's promise not to sell the NTE to states intending to use it as an employment test and asked if he had a similar policy for the SAT. She made careful notes of my questions, read them back to me when I was finished, and promised to call me right away. She never did.

I also called Morgan Stanley's Management Information Services training program. Stanley J. Kay, Jr., manager of college recruiting, had recently written to several college seniors interested in jobs after graduation. "Enclosed is a blank candidate profile," his letter said.

> Also enclosed, are instructions obtaining [sic] your (SAT) Scholastic Aptitude Test scores from the Educational Testing Service. Please bring the completed profile, SAT score report and a copy of

your undergraduate transcript with you when you arrive for your interview.

Please contact ETS *immediately* upon receiving this letter. We will not make any hiring decisions without this information. If you did not take the SATs before entering college, please explain why on the profile and, if possible, provide an equivalent standardized aptitude rating on the profile. The cost of obtaining your SAT scores and transcript will be paid as part of your expenses.

The attached profile contained blanks for "scores on standard test," "SAT's," and "other," but there was no space for the names of the tests, descriptions of what they measured, or explanations of how they had been scored.

The person I was referred to at Morgan Stanley told me he would call me back with answers to my questions. He never did. Nor did he return my follow-up call. I finally reached him on his direct line. "I applied for permission to talk to you and was denied," he said. "I was told that we do not wish to pursue the discussion."

About two weeks later, I received a note from Joy McIntyre of ETS. "Because, as you know, the College Board is responsible for policies regarding the SAT," she wrote, "we referred your question about businesses requiring the SAT there." Attached was a "response to Mr. Owen's inquiry" from Bob Seaver, a vice president. "If you have further information," McIntyre continued, "Mr. Seaver asks that you contact him directly so he can pursue this issue." Seaver's memo read:

> The College Board does not encourage nor [sic] approve using SAT scores in considering candidates for employment for several reasons. Scores are typically several years old and do not reflect the changes over time which most individuals' skills display, nor the effect of intervening education or experience on the individual. Performance in college or other work experience is a much better indicator of such developments. Even where the candidate is a recent high school graduate, it seems highly questionable whether scores intended to help predict performance in college would be appropriate predictors of performance on the job, where many other factors may come into play and many other skills are requisite. So the Board does not permit assignment of "designated institution" codes to businesses or corporations to receive score reports for these purposes; it advises such organizations against using

scores for employment purposes; and it follows up actively to dissuade them from such use where such practice is brought to its attention.

This sounded very reasonable to me. I called Seaver two weeks later. He sounded quite surprised to hear from me. Perhaps he had forgotten that he had asked me, through McIntyre, to contact him directly. I asked him how his follow-up investigation was going.

"I honestly don't know," he said. "I did what — I think our query to ETS was, Can you tell us what the source of the allegation was, or who it was specifically within the organizations who were supposed to be using it? And I think that we haven't heard back from ETS on that."

And probably never would, since ETS had already said that the problem was the College Board's. It would have been much simpler for Seaver to call me and ask me to repeat the information I had already given ETS. But he hadn't done so. I asked him how big a problem the misuse of scores by employers was.

"We do not have a sense that it is a problem of *any* size," he said. "We do — I think we mentioned that whenever we hear about this thing we try to follow up, and there's not very much to follow up."

"How many companies a year?"

"I don't have a count."

"Any?"

"I honestly don't know. I'll ask the program officer. I'd be happy to."

"More than one? Or you don't have any idea?"

"It's not something that I generally deal with. My impression in talking with the program service officer was that this is an extremely rare occurrence, so rare in fact that she could follow up personally on those where it comes to our attention — less than once a year. But I don't know. If you want me to get that information, I'll be happy to."

I never heard from him again. And no one from the Board or ETS ever followed up on the program at Morgan Stanley. I later called ETS and asked a candidate information officer whether it was all right for a company to require SAT scores. She said it was and that "a lot" of companies had such a requirement. Then she told me how to order a copy of my scores.

Notes

Introduction: High Anxiety

1. Banesh Hoffmann, *The Tyranny of Testing* (New York: Collier Books, 1964).
2. Banesh Hoffmann, "The Tyranny of Multiple-Choice Tests," *Harper's*, March 1961; " 'Best' Answers or Better Minds," *American Scholar*, Spring 1959.
3. Hoffmann, *Tyranny of Testing*, p. 17.
4. Ibid., p. 18.
5. David Wechsler, *Manual for the Wechsler Intelligence Scale for Children — Revised* (New York: Psychological Corporation, 1974), p. 183.
6. Victor H. Noll, Dale P. Scannell, and Robert C. Craig, eds., *Introduction to Educational Measurement,* 4th ed. (Boston: Houghton Mifflin, 1979), p. 271.
7. Patrice Horn, "California's Declining SATs: Is It the Weather?" *Psychology Today,* March 1983, pp. 76–77.
8. College Entrance Examination Board, *On Further Examination: Report of the Advisory Panel on the Scholastic Aptitude Test Score Decline,* Willard Wirtz, chairman (New York: College Entrance Examination Board, 1977), p. 35.
9. Most of these possibilities are discussed, at least in passing, in the work just cited and in *Appendixes to On Further Examination* (New York: College Entrance Examination Board, 1977). See also Lawrence Lipsitz, ed., *The Test Score Decline* (Englewood Cliffs, N.J.: Educational Technology Publications, 1977); Landon Y. Jones, *Great Expectations* (New York: Coward, McCann & Geoghegan, 1980).

10. Quoted in Ann Hulbert, "S.A.T.s Aren't So Smart," *New Republic,* December 20, 1982, pp. 12–13.
11. Associated Press, "Pupil signals mixed on aptitude scores," *Kansas City Star,* September 18, 1983.
12. Lawrence Feinberg and Leon Wynter, "P.G.'s Roosevelt Tops Area Schools in SAT Averages," *Washington Post,* October 22, 1983.
13. Associated Press, "Unusual Incentives in Florida Schools Hailed," *New York Times,* October 11, 1983, p. A19.
14. ETS, *1983 Annual Report,* p. 28.
15. This figure is from the ETS Test Collection, a compilation of tests from around the world.

1: The Kettle Defense

1. *The Henry Chauncey Conference Center Welcomes You* (Princeton, N.J.: ETS, undated).
2. Ibid.
3. See, for example, Steven Brill, "The Secrecy Behind the College Boards," *New York,* October 7, 1974, p. 67.
4. Allan Nairn and Associates, *The Reign of ETS: The Corporation That Makes Up Minds* (Washington, D.C.: Learning Research Project, 1980), p. 28.
5. Until 1982, ETS included a list of clients in its annual report. Unfortunately, this extremely entertaining feature has been dropped. Most of the customers listed here are taken from the 1981 report; several others are from a 1983 promotional brochure for ETS's Center for Occupational and Professional Assessment (COPA).
6. ETS, *1981 Annual Report,* p. 16.
7. Brill, "Secrecy Behind the College Boards," p. 68; Frank Caplan, *The First Twelve Months of Life* (New York: Bantam Books, 1981), p. 75.
8. ETS, *1983 Annual Report,* p. 12.
9. College Entrance Examination Board, statement of 1982 revenues with projections for 1983.
10. ETS, *1983–84 Reference Guide: Student Search Service* (New York: College Board, 1983).
11. See *New York,* March 9, 1981.
12. ETS, 1983–84 *Student Bulletin,* p. 4.
13. See various College Board statements of revenues.
14. ETS, 1983–84 *Student Bulletin,* pp. 8–9.
15. ETS, 1983–84 SSS *Reference Guide.*

16. Brill, "Secrecy Behind the College Boards," p. 77. The speaker is former College Board president Sydney Marland.

17. This information is taken from "AGREEMENT dated as of January 1, 1979," etc., between ETS and the College Board. I obtained a copy from the public trial record of a lawsuit. (*Denburg v. ETS,* Superior Court of New Jersey, Chancery Division, Middlesex County, Docket Number C-1715-83. So far as I can tell, this is the only court case ever in which ETS has failed to win a protective order covering exhibits and other materials. The trial record is a treasure trove of information about ETS that is available nowhere else.) The 1979 agreement remained in effect until about 1983. I asked ETS for a copy of the new contract, but my request was denied.

18. Ibid.

19. William H. Angoff (of ETS), ed., *The College Board Admissions Testing Program: A Technical Report on Research and Development Activities Relating to the Scholastic Aptitude Test and Achievement Tests* (New York: College Entrance Examination Board, 1971), p. 15 (hereafter cited as *Technical Report*).

20. ETS, *1983 Annual Report,* p. 28.

21. Form 990, Return of Organization Exempt from Income Tax, 1982 (for the fiscal year ended June 30, 1983). Copies of ETS's tax returns can be ordered from Disclosure Office, Brookhaven Service Center, 1040 Waverly Ave., Stop 500, Holtsville, N.Y. 11799; telephone: (516) 654-6481.

22. Carole Gould, "Designing a Benefits Package," *New York Times,* December 11, 1983.

23. Minutes of Proceedings at a Joint Public Hearing of the (New York) Senate and Assembly Standing Committees on Higher Education, May 9, 1979, p. 89 (hereafter cited as New York Minutes).

24. Report of hearings on the Truth in Testing Act of 1979 and the Educational Testing Act of 1979, held in Washington, D.C., July 31, August 1, September 10, September 24, October 10, October 11, 1979, before the Subcommittee on Elementary, Secondary, and Vocational Education of the Committee on Education and Labor of the United States House of Representatives, p. 180.

25. Nairn, *Reign of ETS,* p. 36.

26. Ibid., p. 36 and note.

27. Joy McIntyre to Owen, June 18, 1984, in (non-)response to a letter of mine, dated May 13, 1984, containing nineteen questions about ETS. McIntyre wrote that ETS would provide me with requested information that was "easily and publicly available." When I called

to follow up, she told me that she had assigned "a couple of people" to look for answers and that she was "trying to find out now what the status of the search is." She said she would call me back on Monday. On Tuesday she called to say ETS wouldn't answer any of my questions. Since I had sent a copy of these questions to President Anrig, I assume that he instructed her not to cooperate.

28. Brill, "Secrecy Behind the College Boards," p. 67.
29. From an unpublished list of fifty-five "corrections" prepared by ETS in response to Brill's article.
30. *The Henry Chauncey Conference Center* (Princeton, N.J.: ETS, undated).
31. "ETS to appeal property tax ruling," ETS *Examiner,* November 21, 1974.
32. ETS, *1982 Annual Report,* p. ii.
33. "1983 Comparative Performance Study," *Business Officer,* news magazine of the National Association of College and University Business Officers, March 1984, pp. 19–20.
34. ETS, *1983 Annual Report,* p. 28.
35. ETS vice president Alice J. Irby to the Honorable Carl D. Perkins, U.S. House of Representatives, November 28, 1979, p. 6.
36. This is what Anrig told me the study cost. The exact figure ought to be listed in ETS's federal tax return (Form 990) for the fiscal year ended June 30, 1982. This is the only recent ETS tax return I was unable to obtain from the IRS.
37. There was a series of articles on this theme in the ETS *Examiner.* See in particular "ETS teams to address revenue growth areas," May 6, 1982.
38. "The Corporate Plan of Educational Testing Service for Fiscal Year 1983," July 27, 1982.
39. Nairn, *Reign of ETS,* p. 70.
40. Brill, "Secrecy Behind the College Boards," p. 67.
41. William W. Turnbull, "Public and Professional Attitudes Toward Testing and ETS: Relations with Key Publics," unpublished typescript, August 14, 1978, p. 2.
42. See Chapter 6.
43. Nairn, *Reign of ETS.*
44. Warner V. Slack and Douglas Porter, "The Scholastic Aptitude Test: A Critical Appraisal," *Harvard Educational Review* 50 (May 1980): 154–75.
45. Barbara Lerner (of ETS), *The War on Testing* (Princeton, N.J.: ETS, 1979), p. 1.

46. Memorandum from Lois D. Rice of ETS to U.S. Congresswoman Shirley Chisholm, July 23, 1979.
47. Robert J. Kingston, "Memorandum for Chief Executive Officers of N.Y. State Colleges and Universities," etc., June 8, 1979.
48. ETS, "Memorandum of Opposition," undated.
49. Turnbull, "Relations with Key Publics," p. 17.
50. IRS Form 990, 1978, 1979, 1980.
51. Turnbull, "Relations with Key Publics," p. 10.
52. Barbara Demick, "Evening the Score," *New Republic,* August 25, 1979, p. 12.
53. New York Minutes, May 9, 1979, p. 129.
54. From an ETS computer study, "Project Operating Statement by Pos. — Category/Project, Period Ending 3/31/77," reported in *Testing Digest,* Fall 1979, p. 5.
55. Pike to Lavalle, June 12, 1979.
56. ETS, "Memorandum of Opposition," undated.
57. New York Minutes, May 9, 1979, p. 131A. See notation.
58. Memorandum quoted in press release of New York Public Interest Research Group, May 18, 1979, p. 3.
59. New York Minutes, May 9, 1979, p. 103.
60. ETS, "Memorandum of Opposition," undated, p. 2.
61. Allan Nairn, rebuttal to ETS, New York Public Interest Research Group, May 17, 1979, p. 5.
62. New York Minutes, May 9, 1979, p. 134A.
63. Richard D. Rooney, "Memorandum for CEEB Representatives and Alternates," etc., May 11, 1979.
64. Frederick H. Dietrich, memorandum to "Those Concerned with Standardized Tests and Testing in the State of California," May 19, 1978.
65. "Statement of the College Board in opposition to Senate Bill 5200/ Assembly Bill 7668," May 1, 1979.
66. Press release of New York Public Interest Research Group, May 17, 1979.
67. The New York surcharge total is based on 213,264 SAT-takers in New York State in 1982–83; figure provided by College Board. Lobbying expense from IRS Form 990, 1982.
68. Letter to the editor, *New Republic,* September 29, 1979, p. 7.
69. IRS Form 990, 1979, 1980.
70. [Robert J. Solomon], *20 Questions: The Truth about Truth-in-Testing* (Princeton, N.J.: ETS, 1981).
71. Brill, "Secrecy Behind the College Boards."

72. David Owen, "1983 The Last Days of ETS," *Harper's,* May 1983, pp. 21–37.
73. Gregory R. Anrig, "Memorandum for: EXECUTIVE ADVISORY BOARD," May 25, 1983.

2: *Holistic Grading*

1. Claud M. Fuess, *The College Board: Its First Fifty Years* (New York: Columbia University Press, 1950), pp. 157–58 (hereafter cited as *First Fifty Years*).
2. Henry S. Dyer and Richard G. King (both of ETS), *College Board Scores: Their Use and Interpretation* (Princeton, N.J.: College Entrance Examination Board, 1955), p. 3.
3. Fuess, *First Fifty Years,* p. 158.
4. Angoff, *Technical Report,* p. 52.
5. Hoffmann, *Tyranny of Testing,* p. 115.
6. Ibid., p. 118.
7. Orville Palmer (of ETS), "Sense or Nonsense? The Objective Testing of English Composition," in *Readings in Educational and Psychological Measurement,* edited by Clinton I. Chase and H. Glenn Ludlow (Boston: Houghton Mifflin, 1966), p. 288.
8. Banesh Hoffmann, "The College Boards Fail the Test," *New York Times Magazine,* October 24, 1965.
9. Fred I. Godshalk, Frances Swineford, and William E. Coffman (all of ETS), *The Measurement of Writing Ability* (New York: College Entrance Examination Board, 1966), p. v.
10. William R. Shane (of ETS) et al., *LSAT Handbook* (Princeton, N.J.: ETS, 1964), pp. 14–15.
11. James Fallows, "The Tests and the 'Brightest': How Fair Are the College Boards?," *The Atlantic,* February 1981, p. 40.
12. ETS, *The College Board Achievement Tests* (New York: College Entrance Examination Board, 1983), p. 21.
13. Ibid.
14. ETS, *The English Composition Test with Essay,* "a report prepared in collaboration with Marjorie Kirrie, the chief reader," etc. (New York: College Entrance Examination Board, 1979), p. 4.
15. Ibid.
16. Ibid., p. 6.
17. Hunter M. Breland and Robert J. Jones (both of ETS), *Perceptions of Writing Skills,* College Board Report no. 82-4 (New York: College Entrance Examination Board, 1982), p. 12.

18. Ibid., p. 3.
19. Ibid., p. 30.
20. ETS, *1983–84 ATP Guide for High Schools and Colleges* (New York: College Entrance Examination Board, 1983), p. 12.
21. Arthur Bishop (of ETS), *The Concern for Writing,* ETS Focus 5 (Princeton, N.J.: ETS, 1980), p. 9.
22. Sherrye Henry show, WOR, New York City, April 17, 1984.
23. C. Fred Main, professor of English at Rutgers, quoted in *College Board News,* September 1979, p. 4.
24. Fuess, *First Fifty Years,* p. 13.
25. Jim Vopat, "Guilty Secrets of an ETS Grader," *Washington Monthly,* November 1982, p. 45.
26. Ibid., p. 46.
27. Ibid., p. 47.
28. ETS, *A Guide to the Advanced Placement Program, For May 1984* (New York: College Entrance Examination Board, 1983), p. 29.
29. Vopat, "Guilty Secrets," p. 47.
30. ETS, *Guide to the CLEP Examinations* (New York: College Entrance Examination Board, 1982), p. vii.
31. Ellis B. Page, "Grading Essays by Computer: Progress Report," in ETS, *Proceedings of the 1966 Invitational Conference on Testing Problems* (Princeton, N.J.: ETS, 1967), p. 87.
32. Ibid., p. 99.
33. Ibid., p. 89.
34. Ibid.

3: Multiple Guess

1. Edward B. Fiske, "Youth Outwits Merit Exam, Raising 240,000 Scores," *New York Times,* March 17, 1981, p. A1.
2. Robert J. Solomon, " 'Truth-in-Testing' Is: (A) (B) (C)," *New York Times,* March 10, 1981, p. A19.
3. Linda Heacock, "Memorandum for: Secondary School Principals," February 9, 1981.
4. Edward B. Fiske, "Pyramids of Test Question 44 Open a Pandora's Box," *New York Times,* April 14, 1981, p. C3.
5. Ibid.
6. Ibid.
7. "Transcript of the Committee on Review Hearing on the Appeal of Frederick R. Kling, July 9, 12, 13 — 1982," confidential unpublished typescript, ETS.

8. Edward B. Fiske, "A Second Student Wins Challenge on Answer to Math Exam Problem," *New York Times,* March 24, 1981.

9. Robert L. Jacobson, "Discovery of Second Error Poses Threat to Test, College Board Chairman Says," *Chronicle of Higher Education,* April 5, 1981.

10. [Paul Hoffman], "The SAT Snafu," *Science Digest,* January 1983, pp. 84–86.

11. ETS, *10 SATs* (New York: College Entrance Examination Board, 1983), p. 222.

12. Walt Haney and Laurie Scott, "Talking with Children About Tests: A Pilot Study of Test Item Ambiguity," National Consortium on Testing Staff Circular No. 7 (Cambridge, Mass.: Huron Institute, August 1980), p. 68.

13. ETS, *6 SATs* (New York: College Entrance Examination Board, 1982).

14. Ibid., p. 12.

15. Ibid.

16. Ibid., p. 11.

17. Ibid., p. 12.

18. ETS, *Preparing for Tests,* undated pamphlet.

19. *Scholastic Aptitude Test* (New York: College Entrance Examination Board, 1926), Form A, Sub-test Seven, p. 15.

20. Hoffmann, *Tyranny of Testing,* pp. 185–88.

21. Ibid.

22. ETS, *An Explanation of Multiple-Choice Testing* (Princeton, N.J.: ETS, 1961), quoted in Hoffmann, *Tyranny of Testing,* p. 186.

23. Hoffmann, *Tyranny of Testing,* p. 187.

24. ETS, *1982 Annual Report,* p. ii.

25. Ibid., p. vi.

26. Joy McIntyre to Owen, June 18, 1984.

27. Owen to Anrig, May 10, 1983.

28. Gregory R. Anrig, "Memorandum for: EXECUTIVE ADVISORY BOARD," May 25, 1983.

29. Anrig to Owen, May 25, 1983.

30. McIntyre to Owen, May 3, 1984; idem, June 18, 1984.

31. Vernyce Danells to *Harper's,* August 8, 1983.

32. Owen to ETS Board, etc., June 9, 1983.

33. Hanford to Owen, June 21, 1983.

34. Stewart to Owen, June 28, 1983.

35. Ibid.

36. Kimmel to Owen, Aug. 4, 1983.

37. Fiske, "Youth Outwits Merit Exam," p. A1.

38. Owen to Kimmel, September 8, 1983.
39. Kimmel to Owen, September 26, 1983.
40. Nicholas Von Hoffman, "Tests Test Ability of the Testee to Please the Tester," *Philadelphia Daily News,* April 29, 1983.

4: Numbers

1. Matthew T. Downey, *Carl Campbell Brigham: Scientist and Educator* (Princeton, N.J.: ETS, 1961), p. 35.
2. "Test Analysis of College Board Scholastic Aptitude Test May 1982 Administration 3ESA05," confidential unpublished statistical report (Princeton, N.J.: ETS, December 1982), p. A3.
3. Angoff, *Technical Report,* pp. 34–36.
4. Ibid., p. 32.
5. From an unpublished list of fifty-five "corrections" prepared by ETS in response to Brill, "Secrecy Behind the College Boards."
6. Angoff, *Technical Report,* pp. 22–23; [James Braswell], "Overview of the Scholastic Aptitude Test," unpublished typescript, prepared February 19, 1980, for South Carolina Task Force Committee on SAT scores.
7. ETS, *A Description of the College Board Achievement Tests* (New York: College Entrance Examination Board, 1962), p. 12.
8. Angoff, *Technical Report,* p. 9.
9. Ibid., pp. 26–27; confidential unpublished computer analysis of SAT form ESA05410, June 18, 1982.
10. Edward B. Fiske, "College Board, Under Criticism, Revises Test Guidelines," *New York Times,* February 2, 1977.
11. ETS, *1983–84 ATP Guide,* p. 11.
12. From an unpublished list of fifty-five "corrections" prepared by ETS in response to Brill, "Secrecy Behind the College Boards," p. 7.
13. ETS, *1983–84 ATP Guide,* p. 10.
14. Ibid.: "Internal consistency estimates tend to be somewhat inflated if the test is speeded. . . ."
15. Letter to the editor, *Harper's,* June 1961, p. 7.
16. Hoffmann, *Tyranny of Testing,* p. 171.
17. ETS, *10 SATs,* p. 175. Four missed questions equal five raw points. The difference between raw scores of 5 and 0 on this test is 10 scaled points; the difference between raw scores of 85 and 80 is 70 scaled points.
18. Ibid.

19. Edward B. Fiske, *Selective Guide to Colleges* (New York: Times Books, 1983).
20. See Leonard Ramist and Solomon Arbeiter (both of ETS), *Profiles, College-Bound Seniors, 1983* (New York: College Entrance Examination Board, 1984), and ETS, *Your Score Report for the SAT and Achievement Tests 1983–84* (New York: College Entrance Examination Board, 1983).
21. Angoff, *Technical Report*, p. 16.
22. Ibid., p. 26.
23. See, among other things, ETS, *10 SATs;* idem, *Profiles, College-Bound Seniors, 1983.*
24. Information about this method of detecting cheating is available in various places. It has never been clear to me whether ETS's scanners actually are programmed to kick out the answer sheets of students whose scores *drop* by 250 points. ETS won't answer my questions about this; perhaps they will answer yours.

5: Tempting the Medicine Freaks

1. ETS, *The College Board Achievement Tests*, p. 80.
2. This is *Denburg v. ETS.* See note 17, Chapter 1.
3. Angoff, *Technical Report*, p. 20.
4. Following are the members of the 1982–83 SAT Committee as they are listed in ETS, *Taking the SAT* (New York: College Entrance Examination Board, 1983), p. 4: Willie May, Wendell Phillips High School, Chicago, Illinois, *chairman;* James R. Buch, University of Oregon, Eugene, Oregon; Nancy S. Cole, University of Pittsburgh, Pittsburgh, Pennsylvania; William Controvillas, Farmington High School, Farmington, Connecticut; Margaret Fleming, Cleveland Public Schools, Cleveland, Ohio; Lynn H. Fox, Johns Hopkins University, Baltimore, Maryland; Jeanette B. Hersey, Connecticut College, New London, Connecticut; Robert S. Moore, South Carolina State Department of Education, Columbia, South Carolina; Allen Parducci, University of California–Los Angeles, Los Angeles, California; and Hammett Worthington-Smith, Albright College, Reading, Pennsylvania.
5. Following is the "Charge to SAT Committee," the College Board's instructions to members:

> The purpose of the committee is to advise the College Board on the various aspects of the SAT and to work with the test development staff of Educational

Testing Service on the development of the test. The more specific responsibilities of the committee are: (1) to become thoroughly familiar with the SAT — its purpose, *rationale*, content specifications, and psychometric properties; (2) to review test specifications and recommend changes if needed; (3) to monitor the effectiveness of the test for its purpose; (4) to consider policy questions related to the test and to make recommendations; (5) to recommend needed research; (6) to review the results of special studies of potential changes in the test and advise on their implementation; (7) to advise on improving communications with the public with respect to the test and its proper interpretation and use; and (8) to review two forms of the test each year by mail.

6. ETS, "Test Development Cycle Narrative," unsigned typescript, undated, p. 4.

6: *Coaching*

1. Dyer and King, *College Board Scores,* p. 46.
2. ETS, *Effects of Coaching on Scholastic Aptitude Test Scores* (New York: College Entrance Examination Board, 1965), p. 4.
3. *Report of the Commission on Tests,* vol. 1 (New York: College Entrance Examination Board, 1970).
4. Fuess, *First Fifty Years,* p. 85.
5. Angoff, *Technical Report,* p. 2.
6. Fuess, *First Fifty Years,* p. 101.
7. For a discussion of changes made in the early SAT to reduce its coachability, see Angoff, *Technical Report,* p. 16.
8. College Entrance Examination Board, *54th Report of the Director,* 1955.
9. Dean K. Whitla, "Effect of Tutoring on Scholastic Aptitude Test Scores," *Personnel and Guidance Journal,* 41 (1962): 32–37.
10. Angoff, *Technical Report,* p. 147.
11. ETS, "PSAT/NMSQT Summary of Answers, Form 1," unpublished report, October 27, 1981.
12. ETS, *Taking the SAT,* 1983, p. 7.
13. Angoff, *Technical Report,* p. 148.
14. Lewis W. Pike and Franklin R. Evans (both of ETS), *Effects of Special Instruction for Three Kinds of Mathematics Aptitude Items* (New York: College Entrance Examination Board, 1972), p. 29.
15. Ibid., p. vi.
16. Lewis W. Pike (of ETS), *Short-Term Instruction, Testwiseness, and the Scholastic Aptitude Test* (New York: College Entrance Examination Board, 1978; reprinted 1979).

17. Ibid., p. 34.
18. *College Board Review,* September 1979, p. 6.
19. Steven Levy, "E.T.S. and the 'Coaching' Cover-Up," *New Jersey Monthly,* March 1979, p. 82.
20. William W. Turnbull, "Memorandum for: SENIOR STAFF FORUM," March 6, 1979, p. 1.
21. Owen to Joy McIntyre, May 13, 1984; request denied by telephone.
22. ETS, *Effects of Coaching,* 1965, 1968. This statement has been cited by ETS on many occasions, in this case in an unpublished response to Brill, "Secrecy Behind the College Boards," p. 3.
23. Slack and Porter, "Critical Appraisal," p. 155.
24. Ibid., references deleted, p. 163.
25. Rex Jackson, "The Scholastic Aptitude Test: A Response to Slack and Porter's 'Critical Appraisal,' " *Harvard Educational Review,* 50 (August 1980): 382. Jackson's title at ETS was assistant vice president. "His main areas of concern," according to a note in the *Review,* "are educational measurement and educational research and development" (p. 456).
26. Ibid., p. 384.
27. Ibid., p. 385.
28. "The Effects of Coaching on Standardized Admission Examinations," Staff Memorandum of the Boston Regional Office of the Federal Trade Commission, September 1978, p. 1.
29. Ibid., p. 4.
30. Jackson, "Response to Slack and Porter," p. 384.
31. Warner V. Slack and Douglas Porter, "Training, Validity, and the Issue of Aptitude: A Reply to Jackson," *Harvard Educational Review,* 50 (August 1980): 394.
32. Donald E. Powers and Donald L. Alderman (both of ETS), *The Use, Acceptance, and Impact of* Taking the SAT — *A Test Familiarization Booklet,* College Entrance Examination Board Research and Development Report RDR 78-79, No. 6 (Princeton, N.J.: ETS, February 1979), p. 1.
33. ETS officials cited Powers and Alderman as proof that coaching didn't work in a seminar on coaching at an open house for College Board members at ETS in the fall of 1982.
34. Lawrence J. Stricker (of ETS), *Test Disclosure and Retest Performance on the Scholastic Aptitude Test,* College Board Report No. 82-7 (New York: College Entrance Examination Board, 1982).
35. Ibid., p. 10.
36. Samuel J. Messick (of ETS), *The Effectiveness of Coaching for the*

SAT: Review and Reanalysis of Research from the Fifties to the FTC (Princeton, N.J.: ETS, 1980).

37. ETS, *Taking the SAT,* 1983, p. 5.
38. Messick, *Effectiveness of Coaching,* p. 44.
39. Ibid., p. 19.
40. Ibid., pp. 7–8.
41. Angoff, *Technical Report,* p. 7.
42. Assembled by ETS and published by the College Board in, respectively, 1980, 1981, and 1982.
43. George Hanford, Memorandum "To College Board Member Representatives and Committee Members in Ohio," November 2, 1979.
44. At $8.95, *10 SATs* is just about the most expensive SAT coaching book on the market. The price seems even higher when you realize that assembling it must have cost virtually nothing.
45. ETS, *A Little Anxiety,* promotional brochure, undated.
46. ETS, *It's Good To Know,* promotional brochure, 1983. In the Summer 1983 issue of *ETS Developments,* ETS employee Billie Slaughter is quoted as saying that after using *A Little Anxiety,* elementary school students will earn test scores that will be "more reflective of their knowledge and skills rather than their feelings about testing." In other words, they will be higher?
47. ETS, *Taking the SAT,* 1983, p. 6.

7: Beating the Test

1. Stanley H. Kaplan Educational Center, 1983 brochure, p. 9.
2. Pike and Evans, *Special Instruction,* p. 10 and elsewhere.
3. Morton Selub and Doris Selub, *How to Prepare for the Scholastic Aptitude Test* (New York: Harcourt Brace Jovanovich, 1981), p. 316.
4. Ibid., p. 270.
5. Ibid., p. 299.
6. Samuel C. Brownstein and Mitchel Weiner, *How to Prepare for the Scholastic Aptitude Test,* 11th ed., (Woodbury, N.Y.: Barron's Educational Series, 1982), p. 423.
7. Robert L. Bailey, et al., *Preparation for the College Entrance Examination SAT* (New York: Arco, 1982), p. 229.
8. Edward C. Gruber and Morris Branson, *Monarch's Preparation for the SAT* (New York: Monarch Press, 1980), p. 1.
9. Michael Donner, *How to Beat the S.A.T.* (New York: Workman, 1981), p. 17.

10. Ibid., pp. 29–30.
11. Constance Garcia-Barrio, "Standardized Tests: How to Beat the Odds," *Essence,* December 1982, p. 35. Garcia-Barrio was quoting from advice given by a coaching school called Plan B's Test Preparation Center.
12. *Computer SAT.*
13. *Barron's Computer SAT.*
14. Gary Gruber, *Inside Strategies for the S.A.T.* (New York: Educational Design, 1982), p. 125.
15. Ibid., p. 126.
16. Ibid.
17. ETS, *1983–84 ATP Guide,* p. 12.
18. [James S. Braswell], "Overview of the Scholastic Aptitude Test," unpublished typescript, prepared February 19, 1980, for South Carolina Task Force Committee on SAT scores, p. 9.
19. Ibid., p. 1.
20. James S. Braswell (of ETS), "The College Board Scholastic Aptitude Test: An Overview of the Mathematical Portion," reprinted by the College Board from *Mathematics Teacher,* 71 (March 1978): 168–80.
21. ETS, *10 SATs,* p. 160.
22. Ibid., p. 55.
23. ETS, *6 SATs,* p. 64.
24. Ibid., p. 87.
25. ETS, *10 SATs,* p. 143.
26. ETS, *Taking the SAT,* 1983, p. 18.
27. ETS, *10 SATs,* pp. 44 and 91.
28. ETS, *1983–84 ATP Guide,* p. 11.
29. Answers: 1. E   2. C   3. A   4. E   5. B
30. ETS, *An SAT: Test and Technical Data for the Scholastic Aptitude Test Administered in April 1981* (New York: College Entrance Examination Board, 1981), p. 7.
31. ETS, "Six Points About Special Preparation for the SAT." Reprinted in various places, including ETS, *Taking the SAT,* 1983, p. 6.
32. Hanford to Owen, May 8, 1984.

8: Test Security

1. ETS, *1983–84 Student Bulletin for the SAT and Achievement Tests* (New York: College Entrance Examination Board, 1983), p. 12.
2. Owen to ETS, January 15, 1984.

3. Goccia to Owen, March 6, 1984.
4. ETS, "Briefing Paper to Stimulate Discussion of the Philosophy and Objectives of Test Security," unpublished typescript, September 10, 1980.
5. ETS, *1983–84 ATP Guide,* p. 5.
6. This is *Denburg v. ETS.* See note 17 for Chapter One. Most of the information in this chapter comes from the court record, including depositions from various witnesses, exhibits, briefs, the judge's opinion, and other documents.
7. Deposition of Jeffrey Leen, p. 9.
8. Ibid., p. 13.
9. Ibid., p. 60.
10. Ibid., p. 79.
11. Ibid., p. 62.
12. "External Inquiry," ETS handwritten document, January 7, 1983.
13. Deposition of Jeffrey Leen, p. 68.
14. Deposition of Stephen Haskin, p. 173.
15. Deposition of Jeffrey Leen, p. 18.
16. "Transcript of the Committee on Review Hearing on the Appeal of Frederick R. Kling, July 9, 12, 13 — 1982," confidential unpublished typescript, ETS (hereafter cited as "Kling Hearing").
17. [Frederick R. Kling], "Precis: Program of Research in the Detection of Copying," unpublished typescript, ETS, July 19, 1978, p. 4.
18. "Kling Hearing."
19. F. Kling, "Memorandum for Mr. F. Smith, Thoughts on a Radical New Approach to Copying Indices," unpublished typescript, ETS, October 1, 1976.
20. "Kling Hearing."
21. Ibid., p. 15.
22. Joyce Purnick, "4 Jersey Students Lose Suit on Invalidated S.A.T. Scores," *New York Times,* August 5, 1983, p. 1.
23. Haskin to Antonia Rosenbaum, March 25, 1983.
24. H. Siegel to Rosenbaum, March 28, 1983.
25. N. Siegel to Rosenbaum, March 29, 1983.
26. Sworn statement of Louis Zuckerman, March 28, 1983.
27. Andre Balazs, "The ETS/CEEB Anti-Trust Suit," *Testing Digest,* Fall 1979, p. 1.
28. Deposition of Neal Vasarkovy, p. 14.
29. Deposition of Stephen Haskin, pp. 19–20 (typing and spelling errors not corrected from transcript).
30. Deposition of David Owen, p. 85.

31. Deposition of Paul Holland, p. 174.
32. Deposition of Protase Woodford, p. 196.
33. Deposition of Shirley Kane-Orr, p. 41.
34. Deposition of Thelma Spencer, p. 99.
35. Deposition of Aileen Cramer, p. 46.
36. Deposition of Lawrence E. Wightman, p. 48.
37. Deposition of Aileen Cramer, p. 52.
38. Ibid., p. 43.
39. Ibid., p. 45.
40. Downey, *Carl Campbell Brigham,* p. 28; Brigham's paper was "A Study of Error," published by the College Board in 1932.
41. Angoff, *Technical Report,* p. 172.
42. Thomsas F. Donlon (of ETS), "The SAT in a Diverse Society," *College Board Review,* Winter 1981–82, p. 31.
43. Deposition of Paul Holland, May 20, 1983, p. 88.
44. Deposition of Paul Holland, [no date], p. 88.
45. Deposition of Aileen Cramer, p. 59.
46. Civil action opinion of Judge Richard S. Cohen, Superior Court of New Jersey, Chancery Division, Middlesex County, Docket Number C-1715-83, August 4, 1983, pp. 47–48.
47. Ibid., p. 42.
48. Ibid., p. 47 and elsewhere.
49. Ibid., p. 29.
50. IRS Form 990, 1982, Schedule A.
51. ETS, "Briefing Paper to Stimulate Discussion of the Philosophy and Objectives of Test Security," unpublished typescript, September 10, 1980, p. 1.

9: *The Cult of Mental Measurement*

1. Carl C. Brigham, *A Study of American Intelligence* (Princeton, N.J.: Princeton University Press, 1923), p. 209.
2. Ibid.
3. Ibid., p. 210.
4. General history of mental measurement drawn mostly from Stephen Jay Gould, *The Mismeasure of Man* (New York: Norton, 1981); Lewis M. Terman, *The Measurement of Intelligence* (Boston: Houghton Mifflin, 1916); Henry Chauncey and John E. Dobbin, *Testing: Its Place in Education Today* (New York: Harper & Row, 1963).

5. Gould, *Mismeasure of Man,* pp. 148–55.
6. Henry Goddard, *Feeble-Mindedness: Its Causes and Consequences* (New York: Macmillan, 1914), p. 561, quoted in Gould, *Mismeasure of Man,* p. 163.
7. Quoted in Gould, *Mismeasure of Man,* p. 161.
8. Terman, *Measurement of Intelligence,* pp. 6–7.
9. Ibid., p. 17.
10. Brigham, *American Intelligence,* p. v.
11. Ibid., pp. 33–36.
12. Ibid., p. 189.
13. Fuess, *First Fifty Years,* p. 103.
14. Brigham, *American Intelligence,* p. 197.
15. Ibid., p. 208.
16. Ibid., p. xxi.
17. Ibid., p. xix.
18. Edwin G. Conklin, *The Direction of Human Evolution* (New York, 1921), p. 52, quoted in Brigham, *American Intelligence,* p. 206.
19. Brigham, *American Intelligence,* p. 208.
20. Downey, *Carl Campbell Brigham,* p. 5.
21. Ibid., p. 6.
22. Ibid., p. 11.
23. Brigham, "Psychological Tests at Princeton," *Princeton Alumni Weekly,* November 28, 1923, p. 185.
24. Fuess, *First Fifty Years,* p. 105.
25. Downey, *Carl Campbell Brigham,* p. 13.
26. Ibid., p. 14.
27. Ibid.
28. Brigham, *American Intelligence,* pp. vii–viii.
29. Carl C. Brigham, "Intelligence Tests of Immigrant Groups," *Psychological Review,* 37 (March 1930): 158–65.
30. Ibid., p. 164.
31. Ibid., p. 165.
32. Downey, *Carl Campbell Brigham,* p. 27.
33. Brigham, "Immigrant Groups," p. 165.
34. Carl C. Brigham, "Army Tests by States," *Eugenical News,* 13 (1928): 67–69; Adolf Hitler, "Text of the German Sterilization Statute," September-October 1933, pp. 89–90.
35. Gould, *Mismeasure of Man,* p. 233; Leon J. Kamin, *The Science and Politics of I.Q.* (Potomac, Md.: Erlbaum, 1974), p. 27.
36. Mark Snyderman and R. J. Herrnstein, "Intelligence Tests and the Immigration Act of 1924," *American Psychologist,* September 1983, pp. 986–95.

37. Ibid., p. 990.
38. Ibid., p. 986.
39. First quote from Carl C. Brigham, "Intelligence Tests," *Princeton Alumni Weekly,* May 5, 1926, p. 1; second quote from Brigham, "Psychological Tests at Princeton," p. 185.
40. Fuess, *First Fifty Years,* p. 121.
41. College Entrance Examination Board, *1932 Annual Report,* quoted in Fuess, *First Fifty Years,* p. 122.
42. Brigham to Holdridge, May 31, 1940, quoted in Downey, *Carl Campbell Brigham,* p. 40.
43. Fuess, *First Fifty Years,* pp. 152–53.
44. Ibid., p. 147.
45. Ibid., pp. 164–66.
46. Ibid., p. 168.
47. Ibid., p. 182.
48. Ibid., p. 171.
49. Downey, *Carl Campbell Brigham,* p. 45.
50. Edward Yahraes, "They Know All the Answers," *Collier's,* May 19, 1951, p. 53.
51. Ibid., p. 23.
52. Ibid., p. 54.
53. Ibid.
54. *The Farmhouse at ETS* (Princeton, N.J.: ETS, 1977).
55. Henry Chauncey, *Fiftieth Anniversary Report,* Harvard College, 1978, p. 120.
56. Chauncey and Dobbin, *Testing,* p. 7.
57. Ibid., p. 3.
58. ETS, *1949–50 Annual Report,* quoted in Nairn, *Reign of ETS,* p. 3.
59. Ibid., p. 4.
60. "Kling Hearing."
61. Ibid.
62. Quoted in Nairn, *Reign of ETS,* p. 198.
63. ETS, *Annual Report to the Board of Trustees, 1950–51,* p. 10.
64. Fallows, "Tests and the 'Brightest,' " p. 43. *Meritocracy* was first used in Michael Young, *The Rise of the Meritocracy* (London: Thames and Hudson, 1958).

10: Brains

1. Chauncey and Dobbins, *Testing,* p. 31.
2. ETS Test Collection, list of bibliographies, undated.

3. Alexandra K. Wigdor and Wendell R. Garner, eds., *Ability Testing: Uses, Consequences, and Controversies* (Washington, D.C.: National Academy Press, 1982), vol. 1, p. 10. ETS cites this book on a variety of matters. I received my copy from Gregory Anrig.
4. Ibid., p. 26.
5. Angoff, *Technical Report*, p. 16.
6. Walter M. Haney, "Disabilities of Committee Testing: A Review," *Educational Measurement*, Fall 1982, p. 18.
7. Ibid., p. 15.
8. Samuel Messick (of ETS), "Abilities and Knowledge in Educational Achievement Testing: The Assessment of Dynamic Cognitive Structures" (Princeton, N.J.: ETS, 1982), p. 10.
9. Ibid., p. 13.
10. Ibid., p. 19.
11. Ibid., p. 21.
12. Martin R. Katz (of ETS), *YOU: Today and Tomorrow* (Princeton, N.J.: ETS, 1959), quoted from Nairn, *Reign of ETS*, p. 213, and Christopher Jencks and James Crouse, "Should We Relabel the SAT . . . Or Replace It?" *Phi Delta Kappan*, June 1982, p. 660. I requested a copy of the Katz booklet from ETS but was told I couldn't have one.
13. ETS, *Taking the SAT*, 1983, p. 3.
14. "A Roundtable: Scoring the SAT," *New York Times*, October 21, 1982, p. B22.
15. ETS, *Guide to the College Board Validity Study Service* (New York: College Entrance Examination Board, 1982), p. 38.
16. ETS, *Test Use and Validity* (Princeton, N.J.: ETS, 1980), p. 16 note and p. 20.
17. Slack and Porter, "Critical Appraisal," p. 165.
18. Gould, *Mismeasure of Man*, p. 242.
19. Nairn, *Reign of ETS*.
20. ETS, *Test Scores and Family Income* (Princeton, N.J.: ETS, 1980), p. 9.
21. ETS, *Test Use and Validity*, p. 16.
22. Ramist and Arbeiter, *Profiles, College-Bound Seniors, 1983*, p. 7.
23. Hoffmann, *Tyranny of Testing*, p. 139.
24. From a draft copy of a talk given by Fred Hargadon at the 1983 ETS Invitational Conference on Testing Problems (typographical error corrected), p. 8.
25. Ibid., p. 9.
26. Shane et al., *LSAT Handbook*, 1964, pp. 44–45.

27. ETS, *Taking the SAT,* 1983, and elsewhere.

28. ETS, *1983–84 ATP Guide,* p. 8.

29. Ibid., p. 10.

30. Ibid.

31. Martha Carmody to Owen, July 9, 1984.

32. ETS, *1983–84 ATP Guide,* p. 10.

33. Ibid., p. 11.

34. Ibid., p. 10.

35. Sherrye Henry radio show, WOR, New York, April 17, 1984.

36. Deposition of George Hanford, *Denburg v. ETS,* p. 32.

37. ETS, *Undergraduate Admissions* (New York: College Entrance Examination Board, 1980), p. 24.

38. Fallows, "Tests and the 'Brightest,' " p. 44.

39. ETS, *Annual Report to the Board of Trustees, 1960–1961,* pp. 25–26.

40. ETS, *Profiles, College-Bound Seniors, 1981* (New York: College Entrance Examination Board, 1982).

41. Ramist and Arbeiter, *Profiles, College-Bound Seniors, 1983.*

42. *Developing a Test* (Princeton, N.J.: ETS, 1981).

43. This "sensitivity review" was an exhibit in *Denburg v. ETS.*

44. Brill, "Secrecy Behind the College Boards."

45. Daniel Seligman, "The Rich Are Different," *Fortune,* May 5, 1980, p. 84.

46. See, for example, Arthur R. Jensen, *Straight Talk About Mental Tests* (New York: Free Press, 1981), p. 61.

47. Edward B. Fiske, "U.S. Pupils Lag from Grade 1, Study Finds," *New York Times,* June 17, 1984, p. 1.

48. Thomas F. Donlon (of ETS), "The SAT in a Diverse Society," *College Board Review,* Winter 1981–82, pp. 16–17.

49. Ibid., p. 20.

50. Ibid.

51. College Entrance Examination Board, *The Work of the College Entrance Examination Board* (Boston: Ginn, 1926), p. 51.

52. Miriam Conrad, "Stress on standardized test results could harm education, critics say," *Kansas City Times,* November 26, 1983.

53. ETS, *Test Scores and Family Income,* p. 10.

54. Fred Hargadon, *Two Cheers* (Princeton, N.J.: College Board Publications Office, 1980), quoted in Walt Haney, "Validity, Vaudeville, and Values," *American Psychologist,* 36 (October 1981): 1028.

55. ETS, *Test Scores and Family Income,* p. 9.

56. Ibid., p. 10.

57. Reginald Stuart, "Black Colleges Survive, But Students Are Fewer," *New York Times,* February 1, 1984, p. A18.
58. Michael S. Schudson, "Organizing the 'Meritocracy': A History of the College Entrance Examination Board," *Harvard Educational Review,* 42 (February 1972): 58.
59. Ibid., p. 59.
60. Kenneth B. Clark, "Black S.A.T. Scores," *New York Times,* October 12, 1982.
61. Harris Dienstry, "How to Promote Sophomore Surge," *Psychology Today,* September 1982.
62. Confidential unpublished memorandum dated May 25, 1979.
63. EEO-1 Employee Summary, January 6, 1983; figures as of December 31, 1982.

11: Mythology

1. Rodney T. Hartnett and Robert A. Feldmesser (both of ETS), "College Admissions Testing and the Myth of Selectivity," *AAHE Bulletin,* 32 (March 1980).
2. Ibid., p. 4.
3. ETS, *Test Scores and Family Income,* p. 9.
4. Robert L. Linn (formerly of ETS), "Admissions Testing on Trial," *American Psychologist,* 37 (March 1982): 279.
5. From the ETS/College Board 1979 contract.
6. IRS Form 990, 1982.
7. McIntyre to Owen, June 18, 1984.
8. "Kling Hearing."
9. James Crouse, "From the SAT to Achievement Tests," draft for critical comments only, January 18, 1982, p. 5, quoted by permission.
10. Crouse, "Does the SAT Help Colleges Make Better Selection Decisions?" draft for critical comments only, January 9, 1984, p. 15; quoted by permission. Crouse's data were from the National Longitudinal Survey of the high school class of 1972.
11. Ibid., pp. 32–35, and conversation.
12. Ibid., pp. 18–27.
13. Ibid.
14. ETS, *Guidelines on the Uses of College Board Test Scores and Related Data* (New York: College Entrance Examination Board, 1981).

15. Unpublished, unsigned, undated ETS response to Brill, "Secrecy Behind the College Boards," p. 7.
16. Bowdoin *Viewbook,* 1984–85, in press.
17. Edward B. Fiske, "Some Colleges Question Usefulness of S.A.T.'s," *New York Times,* October 9, 1984, p. C1.

12: *Testing and Teachers*

1. Edward B. Fiske, "Test Misuse Is Charged," *New York Times,* November 29, 1983, p. C1.
2. Ibid. Anrig was speaking at the Annual Meeting of the Council of Chief State School Officers, Little Rock, Arkansas, November 22, 1983.
3. Anrig, "Identifying and Rewarding Excellence in Individuals," speech cited above; ETS, *NTE: Guidelines for Proper Use of NTE Tests* (Princeton, N.J.: ETS, 1983), p. 7.
4. National Commission on Excellence in Education, *A Nation at Risk: The Imperative for Educational Reform* (Washington, D.C.: U.S. Department of Education, April 1983).
5. Ernest L. Boyer, *High School, A Report on Secondary Education in America by the Carnegie Foundation for the Advancement of Teaching* (New York: Harper & Row, 1983).
6. Diane Ravitch, "Scapegoating the Teachers," *New Republic,* November 7, 1983, p. 27.
7. "The Corporate Plan of Educational Testing Service for Fiscal Year 1983," confidential internal memorandum, July 27, 1982, p. 2.
8. Fiske, "Test Misuse Is Charged," p. C11.
9. ETS, *NTE Guidelines,* p. 8 and elsewhere.
10. Fiske, "Test Misuse Is Charged," p. C1.
11. ETS, *NTE Programs: Core Battery and Specialty Area Tests* (Princeton, N.J.: ETS, 1983), p. 19. ETS also publishes each section of this book as a separate pamphlet. See also *A Guide to the NTE Core Battery Tests* (Princeton, N.J.: ETS, 1984).
12. ETS, *NTE Programs,* p. 20.
13. Ibid., p. 66.
14. Ibid., p. 80.
15. Ibid., p. 51.
16. Ibid., p. 90.
17. Ibid., p. 123.
18. *Bulletin of Information* (Princeton, N.J.: ETS, 1983), p. 5; ETS, *NTE Programs,* passim.

19. ETS, *NTE Programs,* p. 82.
20. Ibid., p. 83.
21. ETS, *NTE Guidelines,* pp. 5–7 and elsewhere.
22. ETS, *Bulletin of Information,* p. 5.
23. Gary Echternacht (of ETS), "The Validity and Passing Standard of the Pre Professional Skills Tests as a Certification Test for Delaware Teachers" (Princeton, N.J.: ETS, undated), 14-page unpublished typescript, p. 1 (hereafter cited as "Delaware Validity").
24. ETS, *NTE Programs,* p. 9.
25. ETS, *PPST 1983 Bulletin of Information* (Princeton, N.J.: ETS, 1983), p. 22.
26. Echternacht, "Delaware Validity," p. 13.
27. Ibid., p. 2.
28. Ibid., pp. 2–4.
29. Ibid., p. 4. See also Samuel A. Livingston and Michael J. Zieky (both of ETS), *Passing Scores* (Princeton, N.J.: ETS, 1982).
30. Echternacht, "Delaware Validity," pp. 4–13.
31. Ibid., p. 4.
32. Ibid., pp. 4–13.
33. Ibid., p. 1.
34. Murray to Keene, May 31, 1983.
35. "The Corporate Plan of Educational Testing Service for Fiscal Year 1983," July 27, 1982.
36. ETS promotional flier, undated.
37. Angelo John Lewis, *Making the Public Schools Work,* Focus 9 (Princeton, N.J.: ETS, 1982), pp. 11–12.
38. The name was changed on July 1, 1982. See ETS, *1982 Annual Report,* p. 19.
39. Walt Haney and George Madaus, "Making Sense of the Competency Testing Movement," *Harvard Educational Review,* 1978, p. 475.
40. David Owen, "Testing, Testing," *New Republic,* June 4, 1984, pp. 12–14.
41. McIntyre to Owen, June 18, 1984.
42. There was a series of articles on this theme in the ETS *Examiner.* See in particular "ETS teams to address revenue growth areas," May 6, 1982.
43. "The Corporate Plan of Educational Testing Service for Fiscal Year 1984," July 1, 1983.
44. Ibid., p. 2.
45. ETS, *The Center for Occupational & Professional Assessment* (Princeton, N.J.: ETS, 1983).
46. Internal memorandum from David A. Martz, December 30.

13: *Testing and Society: What Can Be Done?*

1. Thomas P. Rohlen, *Japan's High Schools* (Berkeley: University of California Press, 1983), p. 102. This is an absolutely fascinating book. All the other information in this paragraph, and most of the information about Japan in succeeding paragraphs, is taken from it.
2. Ibid., pp. 96 and 99.
3. Ibid., p. 98.
4. Ibid., p. 96.
5. Edward B. Fiske, "Japan's Schools: Exam Ordeal Rules Each Student's Destiny," *New York Times,* July 12, 1983, p. A1.
6. Fuess, *First Fifty Years,* p. 85.
7. Owen, *High School: Undercover with the Class of '80* (New York: Viking, 1981).
8. These figures are my own guesstimations.
9. Fred Hargadon, "Test Use in Higher Education," draft of a speech given at the 1983 ETS Invitational Conference on Testing Problems, October 29, 1983, p. 9.
10. [Robert J. Solomon], *20 Questions: The Truth about Truth in Testing* (Princeton, N.J.: ETS, 1981).
11. ETS, "What the Polls Say . . .," undated brochure.
12. Jencks and Crouse, "Should We Relabel the SAT?" p. 662.
13. Ibid., p. 660.
14. ETS, *The College Board Achievement Tests,* p. 374.
15. Ibid., p. 163.
16. Ibid., p. 184.
17. Ibid., p. 242.
18. Promotional leaflet, 1981.
19. Ibid.
20. Ibid.
21. Ibid.
22. Clinton I. Chase and H. Glenn Ludlow, eds., *Readings in Educational and Psychological Measurement* (Boston: Houghton Mifflin, 1966), p. 59.
23. ETS, *The Center for Occupational & Professional Assessment,* 1983.
24. In addition to the million dollars or so reported in ETS federal tax returns, the company devotes a great deal of money and staff time to promoting its side in various testing disputes.
25. ETS, *The Center for Occupational & Professional Assessment,* 1983.
26. ETS promotional brochure, undated.

27. Ibid.
28. EE0-1, Employee Summary, January 6, 1983.
29. PPST brochure.

Appendix A: A Poisoned Question

1. Scholastic Aptitude Test administered May 1984, p. 4.
2. Owen to ETS, June 18, 1984.
3. Konstantakis to Owen, July 17, 1984.

Index